To leisure

To leisure:
an introduction

JOHN NEULINGER

*The City College
of the
City University of New York*

ALLYN AND BACON, INC.
Boston   London   Sydney   Toronto

Library of Congress Cataloging in Publication Data

Neulinger, John.
  To leisure: an introduction.

  Bibliography: p.
  Includes index.
    1. Leisure. 2. Leisure–Social aspects.
  1. Title.
GV14.N39   790'.01'35   80–36804
ISBN 0–205–06936–3

Series Editor: Hiram Howard

Printed in the United States of America

Contents

Foreword

It does not occur frequently that one reads the manuscript of a forth-coming book on leisure, immediately flies to Jersualem for an international gathering on "Leisure Policy," appears on the program with book's author and hears him expound ideas, then returns to read the manuscript with better understanding to write its Foreword. Perhaps I should have begun with, "A funny thing happened on the way . . ."

The readers should know that John Neulinger is not just your detached scholar—he can be that—but also a warm human being, concerned deeply with the *quality of life* he writes about. Jerusalem discourse is colored with passion, and so it was as we met for three days at the recreational park in the forest overlooking Ein Kerem, the birthplace of John the Baptist and the village that Mary visited before the birth of Jesus. Here another, contemporary John fulfilled the spirit of this legacy and the current need for eloquence, clarity, and enlightenment.

For as I view this book, it will take its signficant place in literature as both a scientific analysis and a humanistic document. The approaches interweave creatively into a polyphonic composition with an enthusiasm rarely explicit among social scientists, who too often write with "objective restraint"—as one can hear at a Leinsdorf performance—for the applause of their colleagues. No, John of today, bearded and prophetic, writes for the world to hear and to take heart.

The very first sentence of the Preface takes off with the phrase, "leisure within the context of the quality of life." Then he presses forward with the "many faces of leisure" (chapter 1); "leisure as a state of mind or an experience" (chapter 2); "quality becomes the primary concern: the type and nature of the experience, its characteristics, its intensity, its depth. . . ." (chapter 3). Consistently the theme appears with its variations and growing intensity, as if to remind us that it was Toscanini who conducted the first concerts of the Israel Philharmonic.

Yet this is not a mere polemic or series of conjectures. It is all carefully developed, with an experienced craft that draws on many instruments: he summarizes at length the theories of others; he opens his own concepts to detail and example; he evaluates other disciplines beyond psychology; and he presents the results. of research, his own and others. His discussions of attitudes, needs, perceptions and motivations are authoritative; his sensitivity to emerging trends, such as flexitime, is reliable; his observations on stages of personal growth in the family context supplement the Rapoport studies in England; his concern with leisure counseling is practical in a time when his own files (and mine). bulge with pleas for instant education from would-be "leisure consultants." Finally, Neulinger ends, not with a traditional sigh for more research, but with a call for consumer advocacy, for ways of making "technological innovations benefit the worker and consumer," and for controls over politicians. As to the last, he says, "Make them discuss basic political-philosophical-moral problems and issues, and address themselves explicitly and concretely to issues of leisure and the quality of life. A leisure society will not come to us through empty slogans and empty gestures."

Where, then, will this volume fall in the expanding stream of research and politics of leisure? Purists will argue that research and politics are incompatible goals. Eric Fromm (who finds himself in the present volume) was criticized for attempting both in his *Sane Society;* but he is a philosopher-psychiatrist! Pitirim Sorokin was scored for his subjective stance in his *Social and Cultural Dynamics;* but was he a sociologist? Now comes Neulinger, going beyond neat, positivistic psychological simplicity with his "leisure as a state of mind" conception. Well, my own approach—to which John is generous—includes what I (and before me, my mentor Florian Znaniecki) call the "humanistic coefficient," i.e., a reminder that human actions and experiences spin off from the actor's perceptions, not from those of the observing scientist. Few of us have Neulinger's brand of courage, and for that his book will help to rescue leisure analysis from where it has lain, in the sociological rushes, waiting to be found and nourished by other sciences. The Holy Land was a fruitful environment to hear John bare his mind and soul; other cultures moving toward rapid industrialization will have much to learn as well.

Max Kaplan

Preface

The overriding theme of this book is the role of leisure within the context of the quality of life. Leisure . . . a word with many meanings. And the quality of life? Perhaps a word without any meaning. I have centered on one particular form of leisure: leisure as a state of mind. And I have shown how this conceptualization puts leisure right in the middle of the quality-of-life controversy. Are things getting better or are they getting worse? Leisure is the criterion by which to judge.

The book is written for two major audiences. The first consists of students, primarily in recreation and leisure studies, but also in sociology, psychology, nursing, counseling, gerontology, future studies, in fact, any area that is specifically concerned with the improvement of the quality of life. The second audience is made up of the professionals involved in these areas, not only as teachers but as practitioners: in hospitals, nursing homes or homes for the elderly, community centers, playgrounds, and departments of parks and recreation. The book is relevant to those who design our physical environment (engineers and architects) as well as to those who shape our social one (educators, lawyers, and politicians).

The hope of making an impact on this rather wide audience brought me to write this book. The more one pursues the implications of leisure, the more imperative it becomes that one attempt to help bring about in all areas of life the conditions that will make that experience possible. I was very much brought to this realization by my students in a course I taught at The City College of New York, entitled "The Quality of Life: A Psychological Perspective." I am indebted to them for many thoughtful suggestions and interactions.

Let me offer appreciation to several other sources of inspiration and support. I am grateful to William Crain, Douglas Kimmel and Jerry Siegel, colleagues at The City College of New York, for their contributions of stimulating ideas and creative criticism. To Gary Paluba go thanks for his cooperation in the development of leisure-counseling programs.

My debt to the professionals in the leisure domain is hard to pinpoint. In writing a book like this, one has to immerse oneself in the thoughts of others. It is, then, often difficult to know where their ideas end and one's own begin, or the reverse. I have attempted, however, to identify sources whenever possible and would like to express thanks to the many authors (and publishers) who granted permission to quote freely from their works or paraphrase their thoughts.

For critical readings of the manuscript I am indebted to Gerald Fain and Douglas Sessoms. The final version of this book has benefited greatly from their suggestions. Let me also express true appreciation to my copyeditor Susan Middleton, whose painstaking reading and incisive modifications helped to sharpen many a critical point.

To Max Kaplan, whom I met at the very first leisure conference I ever attended, I feel a special closeness: not only because he wrote a most generous foreword for this book, but also because our approaches to leisure, while quite different in detail, to me express a shared philosophy. I hope we shall perform in many more orchestras together.

Finally, let me express my particular appreciation to the whole Mayhew family—Arthur, Rita, Lisa, Artie, Anne and Kathy—whose presence in my bucolic summer retreat as neighbors, friends, and as people always available to experience leisure with, made the very writing of this work possible.

John Neulinger
Dolgeville, N.Y.

Introduction

This book is designed to be an introduction: to make known widely and formally, to call to the attention, and to help usher in, a philosophy and way of life that may simply be stated as *to leisure*. This author confesses to a strong bias in favor of leisure. But would one not expect a mathematician to have a love of mathematics, a chemist a love of chemistry, and a shoemaker a love of shoes? (And would we not wish that such shoemakers still existed!). This book contains many value statements; but these are identified as such and separated from statements relating to facts or hypotheses.

First, some comments about my use of the word *leisure* as a verb. Even though the verb form of *leisure* is not listed in standard dictionaries, I have used the term in this form since at least 1973 (e.g., Neulinger, 1974a, 1974b), and have had the distinct honor of having the term *to leisure* referred to as "Neulinger's ugly phrase" (Muir, 1975). I started using the term in this way on a rather intuitive basis, feeling that there ought to be such a verb, since leisure is not a thing one has (as one might "have" *free time*), but an experience, a process, an ongoing state of mind. I have recently become aware of a most powerful rationale for the use of the term *leisure* as a verb. I am referring to Erich Fromm's (1976) book, *To Have or to Be?* Let me quote:

> A noun is the proper denotation for a thing. I can say that I *have* things: for instance that I have a table, a house, a book, a car. The proper denotation for an activity, a process, is a verb: for instance I am, I love, I desire, I hate, etc. Yet ever more frequently an *activity* is expressed in terms of *having*; that is, a noun is used instead of a verb. But to express an activity by *to have* in connec-

tion with a noun is an erroneous use of language, because processes and activities cannot be possessed; they can only be experienced. (P. 20.)

The above quote deserves this prominent position since it deals
with the very essence of what is important in our conception of
leisure: the difference between leisure as a thing, and leisure as an
experience; between a leisure society based on consumption and the
accumulation of possessions, and one based on individual growth and
the experiencing of self and others. It may make the difference between a world that will collapse and destroy itself through a ruthless
exploitation of all its resources, or one that will grow through genuine
development in harmony with nature.

A word of clarification may be indicated for the traditionalists in
this field, namely the recreation professionals. This book is an introduction to the field of leisure and not to recreation. This does not
imply a derogation of the role of recreation, but is an attempt to free
recreation from its subservient position to work (as traditionally defined). Let us look into the future. The time is near when people will
truly be freed from the necessity of toil, except perhaps for a very
limited number of years within their life span. To define recreation
(or leisure) in opposition to work or as a component of free time
(again defined in opposition to work) will no longer make sense.
Recreation has always been an important aspect of life and will
probably be even more so in the future. But leisure is a broader concept than recreation. It relates to all meaningful activities and recreation is only one of these.

Meaningful activity is *the* crucial aspect of life. But in the past
the most meaningful activity for the majority of people had to be
assuring one's survival. Post-industrial society is about to provide the
conditions that will allow mankind to go beyond this goal. We are
suddenly confronted with a totally new experience and a task for
which we have not been prepared. The leisure professional has the
unique opportunity to become the guide for this arduous but utmost
challenging endeavor. The future will tell whether we shall succeed,
but it is this author's hope that this work will enhance the chances
at least to a minimal degree.

This book, then, is intended as an introduction to the field of
leisure, and to the intimately related issues of the quality of life. It is
organized into three sections. The first (chapters 1 through 3) deals
with questions of "What": What is leisure? What are the ways in
which it has been defined or conceptualized? The second section
(chapters 4 and 5) addresses itself to questions of "How": How do we
approach and study this phenomenon of leisure? How do we deal
with the related issues of the quality of life? The third section (chap-

ters 6 through 9) traces leisure through various areas of life, and concerns itself with questions such as, What shall we do to make leisure flourish, and how shall we go about achieving this goal? Let us take a brief look at each of the chapters.

Chapter 1 presents an overview of the domain of leisure. Issues and areas of relevance are identified and the reader is given some idea of the pervasiveness of leisure in the most diverse aspects of our society. The purpose of this chapter is, in fact, to highlight this diversity. The many ways are shown in which leisure interacts with our daily habits, our customs, our institutions. The word *leisure* is seen to have many different meanings and to be used in many different contexts. The picture is confusing and reflects one of the few commonly recognized psychological principles: life and nearly every single behavioral act is multi-determined.

Chapters 2 and 3 deal with conceptual issues. Given the diversity described in chapter 1, it is imperative to bring order into this chaos if we intend to study the phenomenon of leisure. The issue of definition is treated first, since how one treats a subject is, after all, dependent on one's definition of the subject matter. As there is no commonly accepted definition of leisure, ways of categorizing different views of leisure are presented first, followed by a more detailed description of three specific conceptualizations of leisure. The last of these represents the author's perspective of leisure and sets the tone for the orientation of this volume: leisure perceived as a state of mind, with an emphasis on the psychological aspects of the issues. Chapter 3 covers further conceptual questions, including a historical perspective, and links the topic of leisure with the broader issues of the quality of life. Leisure is recognized as an interdisciplinary concern to which no one discipline has an exclusive hold or prerogative.

Chapters 4 and 5 deal with methodology: how do we come to grips with this evasive topic *leisure?* Research methodology has taken on an ever increasing importance and sophistication, so that today it has become impossible even to approach the topic without at least some understanding of the fundamentals of the scientific method. Chapter 4 centers on objective approaches in the measurement of leisure and the quality of life, as exemplified by social indicators in general, and time-budget studies in particular. Chapter 5 turns to subjective approaches and specific problems related thereto.

Chapters 6 through 9 examine the potential for leisure in various areas of life. This separation into specific areas is of course an artificial one, and the issues and problems discussed in each chapter by necessity overlap. Chapter 6 starts this section with a discussion of leisure during non-free time. This is to highlight the conceptualization of leisure as a state of mind and its consequent relevance even to the work situation. Chapter 7 looks at leisure during free time, and in this context examines groups of people who differ in the nature of their free time. It also explores the changing conditions of free-time environments.

Chapter 8 traces leisure through the life cycle. As we pass the milestones of life, the realization of leisure requires quite different conditions. This fact reflects not only age differences, but also the changing conditions of society. What was functional at one time in history may have become quite dysfunctional at this point. Chapter 9 picks up on this issue and deals with the important question of the preparedness of our society for leisure. Leisure education and leisure counseling are described as means of helping us achieve, as a society and as individuals, the goal of living a life of leisure.

Chapter 10 moves into the social-political arena. While leisure as a state of mind is very much an internal event, the conditions that bring it about are very much public—both social and political. Anyone concerned with leisure, and even more so with the quality of life, will find it impossible to avoid political questions: what are we doing as a society to bring about this desired life of leisure? What ought we to do under ideal conditions, and what could be done within a more realistic context?

As a concluding remark, let me make the following point. In line with my approach to leisure education and counseling, this book has two purposes—one informational and the other motivational. For an introductory text the informational aspect is important, but it is the motivational component that really counts. If this work helps to clarify the role of leisure for the quality of our lives and heightens its value as a positive goal, the aim of this work has been achieved.

To leisure

1

Leisure:

an overview

Increased means and increased leisure are the two civilizers of man.
   Benjamin Disraeli (1872).

More free time means more time to waste. The worker who used to have only
a little time in which to get drunk and beat his wife now has time to get drunk,
beat his wife—and watch TV.
   Robert Hutchins (1970).

By temperament I am a vagabond and a tramp. I don't want money badly enough
to work for it. In my opinion it's a shame that there is so much work in the
world. One of the saddest things is that the thing a man can do for eight hours a
day, day after day, is work. You can't eat eight hours a day nor drink for eight
hours a day nor make love for eight hours—all you can do for eight hours is work.
   James B. Meriwether and Michael Millgate (1968).

. . . There runs a persistent belief that all leisure must be earned by work
and good works. And second, while it is enjoyed it must be seen in a context of
future work and good works.
   Margaret Mead (1957).

The morality of work is the morality of slaves, and the modern world has no
need of slavery.
   Bertrand Russell (1958).

The fundamental principle of equal educational opportunity for all is not discharged
by keeping all in school the same number of years. It requires us to have exactly
the same objectives in mind for all; namely, to prepare all to exercise critical
intelligence in the performance of their duties as citizens, to prepare all to use
their free time in the pursuits of leisure, which are essentially efforts at learning.
   Mortimer J. Adler (1979).

Leisure is a frequently used word. It is part of everyday conversation; it appears in print, in newspapers, magazines, and many books. We hear the word on the radio and on television, within the context of news reports, sports, plays, variety and comedy shows, and on many other occasions. I suspect that a study of the frequency of public usage of the term *leisure* over the past decades would produce an accelerating curve. The word seems to have spread everywhere. We hear of leisure suits, leisure villages, leisure agencies, leisure education, leisure studies departments, and are we not heading into the twenty-first century, to be known as the century of leisure?

Well, are we? What are the chances, and do we actually want to live a life of leisure? Do we even understand what we mean by such a statement? We probably have very different conceptions of what such a life might be like, or how a leisure society might function.

IMPLICATIONS AND CONSEQUENCES OF LABELING

The word *leisure* is used with many different meanings, often quite ambiguous ones, and we are left to choose whatever interpretation we wish to adopt. At the same time, a number of other words are used as if they implied the same meanings as leisure, or as if the term *leisure* were interchangeable with them. We substitute such terms as *free time, play, recreation, relaxation,* and so forth. It is in the nature of language to provide different labels for phenomena that, while similar, are different in certain relevant aspects; and it is in the nature of people to use these labels in ways that are somewhat removed from their original purposes. We call these words synonyms, one of two or more words of the same language that have the same or almost the same meaning in some or all senses.

Does it matter what label we use as long as we all seem to know what we are talking about? It depends on the purpose of our communication. Everyday conversation allows a certain degree of ambiguity. Artistic expression may even welcome an overlap in meaning. If the communication is for purposes of scientific expression, however, or for legal, policy, or other kind of implementative action, specificity becomes crucial. It then becomes important that we know precisely what is implied by the label we use, and that others are in

3

agreement with us in that respect. This concern has led to the emphasis on *operational definitions*.[1]

The issue is further complicated by the fact that the different labels used for the same phenomenon may not only point us to the wrong object or event, but may also carry different surplus meanings. We are well aware of this. Just imagine the implications of addressing an officer of the law as either "Officer" or "cop." The responses you get may not be identical!

There is an additional complication. The meaning of a word may be crucially influenced by that of its antonym, a word of opposite meaning. What we define as cold is determined by what we experience as hot; what we define as bad by what we label as good.

The implications of taking meaning from a concept's antonym are very serious for the term *leisure*. *Work* is commonly seen as the antonym of *leisure*. Work is also commonly viewed as good, desirable, to be striven for, and so on. Since we still tend to define leisure in opposition to work, the implication and consequences are obvious, and most regrettable. Leisure has acquired a negative connotation. We shall show in the following chapters that this has come about largely through the creation of a false and unnecessary work-leisure dichotomy.

We shall conclude, then, that the choice of label is critical when we are referring to the phenomenon of leisure. It will determine not only the direction our thoughts take, but the feelings that will be involved and the actions that may result. In other words, the connotation of the label used to denote the phenomenon of leisure will greatly influence our attitude toward it.

THE MANY FACES OF LEISURE

The following silhouettes of the intersection of leisure with various areas of life and society are offered as examples of the diversity of contexts in which this phenomenon is found. No attempt is made at abstracting the common elements or discovering a unifying theme at this point. Nor are these brief descriptions meant to convey the whole picture in respect to any one area; whole chapters, if not separate books, would be needed to do justice to that. We shall return to some of the topics in later chapters. The purpose here is as stated: to convey the ubiquitousness and multi-faceted appearance of the phenomenon of leisure in our society.

Arts

The *New York Times* Sunday edition has a major section (sec. 2) entitled "Arts and Leisure." It contains what one might vaguely refer to as entertainment information, but goes far beyond that. Every major newspaper in the country has similar special sections providing guidance to the world of arts and leisure. It is interesting to note that on a typical Sunday (September 18, 1977), the *New York Times* used the following breakdown to refer the reader to relevant pages:

Arts: Architecture, Art, Dance, Film, Music, Radio Log, Television, Theater

Leisure: Bridge, Camera, Chess, Gardens, Home Improvement, Numismatics, Stamps

One might ponder the criteria for the separation between arts and leisure, adopted here. One also might wonder what is implied by the fact that these two categories are contained in the same section of the newspaper. Is it that these two areas are merely contiguous subsets of the field of entertainment, or is it that they are overlapping in a deeper sense, sharing critical components of experience?

Another interesting question we might consider is the relationship of leisure to the arts in the traditional sense versus the so-called popular arts, often referred to as mass culture (e.g., Rosenberg and White, 1957). Was the metamorphosis of *leisure* to *free time* (to be discussed in later chapters) perhaps reflected and paralleled in this trend of the arts? And what is the role of leisure in the life of the professional artist who makes a living out of his or her art? This is not the place to answer these questions, but merely to raise them.

Education

Once again, education is undergoing a major change. Long ago, education was reserved for a small elite; only the privileged few were in a position to avail themselves of it. Then changing social-economic-political conditions brought about mass education. Education turned from a privilege to an obligation: compulsory public education. In the twentieth century the school system has become one of the largest social institutions, ranging from pre-kindergarten to postdoctoral training, with formal and informal courses in practically every aspect of life.

Another radical change, however, is taking place in our educational system. The traditional assumption that education is to be primarily designed for and taking place during the early part of one's life cycle is being seriously questioned. Much of education used to be devoted to preparation for a job or a profession before one entered the work place. More and more this pattern is changing. Education, formal and informal, is taking place during and in between one's career, as well as after one completes the work cycle, i.e., after retirement. This is true not only for the so-called adult education courses, frequently designed to help people "fill their free time" constructively, but also for job-related and professional education. Rapid changes in technology and the knowledge base force many to take refresher courses or even develop new careers in midlife. Extended life spans lead the elderly to seek education either as a goal in itself or as a means to further their market value.

Education and leisure have always been associated with each other. As Kando (1975, p. 22) states,

> all encyclopedic definitions of leisure point out that the Greek word for it is *schole,* which leads to the English *school, scholarship.* The significance of this is that it indicates that leisure, traditionally, has incorporated education, scholarship, and philosophy.

In the recent past we may have been aware of this connection mainly through the association of leisure with arts and crafts classes, or with adult education courses. The revolutionary changes taking place in our society are bound to make this connection more visible, not only through such events as the spreading throughout the country of leisure studies departments at universities, but also by once more shifting the goal of education from job preparation to liberal arts education.

Mental Health

"Whatever other labels may seem apt for our time, the 'Age of Leisure' is surely suited for describing the state in which we find ourselves" (Martin, 1967a, p. 3). So wrote a leading psychiatrist and chairman of the American Psychiatric Association Committee on Leisure Time and Its Uses, 1964–1969. The psychiatric recognition of problems related to free time is usually traced to Ferenczi's (1950) description of Sunday neuroses. The value of leisure as a positive experience, however, has also been recognized.

> There are almost as many ways of experiencing leisure as there are people. But all the positive ways seem to have one thing in common, and that is that they contribute to mental health, which I will define as a subjective sense of well being and a capacity for enjoyment and happiness. (Martin, 1967a, p. 6.)

Similarly, self-actualization was seen as the link between leisure and mental health in a testimony before the United States Senate (Neulinger ,1974c). In addition, leisure was said to play a crucial role in our efforts to improve the quality of life. There is some empirical evidence for a positive relationship between mental health and leisure. A relatively healthy group, for example, members of the Mensa society (people with high IQ) reported positive attitudes toward leisure (Neulinger and Raps, 1972); a relatively unhealthy group, for example, alcoholics in treatment, expressed generally negative attitudes toward leisure (Berg and Neulinger, 1976). Another study found that, while an index of mental health did not relate to leisure attitudes, it was related to the respondents' perception of the concept of leisure (Neulinger, 1971). Respondents who rated high on a measure of mental health saw leisure as more full and refreshing, and somewhat more sociable, necessary, and meaningful, than did respondents rating low on that measure. On the other hand, Spreitzer and Snyder (1974), using items from one of Neulinger and Breit's (1969, 1971) leisure attitude dimensions ("self-definition through leisure or work"), found a negative relationship between leisure attitudes and a measure of psychological well-being. That measure, however, related to life satisfaction and happiness rather than mental health, per se. It may indeed be the case that in our work-oriented society the more work-oriented person can experience and express greater life satisfaction.

Physical Health

Leisure has always been associated with a person's physical condition, be it through the recognition that one's physical state affects one's mental state, through the concept of recreation, or in relation to a particular lifestyle that may be deemed healthier. Contemplation, according to Aristotle one of the two forms of pure leisure (the other being music), is said to be helped by assuming certain physical positions, and is practiced in our society by a growing number of people engaging in various forms of Eastern practices, like yoga. A 1976 Gallup Poll (*New York Times*, November 18, 1976) indicated that about 12 percent of a sample of 1553 adults, eighteen years and older, were engaging in some form of meditation, such as mysticism, oriental religions, yoga, Transcendental Meditation, and the charismatic renewal. Interest in these movements is seen as partly due to a desire for finding ways of calming the tensions of modern life.

A leisurely lifestyle, one in which one moves through life in a relaxed manner without undue haste and stress, has long been viewed as a healthier one, be that correct or not. The busy executive is told to slow down to avoid getting an ulcer, and the even more frantic person is sent off on a long vacation. Heart disease is claimed to be related to lifestyles: the person with "hurry sickness" (called Type A behavior in some studies) is one who is overly ambitious, has never enough time for the things to be done, and is prone to coronary heart disease (Friedman and Rosenman, 1975). "Type A behavior is characterized by excesses of competitive achievement striving, time urgency, and aggression and is associated with at least twice the likelihood of heart disease as an opposing Type B behavior pattern" (Weidner and Matthews, 1978).

Finally, an important function of recreation is restoring the body to a healthy condition. "Increasingly, recreation has gained recognition in the United States and Canada as a health-related service which has important implications for both the general population and for those who have physical, mental, or social disabilities" (Kraus, 1978, p. 338). Many different types of so-called therapeutic recreation have been developed for people with special problems.

Recreation

> *Recreation* . . . is frequently defined as an activity one enters into during his leisure time for the satisfaction derived from the experience. However, it is also used to describe the recreation movement and the recreation service or field of work. It is sometimes difficult to determine the use of the term without knowing the context. The problem is further complicated by the various concepts of recreation. Some hold recreation to be a diversionary experience, while others see it as a certain set of activities, those for which one is generally not paid to perform. (Sessoms et al., 1975, p. 17.) [2]

From the middle of the nineteenth century to the middle of the twentieth century the average workweek in the United States dropped from about seventy to about forty hours. The amount of free time increased proportionally, not withstanding certain limitations due to increased travel time from and to work, second jobs, and other factors. This increase in free time has been the concern of both government agencies and recreation and park professionals, and has led to the development of a strong recreation movement.

The challenges of the recreation movement, however, go far beyond the need of coping with increased free time. Kraus (1978, pp. 9–17) has categorized these under the following headings:

> The Challenge of Increased Leisure, . . . of Education for Leisure, The Needs of Special Populations, Environmental and Energy-related Needs, The Challenge of Planning, . . . of Fiscal Support, . . . of Professional Development, . . . of the Cities, . . . of Change.

There is little doubt that the recreation movement, through its various organizations and affiliations, has carried the major burden and responsibility for setting policy and determining the philosophy in respect to free time. Given the rate of change prevailing in post-industrial society, the role of this movement in helping people to adjust to newly emerging lifestyles and social structures is likely to increase even more.

Self-fulfillment

One of the striking developments of the twentieth century has been the emergent cry for self-fulfillment. Self-actualization has become a slogan, a movement that has produced innumerable methods and techniques designed to achieve that goal. Whether this is a reflection of increased living standards, as predicted by Maslow's (1954) concept of a hierarchy of needs, whether it reflects a revolt against materialism or the influx of some other spiritual revival movement, there is no doubt that the majority of people, at least in this country, are starting to look for more than the basic needs in life.

The role of leisure in that goal is recognized by some. "There is no aspect of human behavior which holds greater potential for self-fulfillment than does the use of leisure" (Boyack, 1973). Unfortunately, the author of this statement is compelled to add, "Yet, there is perhaps no other aspect which is less understood or more underrated." Once again, we are confronted with the competing role of work and leisure and the as yet slow recognition that work (that is, paid employment) no longer suffices as the prime source of self-fulfillment.

This demand for personal development is recognized, at least by some, as being here to stay. "In our opinion, to deny the new needs of the personality, which appear with the production of leisure by post-industrial society, is a fantasy" (Dumazedier, 1971, p. 205).[3] Once a person or a society has grasped the potential satisfactions derivable from the freedom from toil, a return to a former state of existence is no longer an acceptable alternative, either in practical or even in moral terms.

Sports

The *New York Times*, again like every major newspaper in the country, has a Sunday edition section on sports (sec. 5). For many, sports are probably linked as closely to leisure as art is for others. And in terms of individual and shared interests, there is probably nothing that can equal sports, at least in this society.

Each morning the American seats himself at the breakfast table, glances at the headlines in his newspaper, and turns quickly to the sports page where what he reads may seem more appealing than the food before him or the woman who serves it. He performs his weekly tasks in perfunctory manner, but when it comes time for sports he comes alive and is transformed by his enthusiasm. Perhaps ours is more nearly the sporting nation than an affluent nation, a capitalist country, a political democracy, or anything else. (Beisser, 1967, pp. 226–227.)

The reader will probably agree with this characterization of the American scene, although one might wonder whether it also applies to the American who seats herself at the breakfast table and looks at the man she shares more than the table with. We shall let our readers come to their own decision on that point. In any case there is no doubt that sports take up a tremendous proportion of our individual and national attention, in terms of time, money, and energy expended.

The Elderly

A strange thing may be happening. The elderly may once more come into a position where they will be viewed as having something worthwhile to teach the younger generation. For a while it has seemed that anything worth knowing has stemmed from the domain of the young: those that are up-to-date on the latest developments and at least one step ahead of obsolescence. Suddenly, however, it is the elderly who are first and foremost experiencing a lifestyle that reflects the future. A life in which the job has lost its meaning: where life cannot be centered around a job and cannot draw meaning from a job; and where free time cannot be defined in terms of a job either. It is the elderly who are learning first how to cope with free time without the resources of a job.

In addition, there are many other problems that the elderly may have experienced and that are in many ways related to the issue of leisure. Most of these are problems of separation: retirement—a separation from one's job; divorce—a separation from one's spouse; widow(er)hood—a similar yet different separation; the "empty nest" phenomenon—one's children leaving the home; and leaving a familiar environment—be it to move into a new job setting in a different town, or to move into an institutional setting because of declining health.

These factors and others lead to the two most common problems of the elderly: loneliness and loss of identity. Leisure counseling for the elderly has become an integral part of many age-oriented social programs, and we see an increasing awareness of the problems of the elderly on all levels of government (e.g., The White House Conference on Aging, 1971). Age-oriented activities and/or enterprises, such as senior citizen centers, "leisure villages," and political and social associations for the elderly are multiplying all across the country.

Tourism and the Leisure Market

Tourism, said to be the world's fastest growing industry, is now Canada's fifth largest earner of foreign revenues.

Tourism receipts in Canada in 1976 reached about $9.2 billion, about 5 per cent of the gross national product. (Tourism is everybody's business, 1977, p. 6.)

Leisure-time activities have become the nation's No. 1 industry, as measured by people's spending. Americans will spend more than 160 billion dollars on leisure and recreation in 1977.

By 1985 the total is expected to climb to 300 billions. (How Americans pursue happiness, 1977, p. 62.)

Tourism is a huge enterprise not only in Canada and the United States but in all other industrialized countries in the world as well. The scope of this industry is truly astonishing and spans (in the United States) such interest groups as the Air Transport Association of America, the American Automobile Association, the American Hotel and Motel Association, the American Society of Travel Agents, the Hotel and Restaurant Employees and Bartenders International Union, the International Association of Convention Bureaus, and many others. When we think of tourism, what comes to mind are travel, vacation, adventure, new and strange places, sunny beaches, quaint restaurants, and so on. And all this is usually thought of as taking place in our free time, or as many put it, "during our leisure." We are also aware of the fact that much business travel is taking on more and more of the flavor of tourism. Anyone who has ever attended a national convention of any kind can attest to that fact.

That people in the United States and other industrialized countries spend record amounts on so-called leisure activities and recreational pursuits is equally well known and documented by economic reports. And the market is bullish. A *U. S. News & World Report* (January 15, 1979) headline reads "Leisure: Where No Recession Is in Sight."

Tourism and the leisure industry are booming, and that is good for the economy and the country; but is it good for the individual? Is tourism always a positive experience? Is it as rewarding as it could be? Are the benefits derived from our "leisure" expenditures equal to the satisfactions gained? Are all the billions spent counterbalanced by the experiences bought at such high stakes? Could and should these resources be utilized in a more effective manner? These and many other similar questions require serious consideration. It is clear that the leisure professional will have an important role to play in this context.

Leisure, indeed, has many faces. We have sketched a number of the more obvious areas that are relevant to leisure. Many more could be added. Leisure truly permeates every sphere of our society as well as our personal lives. This is not only true of the present, but of the past, and even more so of the future. What then are we up against if we intend to study this all-encompassing phenomenon? Can we come to grips with a topic that seems to have no boundaries? Do we have to include every discipline in our efforts to understand the nature of leisure and the issues and problems connected with it? To some degree, the answer must be yes. As Kaplan (1960, p. 289) pointed out, "Ultimately a theory of leisure can be little less than a theory of man and a theory of the emerging culture," and as he reemphasized later, "A theory of leisure is essentially a theory of history" (1975, p. 39).

SUMMARY

A full treatment of the topic of leisure would require an encyclopedic effort. Indeed, a handbook of leisure, to be written by experts in the various related disciplines, is very much called for. The purpose of this chapter has been to convey this fact to the reader, to emphasize the complexity of the issues, and to make it clear that the student of leisure must have a broad perspective and not be restricted by his or her own respective standpoint. Claire Louise Hobbs (1973) used the well-known story of the elephant and the blind men to get this point across.

> The first blind man felt the elephant's leg and said, "The elephant is like a tree." The second blind man felt his tail and said, "The elephant is like a rope." The third blind man felt his trunk and said, "The elephant is like a snake." The fourth blind man felt his side and said, "The elephant is like a wall." And they were all right . . . or were they? Didn't they miss the WHOLE TRUTH?

Is it ever possible to overcome one's individual blindness? In this book I attempt to look at the total phenomenon of leisure; yet I am writing it from a specific perspective. I am dealing primarily with the experience of leisure: the meaning leisure has, how people feel about it or are affected by it, and how they act as a result of these meanings and feelings. Leisure understood as a state of mind will be the unifying thread throughout the following chapters, as we consider areas of theoretical relevance and practical application.

ENDNOTES

[1] "By the operational definition of a concept we mean the ability to measure it objectively, to point to it or identify it unambiguously in the physical environment, or to state the conditions which will bring it about" (Neulinger, 1974a, p. 9. Courtesy of Charles C Thomas, Publisher, Springfield Illinois).

[2] At this point this quote is offered merely to demonstrate further the diversity of contexts to which the term *leisure* relates. In line with our later discussions, however, it is important to note that in a succeeding paragraph the authors "suggest using *recreation* as a noun only when one is describing the recreation experience" and that they state that "as with leisure, the recreation experience can be seen two ways: as a state of mind and as an activity set" (Sessoms et al., 1975, p. 17).

[3] We are using the term *post-industrial society* in this volume with its generally accepted meaning of referring to a society so technologically advanced that the majority of the labor force no longer needs to be involved in the manufacture of goods. Instead the majority is engaged in providing services, such as education, entertainment, government, health care and welfare, and research and development. Two other characteristics usually associated with such societies are the increasing importance of the professional, scientific, and technical occupations and the role of theoretical knowledge in the solution of societal and social problems.

2

Leisure definitions and conceptualizations

Question: *"How do you define it [leisure]?"*
Answer: *"Allow me not to answer this question."*
    Joffre Dumazedier (1974*b*).

The purpose of the first chapter was to make the reader aware of the diversity of circumstances in which we encounter leisure. Leisure is not confined to one or even several areas of life; it may appear at any moment at any place. It is not the concern of one discipline but of many. And it is known under many names; or we might say it is sometimes disguised, taking on many different forms.

In this chapter an attempt will be made to bring order into the universe. The fact that the term *leisure* is being used with many different meanings has obviously not escaped the professionals in this area and quite a number of recent publications have categorized and described different conceptualizations of leisure. Since these sources are relatively available, I shall merely mention a number of them and leave it up to the reader to check them out in detail. I shall then focus on two authors who have established conceptual schemes of their own. Finally, I shall present the conceptualization that both reflects and determines my particular way of looking at the phenomenon of leisure.

CATEGORIES OF LEISURE CONCEPTUALIZATIONS

The fact that the phenomenon of leisure has relevance to so many different spheres of life is reflected in the many ways the term is used. Each systematic user of the term attempts to give it a special flavor, a special set of meanings that relate specifically to the situation dealt with and the user's viewpoint. This is the case with any multidimensional concept. One solution to the problem might be the introduction of subscripts, such as $leisure_1$, $leisure_2$, $leisure_3$, etc. $Leisure_1$ might then refer to the concept as used by the economist, $leisure_2$ by the sociologist, $leisure_3$ by the psychologist, and so on. Or alternatively, $leisure_1$ could stand for free time, $leisure_2$ for a leisure-related activity, $leisure_3$ for a state of mind, and so on. Attempts of this kind have been tried with the concept *intelligence,* but did not seem to catch on. I doubt that they would for leisure.

To state the issue differently, the definition of leisure tends to reflect not so much what leisure "really is," but rather what the philosophy, special area of interest, and intent of the definer are. The following categorizations of leisure viewpoints make this fairly clear.

A Fourfold Categorization (Kraus)

Richard Kraus, a pioneer in the recreation field, outlines four views of leisure (Kraus, 1978, pp. 38–41).

I. The Classical View of Leisure. This view is best represented by Aristotle, who according to Kraus regarded leisure as "a state of being in which activity is performed for its own sake." It reflects the philosophy of an intellectual elite, for whom the modern concept of work did not exist. It is difficult to relate this conceptualization to the modern use of leisure, since the conditions of society are now so totally different. Each term one uses in such comparisons needs first to be defined in terms of both the ancient and the present society. The authors who have managed best to present these views are de Grazia (1962) and Pieper (1963). Probably the most critical aspect of this classical view is the fact that leisure is considered to be "a state of mind," and that this state is brought about through activities engaged in for their own sake. Neulinger's (1974a; 1976a) conceptualization of leisure attempts to phrase these conditions in modern terminology, and may thus be considered a direct offspring of this orientation.

II. Leisure as a Symbol of Social Class. This view of leisure is traced back to Thorstein Veblen's *The Theory of the Leisure Class* (1899), which both described the conditions that brought about this view as well as helped to establish this particular meaning of the term. Leisure here becomes the prerogative of an elite class that uses it to establish and maintain its position through such means as *conspicuous consumption*. It is a negative view of leisure and has, in combination with the teachings of the Protestant Ethic, contributed to the negative image that leisure has achieved.

III. Leisure as a Form of Activity. According to this view, leisure is a nonwork *activity* in which people engage during their free time. This leisure activity may serve specific functions, such as relaxation, entertainment, and personal development (Dumazedier, 1967). The criterion of classification is the nature of the activity engaged in, primarily as it contrasts to that of work.[1]

IV. Leisure as Unobligated Time. Leisure here is viewed as unobligated or discretionary time. This is the most frequently used definition in the sociological literature and is often referred to as the residual definition of leisure: time left over after existence and subsistence needs have been taken care of. The delineation, however, of what existence- and subsistence-related activities are exactly, is not always that simple.

Kraus (1978) recognizes these conceptual difficulties and adds a discussion of "Semi-Leisure" (Dumazedier's concept, to be discussed shortly), of the role of values in leisure, and of the problem of having the definition of leisure depend on the existence of work. We shall postpone a consideration of the advantages and disadvantages of the four conceptualizations presented until the end of this section, at which point the reader will have obtained an overview of the other orientations as well.

A Fivefold Categorization (Murphy)

James F. Murphy (1975; Murphy et al., 1973), a prolific writer involved both in the philosophical and applied aspects of leisure, describes five views of leisure.[2]

The Classical or Traditional View. Same as category I of the Kraus (1978) categorization, with "heavy emphasis upon contemplation, engagement in debate and politics in a search for knowledge and cultural enlightenment" (Murphy et al., 1973, p. 8). De Grazia (1964) and Pieper (1963) are again listed as the main advocates of this position.

The Discretionary-Time Concept. Same as category IV in Kraus (1978), this view holds that "leisure is the portion of time which remains after work and the basic requirements for existence have been satisfied" (Murphy et al., 1973, pp. 8–9).

Leisure as a Social Instrument. Murphy traces this view to Kaplan (1971), a view that sees leisure "as a means of meeting needs of the poor through VISTA and Community Action Programs and as a *threshold* for the disadvantaged to help them actualize social needs and develop self-help skills" (Murphy et al., 1973, p. 9). It could be called a functional view of leisure and is also expressed in Kaplan's later writings where, for example, he speaks of commitment to self-growth as well as to serving others (Kaplan, 1975, p. 394).

The Antiutilitarian View of Leisure. Murphy names Gray (1971) as having identified this view and refers to Walter Kerr's (1962). *The Decline of Pleasure* as an articulation of this position. The antiutilitarian view sees leisure as a state of mind and as an end in itself, needing no further justification or utilitarian function. Quite understandably, such a view would not align itself well with the Protestant Ethic. According to that orientation, a person's deeds are to be relevant to salvation, instrumental in fulfilling one's "calling." Thus, engaging in an activity merely for its own sake or even for self-development could not be viewed positively, unless it also was performed *in order to* come a step closer to salvation. The antiutilitarian view frees leisure of this obligation.

The Holistic Model of Leisure. Murphy quotes the following description of this view: "Leisure in the holistic orientation is seen as a complex of multiple relationships involving certain choices which indicate both societal and individual aspirations as well as life styles" (Hendricks and Burdge, 1972). This view of leisure seems to be an all-encompassing one. Its multidimensional conceptualization attempts to deal with every aspect of the person as well as society. Rather than emphasizing the separation of the different aspects of life and society, it looks at their interaction and sees a resulting fusion, such as between work and nonwork. "According to the holistic concept of leisure, the meanings of work and leisure are inextricably related" (Murphy, 1974, p. 5).

A Sixfold Categorization (Kaplan)

Kaplan (1975), whose own conceptualization of leisure we shall treat shortly, distinguishes six traditions of leisure.*

The Humanistic Model of Leisure. This view corresponds to the classical view as stated in the previous categorizations, and is also seen as represented by de Grazia and Pieper. In addition, however, Kaplan also relates it to contemporary Chinese philosophy, as exemplified by the writings of Lin Yutang (1937). Kaplan presents such tantalizing tidbits of oriental wisdom as "the man who is wisely idle is the most cultured man"; "the wisest man is therefore he who loafs most gracefully"; and "time is useful because it is not being used" (pp. 20, 21). A comparison of Chinese (or oriental) and Western conceptions of leisure certainly would be a most fascinating and worthwhile task, but could not be undertaken in a meaningful manner without a comparison of the total picture of these two types of civilizations.

The Therapeutic Model of Leisure. According to this view leisure is seen as a means, an instrument, or a control. Kaplan includes in this category not only leisure as used for therapeutic purposes, but also Kraus's (1978) "leisure as a symbol of social class," that is, leisure in Thorstein Veblen's sense, and J. Murphy's (1975) "leisure as a social instrument." As an example of the latter he quotes several East European communist theoreticians who ascribe to leisure clearly a functional status, both as it serves the individual personality and as it benefits society at large.

The Quantitative Model of Leisure. This view corresponds to the sociological residual model of leisure, as outlined in the two previous categorizations, and there referred to as "discretionary time." It lends itself well to quantification, as exemplified by the many time-budget studies, but carries serious problems of defining just of what that residual should consist.

The Institutional Conception of Leisure. This view is said to distinguish leisure "from such behavior and value patterns as the religious, marital, educational, or political" (p. 18). In some ways, Dumazedier's recent conception of leisure may fit this category (1974a), as he attempts to give it the "distinctiveness of a special branch of sociology" (p. 208).

The Epistemological Conception of Leisure. According to this view,

> leisure relates activities and meanings to the assumptive, analytic, and aesthetic views of the world: that is, those that repeat and confirm the world, like playing a familiar game; those that examine the world, like a political book; and those that transform the world, like painting a picture or marching in protest. (P. 18.)

Kaplan does not elaborate much on this conception and it does not seem to carry the same weight as the other five.

The Sociological Conception of Leisure. According to this view, "nothing is definable as leisure per se, and almost anything is definable as leisure, given a synthesis of elements as suggested" (p. 19). This is a very broad conception of the term and comes closest to Murphy's (1974) "holistic model of leisure."

A Twofold Categorization (Neulinger)

Neulinger (1974a), in examining various conceptions of leisure, recognizes a functional view of leisure ("what leisure does for the person rather than what it is," p. 7) as well as a multidimensional, quasi-holistic one (for example, Kaplan's 1960 approach). But his two primary categories of leisure conceptualizations are as follows.

The Subjective Definition of Leisure. This view includes the classical or traditional conceptions of leisure, as outlined by de Grazia (1962) and Pieper (1963), and in general any view that portrays leisure as a state of mind. To the degree that the mind, or more appropriately *experience,* is the scientific domain of psychology, this view may also be called a *psychological* one. This is not meant to imply that according to this view leisure is to be investigated by psychologists only. The study of experience, and in a broader sense of the mind, obviously requires an interdisciplinary approach, especially when we deal with the content of experience, such as the religious experience, and so on. However, when dealing with process aspects, psychology is the science that concerns itself with the appropriate methodology.

The Objective Definition of Leisure. This conceptualization includes the views that in the previous categorizations were referred to as the *quantitative, residual,* or *discretionary-time* concepts. As pointed out before, it is the model most frequently used by sociologists until fairly recently. It enables a relatively easy quantification of leisure and has been widely used in survey-type research, such as time-budget studies.

Now for some general remarks regarding these categorizations, as well as the various views of leisure themselves. First, the categorizations: Are mutually exclusive categories used within each system of categorization? Considering the complexity of the topic involved, my answer would be yes. Are the systems themselves exclusive of each other? Obviously not, and the similarities were pointed to in our descriptions of the systems. Are the systems exhaustive? Again, the answer must be no, simply because there never is a limit to the number of possible categorizations. One can always come up with yet another criterion according to which one can order phenomena or viewpoints. The main question is, are they useful to the student of leisure? The answer is undoubtedly yes. They help one to obtain an overview of the field and to recognize each writer's perspective.

As to the various views of leisure themselves, we can ask the question, Is one more valid than another? This is as good a place as any to stress the fact that such a question is as meaningless as asking, Is test X valid? Validity refers to a specific purpose, to a particular criterion, in the case of a test. Thus a test may be valid to predict "typing," or "success in college," or "attendance at outdoor concerts." Without specifying the criterion, we cannot know whether a test is or is not valid.

Similarly, the various conceptualizations of leisure may each be optimal for certain purposes, and quite dysfunctional for others. The question really becomes one of choosing the right view for the given purpose. A proper understanding of each view should help one in this respect.

We shall next deal in some detail with three specific conceptualizations of leisure. They lie on a continuum of approaches from very broad to quite narrow. The first is a truly grand approach that attempts to take it all in. This requires a scheme that covers the whole range of human endeavor, indeed a herculean task. Kaplan's (1975) system is of that type. The second position, that of Dumazedier (1974a), is a more restricted one; it sets a clear limit on the subject boundaries it intends to stay within and the range of phenomena to be covered. Dumazedier limits himself to the sociological domain and even within this tries to establish clear boundaries of what he sees as relevant to leisure, and what not. My own approach (Neulinger, 1974a; 1976a), the third one to be discussed, is an even narrower one. It is restricted to a psychological phenomenon, namely the experience of leisure.

LEISURE AS A THEORY OF HISTORY

> Leisure, we might say, consists of relatively self-determined activity-experience that falls into one's economically free-time roles, that is seen as leisure by participants, that is psychologically pleasant in anticipation and recollection, that potentially covers the whole range of commitment and intensity, that contains characteristic norms and constraints, and that provides opportunities for recreation, personal growth, and service to others. (Kaplan, 1975, p. 26.)* [3]

Compare the above definition (or would it be called a conceptualization? a construct?) of leisure with an example of one that used to be generally accepted by most sociologists not so long ago:

> By leisure, we mean all time beyond the existence and subsistence time. (Clawson, 1964, p. 1.)

There is little doubt that the latter definition seems to make life for the student of leisure much easier. But simplicity can and should never be an end in itself. When the phenomenon studied is complex, so must be its description and explanation. The law of gravitation is indeed a very simple one, and can be expressed in a simple formula, *if* we are applying it to a vacuum. Apply that law to a leaf falling to the ground, and we suddenly have to add a myriad of other factors into our formulation. We are now treating the event within the context of the whole universe. And this is what Kaplan is attempting to do with his construct of leisure.

Just what does the first quote above mean? What does it say, and even more importantly, what does it not say? Kaplan spends the next three pages (and, one might say, the rest of his book) on an elaboration of this statement. The critical and first component is clearly the word *self-determined*. While Kaplan recognizes that self-determination is always a matter of degree, or may even be illusory, it is the one and only condition predicated on all the other qualifications of the construct offered later on. By using the term *activity-experience*, Kaplan attempts to include both behavioral and phenomenological aspects of leisure, opening the door to a multidisciplinary approach.

Leisure is placed into "one's economically free-time roles." This implies that leisure is not necessarily the same as nonwork time or simply equated with free time. But what exactly *is* meant by that phrase?

Leisure must be "seen as leisure by participants." This requirement is circular and raises an interesting question. Do participants already have a definition of leisure, beyond this one, that they can use to determine whether the given behavior-experience is leisure? Or is this implied on an unconscious level, in the sense that animals *know* when they are playing or when they are attacking each other in earnest? I would assume that something of the latter kind is implied.

Leisure is "psychologically pleasant in anticipation and recollection." This qualification affirms the generally agreed-on conception that leisure is a positive experience.

Leisure "potentially covers the whole range of commitment and intensity." This statement raises leisure beyond the level of mere fun, amusement, or even play. Leisure may involve very serious commitments and the full intensity of emotion of which a person may be capable.

Leisure "contains characteristic norms and constraints." This statement emphasizes that the leisure activity-experience takes place within a social context, and is thus subject to the constraints that prevail on any form of behavior-experience. It is another way of saying that the study of leisure must take into account all the interacting factors and forces of society, both physical and social. It is a reminder of the fact that life is complex!

Leisure "provides opportunities for recreation, personal growth, and service to others." This statement also asserts the seriousness of leisure and serves as a clue to the ways in which leisure may supply meaning to a person's life.

This, then, is an outline of a conceptualization of leisure. It treats the topic of leisure clearly in a multidimensional manner and requires a multidisciplinary approach. To come to grips with the actual task of integrating such approaches and providing the framework for testable hypotheses, Kaplan furnishes a model, "a series of fourfold systems

Table 2.1. *Conceptualization of Leisure in Society*

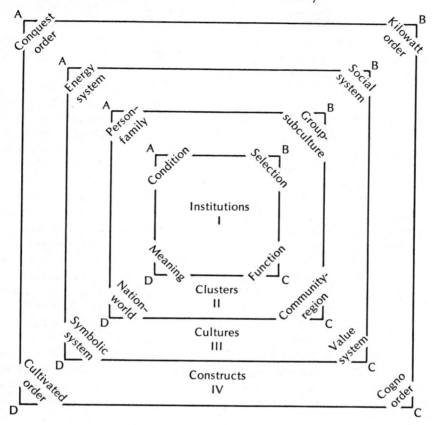

Source: M. Kaplan, *Leisure: Theory and policy.* (New York: Wiley, 1975), p. 33, chart 1. Copyright © 1975 John Wiley & Sons. Reprinted by permission of John Wiley & Sons, Inc.

called institutions, clusters, cultures, and constructs" (p. 30). This model, labeled "Conceptualization of Leisure in Society" (see Table 2.1), is the tool suggested for use in our work with leisure.

It needs to be repeated that the model is not one of leisure per se, but a paradigm that can be applied to any one of several social institutions, such as the religious or the educational. The model consists of a system of four concentric layers (squares), each with four components. The inner layer (*Institutions*) deals with individual and/or intrapsychic components (*Condition, Selection, Function,* and *Meaning*). The next layer (*Clusters*) relates to social groups, ranging from *Person-family* to *Nation-world*. The third layer (*Cultures*) involves societal systems—*Energy, Social, Value,* and *Symbolic*. Finally, the fourth layer (*Constructs*) uses order concepts labeled *Conquest, Kilowatt, Cogno,* and *Cultivated.* Each of the components can be viewed as a variable—or even cluster of variables (e.g., *Conditions* includes age, *sex, income,* etc.)—and the model thus invites the systematic exploration of all possible interactions of these variables as they relate to the institution of leisure.

The model provides an opportunity for input from every conceivable source of influence on behavior-experience, be it personal, societal, or environmental. At this level, the model is primarily descriptive. By that I mean it lists and enumerates the various components. It may be compared to the approach of Lewin (1951), whose theory was often labeled descriptive rather than predictive, and who seemed to have viewed as his main task an exact and detailed elaboration of the life-space. Behavior *B* was seen as a function of the person *P* and the environment *E,* so that $B = f(P,E)$, and the psychologist tries to describe the forces that either pull the person towards goals or restrain him from them. The problem with Lewin's model, and similarly with the present one, is that the model does not, and cannot, include clues as to the valence, either positive or negative, of the various components of the model. In other words, the forces that operate within the model are dependent on the nature of the components, the characteristics of the person involved, and their interaction. A lot of painstaking work is required to establish empirically just what these valences are, and how they will interact with each other.

The presentation of the model here is sketchy. Anyone interested in working with it must obviously consult the original source. My purpose is to make the reader aware of its existence and to encourage its use. The final judgment of its usefulness will result not from a theoretical discussion of its merits but from whether its application leads to new insights, clarifications, and better predictions and policy formulations.

LEISURE AS A SPECIAL BRANCH OF SOCIOLOGY

> I shall call leisure any activity which offers four properties: two "negative" ones, defined by reference to the obligations imposed by social institutions and two "positive" ones, defined by reference to personality needs. . . .
>
> The system of characteristics discussed below . . . constitutes leisure, which would not exist without it. This is my basic tenet.
>
> > *Liberating Character:* . . . Leisure is freedom *from a certain number and from certain kinds of obligations.* . . . freedom from the basic primary obligations derived from the basic units of society: family, socio-political and socio-spiritual institutions.

Disinterested Character: Basically leisure serves no lucrative end, unlike work, no utilitarian end, unlike household duties, no ideological or proselytising end, unlike political or spiritual obligations.

Hedonistic Character: The search for a state of satisfaction is the prime condition of leisure: "this interests me."

Personal Character: It is connected with the realization, either encouraged or hampered, of man's full potential, conceived as an end in itself, whether it is related to social needs or in contradiction with them.

(Three individual needs are satisfied: (1) recovery from physical or nervous strains; (2) entertainment; and (3) freeing of creative powers and going beyond the confines of the self.) (Quoted and paraphrased from Dumazedier, 1974a, pp. 73–76.)

Dumazedier's approach to leisure is scholarly, disciplined, and focused. While he feels that "the time is not yet ripe to devise a sociological theory of leisure . . ." (1974a, p. 3), he sets out at least to identify and justify the sociology of leisure as a distinct branch of sociology (p. 208).

He approaches the question of definition by delineating four types of definitions, and then placing his definition appropriately. Since his is based on the nature of the activities involved, he begins by distinguishing types of activities, as follows:

A) remunerated work, B) family obligations, C) socio-spiritual and socio-political obligations, D) activities external to these institutional obligations and mainly oriented towards self-fulfillment. (Pp. 67, 68.)

He then classifies leisure definitions on the basis of their including one or more of these elements. Definition 1 includes all four categories of behavior. "Any behaviour in each category may represent leisure, even work" (p. 68). This type of definition corresponds to what we have previously identified as a holistic one. Dumazedier sees this type as a psychological rather than sociological definition, and thus rejects it as suitable for his purposes. Definition 2 excludes category A, remunerated work, but includes everything else. It thus equates leisure with nonwork. This definition is said to be most common among economists and found in most of Karl Marx's writings. Dumazedier views this definition as influenced too much by the sociology of work, and "less and less apt to deal with the specific problems of leisure in advanced industrial societies" (p. 69). Definition 3 excludes categories A and B, but still includes C and D. Dumazedier objects to this definition on the basis of the major changes taking place in the nature of sociospiritual and sociocultural obligations. Many obligations seem to be losing their strength, yet the same activities may persist now in response to some personal rather than societal need. Dumazedier feels that "such a definition of leisure covering socio-spiritual and socio-political obligations would merge political sociology and the sociology of religion with the sociology of leisure, letting the former two handle problems for which they are not competent" (p. 70). He suggests that the term *free time* be used to cover this conception, namely, time freed from the double duties of work and family. Such free time would have no normative meaning, and would be distinct from the concept of *leisure*. Definition 4 excludes activities A, B, and C, and includes only D, activities oriented towards self-fulfillment. Dumazedier quite unambiguously states his preference for this type of definition: "I prefer to reserve the word leisure for the time whose content is oriented towards self-fulfillment as an ultimate end" (p. 71). Lest the reader wonder whether Dumazedier is slipping into a psychological definition, be assured he is not. "This available time is not the result of an individual decision, but above all the product of economic and social evolution" (p. 71). "This time is granted to the individual by society, when he has complied with his occupational, family, socio-spiritual and socio-political obligations, in accordance with current social norms" (p. 71).

Dumazedier sees four time periods as specifically related to leisure: the end of the day, the weekend, the end of the year (holidays) and the end of life (retirement). These periods of time are increasingly dominated by the dynamics of leisure, rather than that of work. This is a rather important and often critical point, for example, as it relates to the retired.

Having set the stage, Dumazedier next outlines his specific conceptualization of leisure, which is represented in the quotes at the beginning of this section, and which the reader might wish to reread and ponder at this point.

One important concept needs to be added: *semi-leisure*. Under his discussion of "Disinterested Character," Dumazedier recognizes the fact that the "disinterested character" of an activity may not be absolute, i.e., it may be partial, a matter of degree. The activity may be partially geared toward profit making, a utilitarian end, or some form of commitment. In that case, the activity is defined as *semi-leisure*, "a mixed activity in which leisure mingles with an institutional obligation" (p. 75).

The above constitutes a minimal presentation of Dumazedier's conceptions. The quality of his theorizing and the implications of his insights and observations can only be obtained by a thorough reading of his major work.[4]

LEISURE AS A PSYCHOLOGICAL CONCEPT

> Leisure has one and only one essential criterion, and that is the
> condition of perceived freedom. . . . there are at least two fur-
> ther dimensions that may be useful in distinguishing among dif-
> ferent types of leisure: the *motivation* for the activity (*extrinsic*
> to *intrinsic*), and the goal of the activity (*instrumental* to *final*).
> (Neulinger, 1974a, pp. 15–16.)*
>
> *Pure Leisure:* A state of mind brought about by an activity freely
>   engaged in and done for its own sake.
> *Leisure-Work:* A state of mind brought about by an activity en-
>   gaged in freely, and providing both intrinsic and extrinsic
>   rewards.
> *Leisure-Job:* A state of mind brought about by an activity engaged
>   in freely, but [where] the satisfaction derived stems not from
>   the activity but from its consequences. (Neulinger, 1976a.)

By leisure as a psychological concept I mean leisure conceived
of as a state of mind or an experience.[5] The conceptualization of leisure, in this sense, implies two tasks. One is to define the difference
between *leisure* and *nonleisure,* which in turn means stating the conditions that will bring about either state. The second task is a comparison of different states of mind, including leisure, to determine similarities and differences, amounts of overlap, and perhaps the development
of some hierarchical scheme of states of mind. Some of these other
states might be anxiety, boredom, dissonance, excitement, pleasure,
and happiness. Our present intent is to deal with the first of these tasks.

The model elaborated here was originally developed using three
variables (Neulinger, 1974a), but was later revised by dropping the
variable *goal of activity* (Neulinger, 1976a). It had been stated from the
start that "we do not consider this variable a critical differentiator of
leisure and nonleisure, but see it as useful in strengthening the paradigm's predictive power" (Neulinger, 1974a, p. 20). Other variables had
also been suggested as possible additions to the model.

The purpose of the model is to identify critical variables of the
leisure experience, so that we can understand, predict, and influence
behavior in this domain. The function of the paradigm is to classify
states of mind, and *not* people, activities, or life situations. These states
may be of varying duration—seconds, minutes, hours, or even longer.
Most likely, the person will fluctuate among different states, drift from
one into another. It is important to keep this in mind, since one in-
advertently and, it seems, inevitably falls into the habit of classifying
people, their lifestyles, or their activities into leisure and nonleisure

* Courtesy of Charles C Thomas, Publisher, Springfield, Illinois.

categories. One may want to do this, but then one no longer acts within the framework of leisure as a state of mind.

One other important point. The paradigm is an abstraction from real life. It uses variables in a dichotomous way, an either/or fashion. In concrete situations, however, it is always a question of more or less, a matter of degree. In applying the model, one may wish to compensate for that by creating more than two levels for each variable.

A paradigm of leisure as a psychological concept is presented in Table 2.2. The primary dimension of leisure is *perceived freedom*. Note the emphasis on *perceived*. This helps to avoid the philosophical problem of the definition of freedom, and permits us to focus on a phenomenological level of analysis. Everyone knows the difference between doing something because one has to and doing something because one wants to. We are not concerned with distinguishing whether such a perception of freedom is of "true" freedom, or only the illusion of it. This difference may be irrelevant, as Lefcourt (1973) has

Table 2.2. *A Paradigm of Leisure: A Subjective Definition*

Freedom					
Perceived Freedom			Perceived Constraint		
Motivation			Motivation		
Intrinsic	Intrinsic and Extrinsic	Extrinsic	Intrinsic	Intrinsic and Extrinsic	Extrinsic
(1) Pure Leisure	(2) Leisure-Work	(3) Leisure-Job	(4) Pure Work	(5) Work-Job	(6) Pure Job
Leisure			Nonleisure		

◄──────────── State of Mind ──────────►

Source: Adapted from J. Neulinger, The need for and the implications of a psychological conception of leisure, *Ontario Psychologist*, 1976, 8, no. 2, p. 15.

argued. Illusions too have real consequences, and the crucial consequence of the illusion of freedom is leisure.

A similar relevant issue is the distinction between objective and subjective constraints. An example of the first type is a physical barrier such as a locked door: "I cannot leave this room because the door is locked." My knowledge of this fact influences my perception of the amount of freedom I have in this particular situation. An example of the second type of constraint is a norm, an internalized rule of behavior by which I abide: "I am not supposed to leave this room in the middle of a lecture." Such rules, whether they operate with or without my immediate awareness, will also influence my perception of freedom in any given situation. These two types of constraints may require different approaches if one wishes to deal with them in an individual's case. However, for purposes of exposition of the model, they have been treated as if they were the same.

The model, then, distinguishes between leisure and nonleisure states on the basis of the variable *perceived freedom*. It further qualifies these states in terms of a second variable, namely *motivation*. The behavior involved is categorized as either *intrinsic* or *extrinsic* (or both). If the satisfaction gained stems from the activity and not from a payoff or consequence therefrom, the behavior is judged to be intrinsically motivated. If the satisfaction comes from a payoff—if the activity itself is not the reward but only leads to a reward—then the activity is seen as extrinsically motivated. One engages in extrinsically motivated behavior *in order to*. On the other hand, outcomes are phenomenologically irrelevant for intrinsically motivated behavior. Since most real-life behavior has components of both intrinsic and extrinsic motivation, the model provides for mixed conditions, thus leading to six cells.

Pure Leisure. (cell 1)—a state of mind brought about by an activity freely engaged in and done for its own sake. This is leisure in the classical sense, "not fully realizable, and hence an ideal not alone an idea" (de Grazia, 1962, p. 5). Not only does it require a complete mastery of oneself in terms of total freedom from inner constraints, but it also implies the condition of being able to enjoy the satisfactions derived from intrinsic rewards without having to pay attention to potential extrinsic ones. Implicit is the understanding that the person's basic needs (Maslow, 1954) have been satisfied to such a degree that they no longer represent an issue.

Leisure-Work. (cell 2)—a state of mind brought about by an activity freely engaged in and providing both intrinsic and extrinsic rewards. The sense of leisure is present: one perceives oneself as the origin of one's behavior. The activity, however, is satisfying not only in itself, but also in terms of its consequences or payoffs.

Leisure-Job. (cell 3)—a state of mind brought about by an activity freely engaged in, but providing satisfaction only in terms of its consequences or payoffs. Recreation, in the literal sense, is an example: exercising in order to maintain one's health, not on doctor's orders but simply because one chooses to do so. Playing cards for the sake of winning money (without, however, being in financial need!), is another example.

The three cells above represent different types of leisure experiences. They all share the essential condition of leisure: the person perceives him- or herself as the originator of his or her behavior, as being able to quit whenever desired and of being under no pressure to continue.

Pure Work. (cell 4)—a state of mind characterized by an activity engaged in under constraint, but providing intrinsic rewards only. A state that comes very close to leisure in terms of felt satisfaction, yet lacks the essential ingredient: a sense of freedom. The student "turned on" by a homework assignment who does more than is necessary and a professor steeped in research yet aware of the need for a paycheck may both experience this state.

Work-Job. (cell 5)—a state of mind characterized by an activity engaged in under constraint and providing both intrinsic and extrinsic rewards. The degree of satisfaction will vary as a function of the proportion of intrinsic to extrinsic rewards.[6] But the awareness of constraints is present and thus makes this situation a nonleisure experience, no matter how satisfying. The average employment situation may produce this state, depending on the degree to which one is aware of one's lot as a worker, that is, one's inability to quit if so desired.

Pure Job. (cell 6)—a state of mind characterized by an activity engaged in under constraint and with no reward in and of itself, but only through a payoff resulting from it. This is the extreme opposite of pure leisure. The everyday situation that may produce this state is the job (paid employment) in its most negative connotation: a job one must do to earn a living and that provides no satisfaction whatsoever, except the paycheck.

The last three cells discussed represent nonleisure experiences. They all share a sense of constraint, a lack of perceived freedom, of being a *pawn* rather than an origin (deCharms, 1968).

The above outlines the skeleton of the model. A number of issues will require further consideration. There is the question of the independence or possible confounding of the two independent variables. Operational definitions and ways in which these variables have been investigated need to be discussed. Areas of relevant research have to be outlined. And last but not least, the implications of this model must be spelled out. All this will be done throughout the rest of this book. At this point, the reader is merely given the essentials of the model, so as to be able to make comparisons and have points of reference to the other conceptualizations of leisure presented.

This concludes our discussion of three particular conceptualizations of leisure. As with all models, they need improvements and constant updating. There are, of course, other conceptualizations of leisure (for example, Kelly, 1972, 1976; Nahrstedt, 1972; Parker, 1971, 1976), and many more are bound to spring forth with the recent upsurge of interest in leisure research. We shall also need models designed for specific areas, such as the economic or the political. Eventually, one may dream of the ultimate paradigm that subsumes all of the others. The final test of any such model will remain its usefulness for the understanding, prediction, and control of behavior.

SUMMARY

Recognizing the ubiquitousness of the phenomenon of leisure and the many ways in which the term has been used, we examined first a number of categorizations of leisure conceptualizations. The fourfold, fivefold, and sixfold categorizations, while differing in minor respects, showed considerable overlap and agreement in indicating that there is at least common ground among leisure professionals in their varying perceptions of leisure. Even the twofold categorization tended to encompass classes of the other systems, rather than cut across or through them. We suggested that these groupings reflect not so much what leisure "really is," but what the theoreticians' philosophy, area of specialization, and intent were.

The major leisure viewpoints seem to be the following:

The first is the *classical* or *traditional* conception of leisure—leisure as a state of mind. The origin of this conception was traced to the Greeks (specifically Aristotle); examples of modern advocates of this viewpoint are de Grazia and Pieper. Neulinger's model of leisure attempts to translate this orientation into contemporary scientific language. This conception was also called the *subjective* or *psychological* definition of leisure.

The *quantitative, discretionary time,* or *residual* model of leisure is the second major category. Used primarily by economists and sociologists, this model reflects the conception of most nonprofessionals as well, and tends to lead to an equation of leisure with free time. This model was also referred to as an *objective* one.

The *holistic* model of leisure seems to become more frequently used. It attempts to encompass all of life, and thus uses an eclectic approach, incorporating aspects of the different models as it sees fit.

Other viewpoints listed were *leisure as a symbol of social class, leisure as a form of activity* or the *institutional* conception of leisure, *leisure as a social instrument* or the *therapeutic* model, the *antiutilitarian* view, and the *epistemological* conception of leisure.

Which viewpoint is best or most valid? It was pointed out that an answer to that question requires a specific criterion of intent. What does one want to use the particular conception for? Depending on one's purpose, different viewpoints may be preferred. Three conceptualizations of leisure were then presented, each having quite distinct intents.

Kaplan's model of leisure is designed to deal with all aspects of life, societal and personal. It offers the potential to integrate the complexities of life into one theoretical scheme, useful for purposes of research, applied work, as well as for policy development and implications. For this purpose, leisure is treated as an institution, and the model allows one to examine the effect of different classes of variables on this institution, as well as the effect of that institution, i.e., leisure, on all the different classes of variables in return.

Dumazedier's approach restricts itself to the sociological domain and his intent is to delineate the sociology of leisure within that area as a well-defined discipline. His concern is the study of activities free from institutional obligations and devoted primarily towards self-fulfillment. These activities he sees characterized by certain qualities: *liberating, disinterested, hedonistic,* and *personal.*

Neulinger's model restricts itself to the psychological domain. Leisure as a state of mind is brought about by activities engaged in under conditions of *perceived freedom.* The quality of this leisure is further affected by the *motivation* for the activity, *intrinsic* as opposed to *extrinsic. Pure leisure, leisure-work,* and *leisure-job* are the three subcategories of leisure. *Pure work, work-job,* and *pure job* are three parallel subcategories of nonleisure. Further elaboration of this model and its implications will be found throughout the rest of the book.

The purpose of this chapter was to familiarize the reader with existing and potential frameworks of organization for the leisure domain. A theoretical structure using an approach that is at least consistent to itself is a necessary condition for a serious consideration of the potentials and problems existing in the area of leisure.

ENDNOTES

[1] Note, however, that Dumazedier (1967) excludes obligatory activities related to family and society, as well as nonwork activities.

[2] Murphy (1974) presents a sixfold categorization of leisure by adding the category *leisure as related to social class structure* (similar to Kraus, 1978, category II), and changing the present *leisure as a social instrument* category to *leisure as a nonwork activity,* with certain essential functions, as outlined by Dumazedier (1967). Murphy attempts to incorporate these six views into one "dynamic conceptualization of leisure" (1974, Figure 1, p. 11).

[3] For a review of *Leisure: Theory and Policy,* including a discussion of Kaplan's model of leisure, see Neulinger (1977, pp. 55–57).

[4] The reader may be interested in a comparison of Dumazedier's and Kaplan's conceptions, as seen and written by Kaplan (1975, pp. 44–48).

[5] There might be those who would argue that psychology is primarily concerned with behavior rather than "the mind" or experience. This is not the place to argue this point. Modern behaviorists, however, recognize that the patterns of behavior of the individual organism are critically dependent on its history, which is necessarily stored *in the organism* (Donald Mintz, The City College of New York: personal communication).

[6] This is not to deny the obvious potential satisfaction derived from extrinsic rewards. However, the interaction between intrinsic and extrinsic motivation is complex and as yet little understood. It has been the subject matter of much recent research and will be discussed later on in this volume.

3

Once more: what is leisure?

I have just taken the reader through a chapter which I consider necessary for the serious student of leisure, and which was designed to familiarize one with at least some of the different ways of dealing with the phenomenon. Only a few of the issues involved were presented, however, and there is still much left that has not been touched on and certainly not been resolved. I shall use this chapter to roam freely among the remaining questions and attempt to convey some feeling for the reasons why discrepant orientations exist or why they may have developed. This will be done in terms of a historical perspective as well as of the needs of contemporary society. Our journey will lead us to the concept of the *quality of life,* an issue that will be treated at great length throughout the book. The chapter will conclude with an impressionistic view of leisure that mirrors the issues touched on.

MORE VOICES

Leisure time is that period of time at the complete disposal of an individual, after he has completed his work and fulfilled his other obligations. The uses of this time are of vital importance. (Charter for leisure, 1972, p. 16.)

Whether or not I have successfully grasped the street-corner definition of leisure and recreation, the present analysis will be based on the uncomplicated assumption that leisure is simply and naively *free time* and that among ways it may be spent, one of the commendable ones is in play. (Haun, 1967, pp. 39–49.)

. . . for there should be a purpose or goal inherent in any leisure time activity. (English, 1967, pp. 105–111.)

Spare time is a part of the out-of-work time fund that is used for free activity, i.e., activity free from discharging obligatory duties and satisfying necessary needs. (Bolgov and Kalkei, 1974, p. 1.)

Leisure, it must be clearly understood, is a mental and spiritual attitude—it is not simply the result of external factors, it is not the inevitable result of spare time, a holiday, a week-end or a vacation. (Pieper, 1963, p. 40.)

YET ANOTHER FACE OF LEISURE

Work

> FIRST: The Mill will be put into operation 10 minutes before sunrise at all seasons of the year. The gate will be shut 10 minutes past sunset from the 20th of March to the 20th of September, at 30 minutes past 8 from the 20th of September to the 20th of March. Saturdays at sunset. (From "Rules & Regulations to be observed by all Persons employed in the factory of Amasa Whitney," Laird and Laird, 1964, fig. 13, p. 117.)

The year is 1830 and the working hours are long, from sunrise to sunset. The conditions of work are harsh and do not allow for personal freedom, individual expression or social interaction.

> NINTH: Anything tending to impede the progress of manufacturing in working hours, such as unnecessary conversation, reading, eating fruit, etc. etc., must be avoided.

Such is life in the factory and for an ever increasing number of people, this is to be their lot. One could argue that the farmer also works from sunrise to sunset. He does, and so does his wife and often his children. But there is a difference. The farmer's hours are determined by nature, the cycles of the seasons, the days, the conditions of the weather, and the nature of the task that needs to be accomplished. Within these hours, however, there are breaks; and the quality of the interaction among the farmer's co-workers, be they the family or outside help, is determined largely by the farmer himself.
' Work in the factory knows no natural cycles. There may be seasonal fluctuations brought about by changes in demand and supply but these are man-made and man-controlled. They might lead to layoffs, but hardly to many changes in the everyday work pattern. Work goes on from sunrise to sunset, with but brief breaks for meals, and the sense of personal control is at a minimum.

> FIFTEENTH: The hands will take breakfast, from the 1st of November to the last of March, before going to work—they will take supper from the 1st of May to the last of August, 30 minutes past 5 o'clock P.M.—from the 20th of September to the 20th of March between sundown and dark—25 minutes will be allowed for breakfast, 30 minutes for dinner, and 25 minutes for supper, and no more from the time the gate is shut till started again.

Given these conditions it is not surprising that free time has become a much cherished goal in the nineteenth century. It is the only period in which people working under these circumstances can engage in activities *they* want to do, they enjoy, and which can be an expression of themselves. Free time and leisure (i.e., the chance to do what you want to do, and doing it for its own sake) indeed has become one and the same.

Now let us move about one hundred years ahead.

> I regard the five-day week as an unworthy ideal. . . . More work and better work is a more inspiring and worthier motto than less work and more pay. . . . It is better not to trifle or tamper with God's laws. (John E. Edgerton, President of the National Association of Manufacturers, 1926, quoted by Swados, 1958, p. 353.)

Despite or perhaps because of the conditions described above, the gospel of work is still with us in 1926. Leisure has reached a low point as a value in our society. We live to work; work is the ideal and anything that promotes that ideal is worthy of our support. Anything that distracts from it is to be discouraged and frowned on. Leisure, seen as free time, may have its value as a means of restoring the worker to greater efficiency. But there are limits to the amount of such free time deemed good for the person, and too much free time can only lead to trouble.

It is hard to say at what point in time a statement like the previous quote would have started to sound ridiculous, at least to most of us. Apparently in 1926 a receptive audience could still be found. And this is not to say that you might not find even today any number of sympathetic ears for words of a similar nature.

Recently a new term has been coined for persons who tend to be totally enmeshed in their business or professional activities: *workaholics*. These have been described as "working the 100-hour week—and loving it" (Machlowitz, 1976). Such people have no free time in the usual sense of the word. As to whether they experience leisure, the reader must be aware by now that the answer to this depends on the definition of leisure used. According to a subjective conceptualization, most of such persons' work is likely to be leisure.

Let us conclude this sketch with the following quote, which expresses beautifully the importance of and need for a clarification of the concepts *leisure, work,* and *job.*

> It is often depressing how some men and women of wealth who work with spirit 18 hours a day—but against a background of security with freedom of movement in a hospitable or challenging environment at jobs which they freely choose and which they obviously enjoy—cannot understand how a man can get sick and tired of his dull, routine job after only 8 hours. (Perlis, 1961.)

THE FREE TIME–LEISURE DISTINCTION: IMPLICATIONS

There are three positions one can take on the issue of a free time–leisure distinction. (1) There is no distinction and the two terms may be used interchangeably. (2) There is a distinction which becomes relevant under certain conditions, but when this occurs people know anyhow what we mean, and the whole issue is not worth worrying about. Too much attention is paid to semantics! (3) There is a distinction between these two terms and their improper use has very serious implications.[1] Let us consider each of these positions in turn.

As to the first position, I doubt that there are many professionals left who would argue this case seriously, if pressed against the wall. Even somebody like Haun (1967), whose quote is presented in the section "More Voices" at the beginning of this chapter, does not seem to apply that definition to his own understanding of leisure, but rather to the person at "the street-corner"! And those who prefer to use a residual definition of leisure (for example, "leisure is *time beyond* that which is required for *existence,* the things which we must do, biologically, to stay alive . . . , and *subsistence,* the things we must do to make a living, as in work, or prepare to make a living, as in school," Meyer et al., 1969, p. 29) tend to state quite unambiguously that leisure and discretionary time are not synonymous, although they are related concepts (e.g., Sessoms, 1976).

The problem really lies between positions 2 and 3. Position 2 is the prevalent one, at least so far as one might deduce from professional writings. Most authors profess to draw a distinction between the terms, but then use one when they seem to imply the other. I have often fallen into that trap myself. I used to speak and write of the problem of leisure when I really meant the problem of free time. Leisure, as a positive state of mind, can never be a problem. The case is analogous to that of health. Health is never a problem; it is always the absence of health that constitutes the problem. You can never have too much health, or, to put it more appropriately, you can never be too healthy.[2] Similarly, you can never experience too much leisure, but you certainly can have too much free time. The reader will have no problem locating such inconsistencies in the usage of the terms in the literature, particularly in the recent outpouring of material on leisure education and leisure counseling. For example, we find statements about improving the quality of life *in* leisure, or *during* leisure. What is meant here by leisure? Is it intended to mean free time, or part of free time? Is this all it is supposed to mean, or does the author wish to include more into the meaning of leisure? Is the term used with the same meaning throughout any given article? To borrow some terminology from *The Greening of America* (Reich, 1970), we have reached Consciousness II in terms of our awareness of the free time–leisure distinction, but we are in a state of Unconsciousness III in terms of turning this awareness into action. There may be many reasons for this, not the least of which are probably habit and inertia. But another seems to be the conviction that it really does not matter that much.

Let us turn to position 3, that the improper use of the terms has very serious implications. I myself hold this view. Let me make this position clear: I do not wish to prescribe with what meaning a person ought to use the term *leisure* or the term *free time*. But I would insist that at least in the professional literature one make it clear what that meaning is and then use the term with that meaning, and that meaning only. This is not an easy task and requires constant attention and a well-disciplined style. If, however, we wish to raise the study of leisure to the level of a scientific discipline, the need for taking this step is obvious and hardly needs to be argued again at this point. Enough has been said and written about the requirement of operational definitions in science.[3]

This argument, however, is only part of the reason for taking position 3. If this were all, the worst that could happen would be that our researchers would become even more confused than they already are, and continue to remain so. There is a more potent reason for taking position 3 and that is the social and political implications of equating the terms.

Each period in history, each society, has certain values that it holds dear, that govern all aspects of life, that permeate whatever is done both in public and private life, by society and by the individual. I am not referring to values that are being given lip service only, such as the belief in democracy or the brotherhood of man, and so on. I am referring to values most of us are not even aware of, values that have become part of our everyday-life habits. The particular value I am alluding to is, of course, the *work ethic* or *Protestant Ethic*. It no longer matters what exactly is meant by this ethic, just how it originated, or even whether we publicly profess to be for or against it. To some degree, and probably much more than we would want to believe, all of us are still imbued with that master of our conscience. And the one dictum that this ethic states clearly and unambiguously is that work is good and nonwork is bad. Work is what you ought to do and what you must do to earn your keep and to justify your existence. If you don't work, you ought to feel guilty!

The really serious implication of equating leisure with free time is thus not the potential confusion of scholars and researchers, but that this equation puts leisure in opposition to work. This is the crux of the issue. Such a dichotomy might at one point have served a useful purpose. But conditions in our society have changed. Dumazedier (1974a), who does not utilize a subjective definition of leisure, still recognizes this problem:

> To my mind, the labour/leisure dichotomy which has for forty years (from Elton Mayo to Georges Friedmann) contributed to progress in the observation and in the interpretation of leisure, is now more likely to lead to stagnation. It prompts increasingly stereotyped statements. It detracts from research designs. It conceals the development of mutual relationships whereby leisure is increasingly affected by *all* institutional commitments and/or influences them in turn, often as a challenge to obligations. (P. 209.)

The reason why the work-leisure dichotomy is so potent is the fact that as leisure has become synonymous with free time, meaningful activity has become synonymous with work, or in fact the job or profession. We shall turn to that point in the next section. It is clear, however, that equating meaningful activity with the job—or what is even worse, making the job seem the only really meaningful activity in life—is an obsolete and dysfunctional position for our post-industrial society.

Changing a habit is an arduous business. Consider the efforts presently being expended to change over to a nonsexist language in our professional journals. "Any endeavor to change the language is an awesome task at best" (APA Publication Manual Task Force, 1977). Whether such a change is to be worked for, however, should not depend on the difficulty of the task but on the implications of remaining in a status quo.[4]

My recommendations, then, are as follows. First, be conscious of just what it is one wants to convey and then use the appropriate term, be it *leisure* or *free time*. Second, use the label chosen consistently throughout any one piece of writing, and hopefully, throughout one's professional activities. The further hope prevails that eventually we shall be able to agree on the use of these labels and establish a common "scientific" language of leisure.[5]

FROM LEISURE TO FREE TIME TO LEISURE: A HISTORICAL PERSPECTIVE

Much has been written about the origin of the term *leisure* as a concept as well as an ideal. It is usually traced to ancient Greece. Probably the best source for obtaining a true feeling for the meaning the term once had is de Grazia's much quoted work, *Of time, work and leisure* (1962).[6] De Grazia anchors the meaning of leisure in Aristotle's definition as the state of being free from the necessity of being occupied and as characterized by the performance of activity "for its own sake or as its own end" (p. 13). Only two activities are considered worthy of leisure: music because it cultivates the mind, and contemplation because it leads to truth and true happiness.

Let us take another look at some of the critical features of the classical view that leisure is experienced in contemplation, as described in the following paragraph by de Grazia:

> The man in contemplation is a free man. He needs nothing. Therefore nothing determines or distorts his thought. He does whatever he loves to do, and what he does is done for its own sake. (P. 18.)

The first condition is one of being a free person—"he needs nothing." This does not imply, however, that a person need be like Diogenes who is reported to have been happy sitting naked in his barrel, contemplating life.[7] Aristotle recognized that few of us are capable of that kind of lifestyle. "He needs nothing," not because he desires nothing, but because he has everything, at least as this refers to the necessities of life. One need not worry about where one's daily bread is coming from, whether one has a roof over one's head, or whether one will be able to send the kids through college. This kind of freedom is not one that can be generated for a specific time period, like between twelve and one o'clock, during your lunch hour, or even during the two weeks of your vacation.[8] It is a freedom that requires a long-range state of mind, springing from one's lifestyle. It is not time-bound and it most certainly has nothing to do with *free time,* a concept which in its modern sense did not exist in ancient Greece, or anywhere else before the Industrial Revolution. "Leisure and free time live in two different worlds" (de Grazia, 1962, p. 5).

The second critical condition of leisure—"what he does is done for its own sake"—is really dependent on the first. Only if one is free can one engage in activities for their own sake. Peace of mind and a sense of detachment from the affairs of the everyday realities of the world are required. Thomas Aquinas (1952) recognized this when writing about the *vita contemplativa,* the contemplative life suitable to leisure, rather than the *vita activa,* the active life. He perceived the contemplative life as the more excellent one, and gave as one of the reasons the fact that "the contemplative life is loved more for its own sake, while the active life is directed to something else" (p. 621).

Sometimes we can achieve the necessary freedom only by denying reality, by creating our own universe, our own set of rules. Play has that characteristic. But leisure, contrary to play, is not limited to make-believe situations; it transcends these and must be understood within the context of the "real" world.[9]

It is evident, then, that the idea of leisure as described by the Greeks was not meant for, meaningful for, or attainable by the common person. Is it even meaningful to say that leisure, as we know it today, had existed at that period? There is disagreement on that point. De Grazia thinks that it did, and those accepting a subjective definition of leisure probably feel likewise. On the other hand, Dumazedier takes a different position.

> While spare time, in other words time off work, must obviously be as old as work itself, leisure has distinct characteristics, specific to the civilizations born of the industrial revolution (1974a, p. 13).

Dumazedier sees leisure as a concept ill-fitted to ancient times as well as to preindustrial societies. Two conditions are listed as necessary to make leisure possible for the majority of workers:

> (a) Activities in society are no longer regulated as a whole by ritual obligations prescribed by the community. At least some of them, such as work and leisure, are not covered by collective rituals. Individuals are free to decide how to use their free time, although their choice is socially determined. (b) Remunerated work is demarcated from other activities. Its delineation is arbitrary rather than regulated by nature. Its specific organisation clearly separates it from free time or makes such a separation possible (1974a, p. 15).

Few would argue with the point that "these two conditions exist in conjunction only in industrial and post-industrial societies" (p. 15), and that therefore the concept of leisure, as applied to a society or the majority of the population, is in fact a child of recent times. But then does it follow that leisure as a concept implying a state of mind did not exist for some people in all civilizations, at all times?

The historical development of the modern meaning of leisure is intimately related to the derivation of the residual definition of leisure, and its concomitant equation of leisure with free time. This issue becomes more visible when we look at the way in which the term *leisure* is used in another language, namely German. The prevalent term is *Freizeit* (free time).[10] The translation of the classical term *leisure* is *Musse,* but this term does not represent anything that would correspond to the way free time is used in our society (Scheuch, 1972a, p. 31). Yet, the term *Freizeit* does not cover the range of meanings implied by the term *leisure,* a problem that has led to a suggestion to differentiate between *Freizeit* and *arbeitsfreier Zeit (free time* and *time free from work)* (Scheuch, 1972a, p. 30).[11]

A most comprehensive look at the development of the concept *Freizeit* has been taken by Wolfgang Nahrstedt (1972). Many of the following paragraphs are based on his work *Die Entstehung der Freizeit.*

According to Nahrstedt there are two views on the development of free time *(Freizeit):* (1) free time originated during the second half of the eighteenth century as an outgrowth of the Age of Enlightenment; and (2) free time came about during the second half of the nineteenth century, as a negative residual to industrial work time. Both views consider free time to be basically different from the classical tradition of leisure *(Musse),* and are in this respect in line with Dumazedier's thinking.

The very words *free time (Freizeit)* and *work time (Arbeitszeit)* could not be found in dictionaries until the nineteenth century. As the term *free time* originated within the context of the Age of Enlightenment, it referred to freedom within free time to develop oneself to one's fullest potential. It implied first *freedom from,* that is, freedom from certain obligations, conditions, and restrictions. Thus, it demanded certain rights. It then led to *freedom to,* that is, freedom to self-actualize. Nahrstedt's thesis is that while free time as an idea and an ideal originated during the second half of the eighteenth century out of the philosophy of enlightenment, it only gained a broad social reality through the industrialization of societies during the second half of the nineteenth century.

Nahrstedt does see leisure in the classical sense, that is *Musse,* originating in ancient Greece. This type of leisure, however, developed within a small and leading section of the total population and remained restricted in this way until well into the nineteenth century. It served as the basis of Veblen's (1899) economic theory of the "leisure class." The concept of free time had been introduced to designate a period of time outside that devoted to the business of work (i.e., gainful employment). To the degree that this time period was used for culturally meaningful activities, it was viewed as leisure *(Musse),* and thus acquired a positive connotation. By itself, however, free time became an empty, purely negative concept (Nahrstedt, 1972, p. 25).

Something had happened on the way. The concept of work (referring primarily to remunerated employment) became the dominant and determining theme of the eighteenth and the nineteenth centuries —particularly the nineteenth. The work ethic came into full bloom. *Orare* and *laborare* became the *Leitmotif.* *Freedom to* became freedom to pray and work. Free time, defined in opposition to work (that is, paid employment), lost its positive aspects and took on negative connotations: nonproductiveness, idleness, and even immorality. The word *leisure* had become synonymous with free time when this term still carried positive connotations of self-fulfillment and the pursuit of reason, goals in line with the classical tradition of leisure *(Musse).*

Unfortunately, when free time lost its positive connotation and came to mean simply a period of time opposed to work time, the label *leisure* still stuck to it and fell into similar disgrace. Work had won the battle; leisure lost out!

Such a position may be functional for a society that is still at a low subsistence level. However, as Nahrstedt points out, as a society increases its productive potential and becomes less and less dependent on the producing person and more and more on the consuming one, the very perfection of the religion of work carries within it the need to overcome that religion (p. 292). This, of course, is particularly relevant for any society with an ever increasing number of retired persons for whom the concept of work (as paid employment) is no longer a meaningful reference point.

Nahrstedt concludes that the critical factor that turns free time into leisure is the concept of individual freedom within free time. The emphasis, then, is on freedom rather than on time, and the recognition that this freedom is not just opposed to work (i.e., paid employment), but to other obligations as well, social and otherwise. To say, as Anderson (1961, p. 14) did, that "definitions of leisure vary a great deal, but the chief emphasis is on the time element," is to adopt the nineteenth-century model of leisure. It is the time element in this model that sets it in opposition to the classical conception of leisure (*Musse*). As Nahrstedt puts it "Dies gerade ist das Neue gegenüber der älteren Musse" (p. 57; my translation: this is precisely what is new compared to the older concept of leisure). To the degree that an ever increasing proportion of our population will be freed from the necessity of work (i.e., paid employment) for an ever increasing period of their lives, this nineteenth-century residual type of leisure definition is becoming inadequate and incapable of grasping the conditions of modern life. A conceptualization of leisure is required that takes into account the essence of the phenomenon, namely individual freedom. The subjective type of leisure conceptualization offers this potential, returning us to the classical tradition of leisure (*Musse*), while at the same time accommodating the conditions of post-industrial society.

FROM QUANTITY TO QUALITY:
FROM LEISURE TO THE QUALITY OF LIFE

The preceding two sections dealt with the free-time–leisure distinction and its historical development. Also discussed were the concomitant leisure-work dichotomy and the resultant negative connotation for leisure. Finally, it was suggested that a residual or objective definition of leisure can no longer cope with most of the critical issues of a post-industrial society and that a subjectively oriented conceptualization of leisure is more and more taking its place. This, I believe, does not represent just the biased view of this author, but is also reflected in the writings of others (for example, Dunn, 1973).

A switch to a subjective definition will not only help remove the burden of the work-leisure dichotomy, but will have two other major implications. The first is that it will lead us to emphasize the qualitative rather than quantitative aspects of leisure. As long as leisure is perceived within the framework of time—as free time or any other subset of time—the primary concern of the investigator tends to be a quantitative one. Time is measured in units of seconds, minutes, days, weeks, etc.[12] The content of time may vary; the purpose for which time is used may vary. But time itself is content-free. We may in fact become concerned with that content, but then we end up counting: how often do we do this or that activity? what is the frequency per time unit? and so on.

Once we consider leisure a state of mind, the quantitative aspects become secondary. Duration matters, yes; but the quality of the experience comes first. We have entered a new domain: the domain of subjective, psychological measurements. Quality becomes the primary concern: the type and nature of the experience, its characteristics, its intensity, its depth, and so on.

The second implication is that we shall become aware of the potential ubiquitousness of the leisure experience. The area of concern has suddenly expanded tremendously. Leisure is no longer restricted to a particular time period. Yes, social conditions still delimit the potential for leisure. But within that framework, leisure is now a condition of psychological variables that may bring about this state of mind at any time and at any place. At least the potential exists. Since this state of mind is a positive and highly desirable one, it is a much sought after condition of life. When we consider improving the conditions of life—or as we call it today, the quality of life—we must certainly include the conditions that bring about leisure.

> Any overall policy aimed at enhancing the *quality of life* by a new allocation of time and space ought to begin by reassessing the implications of leisure for all areas of social and personal life (Dumazedier, 1974a, p. 213).

That is not to say that every effort of improving the quality of life needs to be approached from the viewpoint of leisure. When dealing with issues such as improving health services, housing, or public safety, we need not stretch the point to make these issues relevant to leisure. They are obviously important in their own right. But in a broader sense, they *are* relevant to leisure, since certain minimum conditions of existence must prevail before one can afford the freedom to leisure.

If we restrict ourselves to the conditions for leisure in a narrower sense, for example, issues of *perceived freedom* and *intrinsic motivation,* we discover again that these relate to every aspect of personal and societal life. Leisure is no longer just the primary concern of the recreation professional who attempts to turn free hours into productive and *re*-creational activities, nor of the economist who tries to make the best of the consumption potential of these free hours, nor of the sociologist who struggles to find a place for leisure within the larger domain of that particular discipline. Leisure has now become the business and concern of all professions and all disciplines of human endeavor.[13]

LEISURE IS EVERYBODY'S BUSINESS

Kaplan (1975, p. 29), whose multidisciplinary approach to leisure is a clear response to the above facts of life, provides an indication of how the various disciplines relate to his basic formulation of leisure. The following list of disciplines and outlines of respective tasks is a further elaboration on that theme. It is a view of the world from one particular perspective. It is not our intent to be prescriptive, that is, tell each discipline how to carry out their work. On the contrary, we merely hope to stimulate each of them enough to come forth and set out a program of leisure research and policy as seen from their particular viewpoint.

Most of the tasks mentioned here will be discussed in more detail throughout the book, where they fit into the various chapters. A compact listing of these different orientations is nevertheless considered useful as a constant reminder that any particular problem confronting the leisure professional can be viewed from at least this many different angles.

Economics. The residual view of leisure is by its very nature an economic model, since it includes work (that is, paid employment) as a component of its definition of leisure. A state of mind view is linked to economics as well, since perceived freedom is very much a function of one's economic status. The leisure professional has always had to, and continues to, count heavily on information provided by the economist. Essential data include: time spent in paid employment, in volunteer services, or in unemployment; shifts in work patterns and in consumption habits; changes in technology and science as they influence economic life patterns; and many others. The new and real challenge, however, are the economic implications of moving into a post-industrial era. The very dream of a leisure society rests on economic assumptions derived from this development. Thus, we need to develop models that allow us to test the feasibility of such societies. How can we make a social system function in which the production of goods and services is carried out by a minute proportion of the population, where everyone has a guaranteed income, and social services are provided for all? What are the implications of a decrease rather than an increase in product consumption? What if production and services are geared toward quality products and "real" needs rather than the satisfaction of the profit motive? Can we develop an economic theory that is based on the needs of the consumer rather than on those of the producer?

Gerontology. One look at the changing population age distribution of the world, but particularly of post-industrial societies, is enough to convince one of the need for this rapidly growing discipline (see, for example, *Social Indicators, 1973*, p. 283; *Social Indicators, 1976*, p. 20). The proportion of people at the upper end of the life cycle is steadily and dramatically increasing. So is the amount of so-called free time for these people, and the problem of finding meaning in life without being engaged in paid employment is taking on epidemic proportions. The elderly represent a natural setting for many issues related to leisure because they are the first and only large adult group that must exist without having their life anchored to paid employment. What are the implications of this in terms of their understanding of the nature and function of "work" and leisure? of their self-concepts? and their search for meaning in life? Needless to say, leisure education and counseling ought to be a prominent part of any comprehensive gerontology program.

History. Do we—or even can we—learn from history? Opinions are divided on that question. One might argue that our chances of benefiting from historical knowledge are quite limited, since (1) such knowledge always seems distorted, and (2) the present is so radically different from the past that any projection or extrapolation is inappropriate anyhow. While this pessimistic view may have validity in respect to the prediction of future trends or behavior, it seems exaggerated in regard to questions of understanding. For example, we have used an historical approach in throwing light on the meaning of the term *free time*, and its becoming synonymous with the term *leisure*. The domain of leisure is intricately tied in with values, social norms, and political structures, and understanding these relationships will certainly be helped by historical probing and analyses.

Philosophy. Telling philosophers to become concerned with leisure is like carrying coals to Newcastle. Philosophy is concerned with the seeking of wisdom and with the wisdom sought: with process and with content. Leisure is linked with the process of philosophy, as the necessary state of mind to carry out such activity. And leisure as a goal, that which to strive for, requires the elucidation of content, of what *is,* as well as of what is good, moral, and beautiful. Perhaps one of our problems is that nobody listens to philosophers anymore; sophists have taken over—the public-relations expert and the guru. Yet philosophy has so much to contribute to the understanding of leisure. Let us call for a renaissance of rational thought; let us examine the "good life" once more as a philosophical concept, given today's conditions; let us ponder the ethical implications of the "life of leisure"; let us examine Eastern and African visions of leisure, but with a most careful eye toward separating religion from philosophy. Let us not be trapped once again into looking for the good life in our reincarnation or the eternal beyond.

Political Science. The political structure of a society determines to a large degree who will experience leisure, and whether leisure will be attainable by as many as possible or only by the select few. This issue is recognized by all who attempt to depict the future, be they writers of utopias or planners of the future, sponsored by government or by private funds.[14] We stated before that a leisure society requires certain economic assumptions; the same is true of political assumptions. Freedom from economic needs is only a necessary, but not a sufficient condition for leisure. *Freedom to,* by whatever political label it may manifest itself, is the critical variable. Political scientists have a tremendous task. What are the forms of government that can make a leisure society a real possibility? What can be done within the limits of any given system to maximize the conditions for leisure? What are the best ways to achieve these goals? How can we best turn leisure into an acceptable political goal?

Psychiatry. Since psychiatrists are medical doctors, they tend to deal with sickness rather than health, although the latter is always the goal of their endeavors. Not surprisingly, their professional contact with leisure first came about through seeing the negative reactions their patients had to the absence of leisure during free time.[15] Unfortunately, the distinction between free time and leisure was not then recognized, and leisure (rather than free time) was labeled as potentially dangerous. The appropriate distinction is particularly important here, since psychiatrists play a tremendous role in bringing about changes in public institutions such as hospitals, nursing and old-age homes, prisons, and others. The basic task of psychiatry—helping people function at their optimal level, particularly if they are blocked in one way or another by mental (and sometimes physical) problems—is obviously in accordance with the philosophy of leisure, as expressed here. To the degree that psychiatrists are concerned with societal, cultural, and historical factors in their theoretical and practical activities, they must be kept informed most thoroughly about the changing conditions of a post-industrial society. It is a well-known fact that certain personality disorders—or at least symptomatology—relate to specific cultures or time periods. The revolutionary changes taking place in our society as we move into this post-industrial era are bound to have severe consequences for the shaping of our personality character, perhaps on a scale never before experienced.[16]

Psychology. It is hard to explain the extreme disregard that psychologists, until very recently, had of the concept of leisure (see chap. 5, fn. 9). Lest we turn clinician, we shall not attempt to. As we move from the free-time to the state-of-mind conception of leisure, however, psychologists' involvement in leisure will and already has increased.[17] Since we devote parts of chapter 5, and in fact, most of this volume, to this end, the matter need not be discussed here any further. Let us just restate that the study of leisure is ready for the psychologist as an area for theorizing; as a rich field for research; and as an applied area for education, counseling, and therapy.

Recreation. If there is ever a discipline that can lay claim to having been most prominently involved in issues of leisure, then it is recreation. It would be redundant to list here all the ways in which this profession is already engaged in relevant tasks. There are many excellent texts available in that area that provide complete overviews.[18] Recreation, too, is experiencing the impact of our changing society; it has to confront some basic questions and is undergoing some major shifts in orientation and emphasis. There are questions related to recreation and park budgets—how to divide the pie at a time of shrinking financial resources. Similar questions arise from a potential energy shortage, and may encourage the development of less consumptive forms of free-time activities. Then there are also more theoretical issues. For example, should therapeutic recreation perhaps be viewed as belonging in the medical rather than the recreation domain? Which discipline does leisure counseling really fall into? And what are the implications for recreation of the shift in the conception of leisure as a state of mind rather than as a period of time? Perhaps the most critical task, then, may be a redefining of the roles that this discipline will have to assume in our future society.

Sociology. While philosophers pursue the idea of leisure and recreationists institute leisure pursuits, sociologists study the institution of leisure. By that is meant the way society has developed patterns that control leisure behavior. Such control may be achieved in various ways, such as through organizational structures, through norms, or by legislation. Leisure is only one of many institutions that society and the sociologist are concerned with, and one of the tasks of the sociologist is to isolate and interrelate this particular institution of leisure.[19] Since the prime focus of this discipline is society, we call on it for information and understanding of the implications of societal shifts from pre- to industrial and to post-industrial states. The recent development of a social-indicator movement attempts to fill the needs of those who are looking for guidance in policy decisions in societal areas. Sociologists also have a long tradition of active involvement in leisure theorizing and research and are professionally represented in this field through many organizations and journals.

Leisure Studies. And now the ultimate discipline: leisure studies! Placing it at the end of the list is not meant to imply that it is least important, or most important. But there is a special significance to it. Leisure studies as a discipline is on a different level from the ones mentioned before. Not only should it be carried out "in an interdisciplinary context," as for example is the case for sociology (Dumazedier, 1974a, p. 209); it is by its very nature interdisciplinary. It requires a classification on a higher level, and perhaps represents the first of similar kinds of interdisciplinary systems that are bound to develop in the future. Since the days of "the Renaissance man" are gone (when one person could still encompass nearly all of the then extant knowledge), leisure studies may be forced into a permanent teamwork approach. A leisure studies department of the future may resemble a postdoctoral institute where people with training in the previously mentioned disciplines, and others, will work together and continue their studies, but always with the emphasis on cooperation with each other. Now in the 1980s, leisure studies departments still have to function within the limits of conventional boundaries. They tend to evolve from recreation departments and often coexist with or within them. The need exists, however, for a much broader type of department as envisioned here. Note, within this context, the introduction of an accreditation system for park-and-recreation curricula, as described in *Parks & Recreation* ("Council on accreditation lists first accredited departments," 1979): The process is seen as "a means of ensuring educational standards, and of stimulating institutional self-improvement. . . ." Whether, in fact, this step will lead toward the kind of interdisciplinary approach suggested—whether the leisure profession, indeed, is willing and able to take on the challenge and forge ahead with the formulations of such institutions—only the future will tell.

LEISURE AS CONTEMPLATION, LEISURE AS BEING

One can approach the issue of leisure in a scientific manner: theorize about it, research it, write elaborate and logically precise analyses of it, all in an endeavor to convey its meaning and understand its nature. This is one way and the approach I am attempting to follow in this book. There is, of course, another, and that is that of the artist. The artist conveys truth through creating experiences and having us participate in them. The knowledge and understanding gained through this active involvement may not be as ordered, as easily verbalized or communicable, but they tend to be deeper and certainly more directly absorbed into our own being.

I am grateful to a true artist for allowing me to present here an example of his work.

Is leisure the hollandaise of life?
Some Saucy Reflections

By Robert Farrar Capon

It is 7:10 p.m. Whisk in hand, I am beating lumps of butter into hot, thickened egg yolks just off the fire. My wife has arranged the broccoli in a pot, basted the leg of lamb with a cup of leftover coffee (with sugar and cream), thickened the Emperor soup and announced her intention of going upstairs to change before the first guests arrive. She leaves me orders to start the mock oyster pudding at 7:15 and the herring savory at 7:30, to fry some onions for the wild rice, open the wine, check the bar, make up the raw-egg-and-Swedish-anchovy relish if I still really want it, and see if I can find out what time my youngest daughter has in mind to come home tonight or tomorrow morning. It is our first free evening in three weeks, and we are in the last stages of the countdown of a day spent enjoying our leisure by having company for dinner.
Leisure?

"I don't know why," she says to me, "you insist on making hollandaise. Drawn butter is just as good and four times less fussy."

"Wrong!" I retort. "Properly drawn butter is almost never seen in America. What you normally get is separated, melted grease. My hollandaise is as easy as pie, and it never separates unless a certain wife tries to warm it up too fast."

"Speak nicely to me, or I'll make you fix the gravy. I'm going to dress."
Enjoying?

Well, yes, as a matter of fact. To both questions. Oddly, I find all this fuss both leisurely and to my liking. But why, I wonder? It is by no means obvious why two human beings with a normal disdain for gainful employment should be willing to labor all afternoon and half the evening putting together a needlessly elaborate meal for six totally unnecessary guests. Our notion of leisure seems as if it could do with a little philosophical underpinning.

I beat in the lemon juice and cayenne and slip the pot of finished sauce to the back of the counter. What is leisure? As I recall a dictionary definition, it is the state of having time at one's own disposal—free or unoccupied time. But that sheds very little light: it's superficially true and fundamentally unenlightening. It tells you where you can find it, but not what to look for when you get there. And, worst of all, it fails to tell you the one thing you most need to know: how to make a success of it when you've got it. It's like defining hollandaise as an egg-thickened butter sauce: if that's all you can say about it, you'll never make it.

How about a more imaginative definition then? How about: *Leisure as the hollandaise of life?* Ah! That's better. Some nice, enlightening correspondences there: both are unnecessary in any simple sense of the word: neither comes easily to hand in the salt mine of the daily grind; there are almost as many recipes for each as there are cooks: and if you don't keep your eye riveted on what you're doing, either of them will curdle on the spot.

Take the first correspondence, for example: leisure activity is unnecessary activity. My wife and I could meet all the practical obligations of our lives by dining alone on the hamburgers, English muffins and green salad we fed our two daughters at 6:00. Why six guests, a small smorgasbord, leg of lamb, the expense of wild rice, and the health hazard of all that cholesterol in the dozen egg yolks tucked away in soup, sauce, and dessert?

Answer? It has got to be that, somehow, human beings need the unnecessary almost more than the necessary, if they are to go on feeling human. The necessary is the pound of flesh the world extorts from us: it is a drag, a drain, a slow, lifelong nag. The unnecessary is the spontaneous gift we give out of the fullness of our being. Like God making the world out of delight and not necessity. I put hollandaise on my broccoli to express my freedom and my joy. My leisure production is my protest against all the two-bit exactions the world lays on me. I may have to walk around in my slave suit most of the time, but at the center of my being, I know I am king. It is in my free time that I claim my rightful freedom.

Leisure, then, answers to no ordinary necessity. The boss, for example, will not be among my six guests, nor do we have any sensible workaday agenda for our evening. As it happens, we have all planned and plotted in the salt mine on other occasions, but tonight we sit down simply to *be* together. If we had mere business to do, Coke and peanuts would suffice. But we have the fullness of our being to celebrate; therefore we shall have wine and sauces and solve no problems unless they are of cosmic dimensions.

Next, however, consider another correspondence between my leisure and the sauce in my pot: the multiplicity of recipes for it. Many people, even though they have grasped the need to banish ordinary necessity from their leisure activities, proceed nonetheless to ruin their free time by introducing the dogmatic necessity of a single right recipe for doing what they are doing. These are the tiresome souls who, when they give a dinner party, for example, will insist that there is only one proper way to do it, and proceed to bore you with endless rules about the alternation of courses, the succession of wines or the correctness of glasses. They take what might have been an excursion into freedom and turn it into one more episode of bondage. If my leisure is to be leisure indeed, therefore, I must admit into it no standard of judgment other than what pleases me. I must be happy simply that I can do what I am doing without having to provide some superstructure of correctness by which to judge myself. I must learn, in short, to stand on my own feet. That takes, no doubt, more character than I presently have; but if I try to hide behind dogmas, I run the greater risk of ending up with even less.

And that brings up the most important correspondence of all: both leisure and hollandaise are difficult, fragile concoctions. I have to know what it is that curdles the mixture and avoid it scrupulously. And the principal cause of curdling in both cases is not watching what you are doing. The essential difference between gainful activity and leisure is that in the former, the eye is fastened on something other than what is being done, while in the latter, it is the thing in front of you that reigns supreme. True leisure activity is always a form of contemplation, and contemplation is simply a serious word for play. Dinner parties, like bridge, tennis or any other properly unnecessary game, exist only for the playful, contemplative exploration of the things and people at hand. They are not *in order to* anything else; they are entered into *for themselves.* They are simply little diagrams of the biggest thing about us: our ability to create and enjoy goodness for its own sake. Add any other purpose to your leisure—advantage, uplift, ego-massage or repayment of debt—and it will curdle promptly into work.

Above all, however, the one extraneous consideration which must never, under any circumstances, be admitted in leisure activity, the ultimate irrelevancy which must at all costs be barred, is the fear of failure. My leisure must be a time when I exempt myself from the threat of the judgment which hangs over all the rest of my life. If my hollandaise curdles, it curdles. I shall simply do the best I can, blaming no one: add boiling water, run it through the blender—or, *in extremis,* serve curdled hollandaise. But nothing, not even my own pride, must be allowed to interrupt my contemplation. That is not as selfish as it sounds: nobody loves a complaining host full of excuses and recriminations. A party should be, above all, a time for the suspension of blame, a general bestowal of forgiveness in advance for everything. It should be a foretaste, if you will, of the Gospel—of the Good News we never otherwise find ourselves able to believe: that there really is no condemnation, and that, under God we are free.

Fair enough. On with the leisure itself. My hollandaise has gotten me as far as the doctrine of Grace; which, when you think of it, is not bad for an egg-thickened sauce. Time now to fry the onions for the wild rice.

Robert Farrar Capon, Vicar of Christ Church in Port Jefferson, New York. Reprinted from Travel and Leisure, September 1976, 6, no. 9, 24–25. Copyright © 1976 American Express Publishing Corporation.

SUMMARY

The purpose of this chapter was to explore further the complexities of the concept of leisure and to bring to light the scope and broadness of the issues. The person getting involved in the study of leisure is on the threshold of a new discipline: one that must rely heavily on the knowledge and expertise of disciplines already in existence, but one that is bound to make its own unique contributions and eventually transcend the more traditional ones.

Disciplines develop as the needs of societies demand them. For example, psychology emerged as a separate discipline out of philosophy, physiology, and medicine, when each of these was no longer adequate to handle the changing conditions of society and concomitant changes in perspectives on knowledge. Space science has achieved a quite independent status among the traditional sciences, because it deals with completely new parameters that require new methods of approach. The social conditions that are about to break on us as we approach the twenty-first century are no less different from what we had before, than is outer space from mother earth.

Leisure studies may well be the discipline that will take on the task of dealing with these new social conditions. The reader might feel that I am getting carried away, but is it not exciting to be a space explorer?

Back to the mundane. The chapter began by presenting the section "More Voices." These and the ones previously offered have been selected for their divergent views, and it is hoped that the reader will take the time to ponder them and perhaps try to integrate them with the various viewpoints presented throughout the chapters. The short piece on "Work" was to be a reminder of how things used to be; one tends to forget! I then took a strong position on the importance of making a clear distinction between the terms *free time* and *leisure*. I recommended that the leisure professional come to grips with the exact meaning of each term, and then be consistent in their use.

A historical perspective attempted to trace the origin of the free time–leisure equivalence, and the concomitant development of a leisure-work dichotomy. With the rise of the work ethic, leisure consequently acquired its negative connotation.

Differences were further examined between the classical conception of leisure and the modern view, a residual conception which defined leisure primarily in opposition to work (i.e., paid employment). The inadequacy of the residual definition to cope with conditions of post-industrial society makes its demise foreseeable, and a subjective orientation to leisure is increasingly taking its place.

Implications of the subjective definition of leisure are the following. It helps remove the negative connotation of leisure; it leads toward a greater emphasis on qualitative rather than quantitative aspects of leisure; and it expands the leisure domain to all areas of life. Leisure, as a positive idea and a highly desirable goal, becomes part of any effort to improve the quality of life. There may be differences of opinion in regard to this (mainly due to a misunderstanding of the term *leisure!*), but striving for a leisure society is, after all, the ultimate way of improving the quality of life.

A multidisciplinary approach to the investigation of leisure is required by the complexities of the issues involved. Potential contributions and tasks of various, but by no means all, relevant disciplines were listed and leisure studies was seen as a suitable institution to be the future integrating force among all of these efforts. The chapter ended with an impressionistic view of leisure, which conveys all that I have tried to communicate and more.

ENDNOTES

[1] There is a fourth position which, however, does not really make a free time–leisure distinction, but rather includes leisure as one of a number of

free-time categories. If one desires to remain on the sociological level of investigation, this may be a valid position. If, however, one wants to consider the psychological issues of leisure, then taking this approach is not a solution.

[2] I am indebted to Douglas Kimmel for making me aware of this inconsistency in my thinking.

[3] For a further discussion of this issue and the scientific method in general, the reader may want to consult Kerlinger (1973).

[4] For a somewhat related discussion of leisure and free time and implications for the future, see Ewald (1972), pp. 157–168.

[5] I have raised the issue of the indiscriminate use of the terms *leisure* and *free time* before, in a *Leisure Information Newsletter* circulated among leisure professionals. There I posed two questions: (1) do we consider the distinction between leisure and free time meaningful, important, and consequential? (2) Should we establish some convention for the use of the terms? I did not receive any response to my questions, which contributes to my feeling that the issue is not taken very seriously by leisure professionals. (See Neulinger, 1975.)

[6] For further historical references see Neulinger 1974a, chap. 1, and fn. 1, p. 4.

[7] The story is told that Alexander the Great, who admired Diogenes for his wisdom, granted him the chance to wish and obtain whatever he might desire. Upon which Diogenes asked Alexander to step aside, since he was blocking the warming sun.

[8] In this context, also see Green's (1968, p. 71) most cogent analogy to love.

[9] The *perception of freedom,* the critical condition of leisure according to a subjective definition, is seen as adequate even if only an illusion. The illusion is one, however, that the person is not aware of. In play, the player knows the difference between make-believe and reality.

[10] For example, a recent work on various aspects of leisure and free time was entitled *Soziologie der Freizeit* (Scheuch and Meyersohn, 1972).

[11] Also compare this to Dumazedier's (1968) *free time, semi-leisure,* and *leisure* distinction or to Friedmann's (1960) distinction between *spare time* and *free time* as other examples of efforts to deal with the same problem.

[12] There are, of course, those who are interested in the qualitative aspects of time, that is, how we experience time, whether we experience its duration as short or long, whether "time flies" or whether it "seems to stand still," and so on. But here we are on a different plane, the subjective one. For a brief consideration of this issue, see Neulinger, 1974a, pp. 138–141.

[13] Two new concepts appear on the scene: leisure education and leisure counseling. We shall postpone a discussion of these developments, however, until chapter 9, which deals with these issues in great detail.

[14] For a look at some utopias and futurists in this context, see Kaplan, 1975, pp. 386–391.

[15] I am referring here to the phenomenon labeled "Sunday neurosis." It is associated with an increase of symptomatology after experiencing free time. I venture to say that it is obviously not the free time, but the inability to experience leisure during your free time, that is the causative agent.

[16] Note, for example, the suggested inclusion of a new diagnostic category, "Narcissistic Personality Disorder," into the American Psychiatric Association *Diagnostic and Statistical Manual of Mental Disorders (DSM-III)*. Would such a disorder flourish in a society that does not idolize individuality as much as does ours?

[17] For a listing of areas of potential contributions by psychologists to the leisure domain and work accomplished, see Neulinger and Brok, 1974, and Neulinger and Crandall, 1976.

[18] For example, see Carlson et al., 1979; Kraus, 1978; Sessoms et al., 1975. Also note Gray and Greben, 1974.

[19] See Dumazedier, 1974a, pp. 208–209.

4

Research—
the quality of life:
objective approaches

The parks commissioner just had a call from the mayor, a "friendly" call. The mayor had expressed some vague uneasiness about the city park. It seems people were wondering: a lot of money was being spent on the park; there were other projects too; not that there was any real complaint; but people were wondering. What could the commissioner tell him? Was the money spent wisely? Could the commissioner justify the expenditure, give the mayor some figures, you know, a report that could be sent to the newspapers? In other words, did the park contribute to the improvement of the quality of life of the city? "Why don't you let me know next week what you are going to do?" was the mayor's final sentence in the conversation.

The commissioner was lucky. He had just hired a graduate from one of the better leisure studies departments in the country. Little did he know what he had let himself in for when he called in that person for advice: a full two chapters worth!

Let us briefly look at the situation. To justify expenditures to the taxpayers, a parks commissioner might obtain information about park usage, the number of visitors per given period of time (an objective measure). Presumably the larger the number, the better. However, the parks commissioner's responsibility would not end there. Data should also be collected about users' satisfaction with the park in general and specific conditions in particular. The mere fact of attendance does not guarantee satisfaction; there may simply exist an extreme lack of alternatives. Besides, attendance or crowding may itself be a factor in the perception of the park. Some people may prefer a less populated park, some a more populated one, or these feelings may vary for different parts of the park. In a playground area, crowding might be experienced as exciting and leading to desired interactions; in a more serene part of the park, aloneness and sparsity might be the preferred condition. (All of these aspects require subjective measures.)

The purpose of this little sketch is to identify two important aspects of any evaluation process, objective measures and subjective ones. There are many other issues that enter into such a task, but they all concern either one, or the other, or both of these aspects. The following two chapters are organized around this distinction. Our overall intent is to familiarize the reader with some of the issues and problems a researcher of the phenomenon of leisure has to face. Let us begin by laying some groundwork.

Every discipline has developed techniques that are best suited for its purposes, needs, and subject matter. For example, sociologists have perfected highly sophisticated methods of sampling, since survey data form an important source of information for that discipline. Economists have designed mathematical models that predict consumer behavior and employment trends, again areas of special interest to their field. Psychologists have developed techniques for measuring subjective phenomena—such as attitudes, values, or feelings—relevant to their particular concerns. There is a great diversity of approaches and techniques among the various disciplines. Yet all of them, to the degree that they consider themselves part of the domain of science (and that does include the social sciences), share common convictions as to the goals of science and the nature of their general approach in the search of knowledge.

The goals of science are said to be three: understanding, prediction, and control. The first is most relevant to pure science, the second and third to applied science. Note that we may achieve any one of these goals without necessarily achieving the others. For example, we may be able to predict that the sun will rise again tomorrow without fully understanding why; or we might even make a "correct" prediction on the basis of a "wrong" explanation. The third goal, control, makes some people uneasy. Control has negative connotations; it sounds like manipulation. Such considerations, however, miss the point. The scientist wants to develop the capacity for control, the ability to manipulate. Whether such control or manipulation will be carried out, and to what ends, is no longer a scientific but a moral or political question.

The general approach we are referring to is known as *the scientific method.* It is assumed that the reader has at least some basic understanding of this method; in addition, anyone who wishes to pursue independent inquiry will need some knowledge in at least two areas: research design and statistics. The first of these deals with developing and setting up appropriate conditions for collecting information, and the second deals with appropriate ways of analyzing the information gathered and drawing valid inferences from these data.[1]

In the preceding chapters we have demonstrated the interdisciplinary nature of leisure. In terms of methodology, this has obvious consequences. Our overall approach will be dictated by the scientific method, but to the degree that we might approach a specific issue from the orientation of a particular discipline, we may take advantage of techniques developed in that area. Ideally, the leisure professional ought to be conversant with the research methodologies of each of the relevant disciplines, an obviously hopeless task. The solution may be a teamwork approach, with members from different disciplines pooling their knowledge.

The study of leisure involves questions of pure research, such as "What is leisure?" or "How does one develop certain leisure attitudes?" or "What, in fact, is meant by *intrinsic motivation?*" But most issues involve applied aspects and have immediate implications. We see here another analogy between leisure and health. One may be concerned purely with the definition of health, physical or mental, for the sake of obtaining an operational definition; yet there are immediate and unavoidably grave implications to such endeavors. (Note the word *grave* in this context!).

The implications of leisure are most directly reflected in what has come to be known as "the quality of life." Irrespective of what one's definition of leisure is, be it one of free time, of activities, or of a state of mind, the nature of that leisure will affect the person's quality of life which will in turn affect one's leisure. Leisure can be either cause or effect, the independent variable or the dependent variable. Since leisure as a state of mind comes about as a function of the myriad conditions of one's life, its investigation and advancement require as complete a picture of the overall quality of life as possible, including such matters as health, public safety, education, employment, income, housing, and general population trends.[2] To these one would certainly add information about the traditional area of "leisure and recreation."

As we just pointed out, however, leisure is not only determined by the quality of life, but it also determines that quality. It is the goal toward which we strive in most of our activities, and as I shall argue throughout this book, the very criterion of the quality of life. This is one of the reasons why I have placed the discussion of research within the larger context of the study of the quality of life. I see leisure studies as becoming most intimately involved in this issue in all post-industrial societies.

The study of the quality of life and that of leisure reveal a number of similarities. Both deal with objective as well as subjective phenomena, and both were first approached in terms of their objective characteristics; only lately have serious attempts been made to investigate their subjective aspects. The important point to remember is that each approach requires different methodologies, which is why we decided to look at each separately. It should be stressed, however, that in any actual research effort the two aspects—objective and subjective—ought to be examined concurrently, if broader implications for the quality of life are to be inferred. This was the point of the example at the beginning of this chapter.

In the present chapter we shall look primarily at objective methods for studying leisure and the quality of life. This may seem irrelevant since our leisure orientation is a subjective one. Not so! Let's draw once more on our analogy to health. To investigate health, be it physical or mental, one needs a thorough knowledge of the structure and physiology of the body. Similarly, to study leisure as a state of mind, one needs all the information one can get about the conditions that influence that state, and these include the person's overall behavior pattern and societal setting. The latter, in turn, requires a knowledge of the total socioeconomic structure of society with which the person is in constant and unavoidable interaction. We shall turn to subjective methods in the next chapter.

THE QUALITY OF LIFE

Quality is a relative term. What is considered good today may be viewed as bad tomorrow. What is adequate now may seem inadequate next year. Getting from New York to Paris in thirty-three and a half hours was once considered a supreme achievement; today some of us feel that we must have a plane that takes us there in four hours. Not only do our views change with time, they also differ from person to person and from society to society. What is considered desirable by one, may be viewed as undesirable by another, and irrelevant by a third. These are the kind of problems that must be faced by anyone attempting either to measure the quality of life or, what is even more problematic, to improve it.

The situation, however, is not hopeless. There is considerable agreement among individuals, within societies, and even between societies, on what constitutes the good life, at least on some fundamental aspects. And at this point we must be satisfied to deal with basic issues, the essentials of life. By finding out what the values are that people can agree on, we come closer to knowing those on which they disagree. Besides, we as individuals need not agree with the delineated standards of the good life. We may even feel that such standards will lead to the eventual doom of humanity and this planet. But by clarifying what these commonly accepted goals are, we move into a better position to deal with them, and can attempt to change them if that is our desire.

This context also brings to light the real importance of leisure for the quality of life. Leisure is not just a component of the quality of life, but the very essence of it. It is not a neutral state of mind, but a positive, highly desirable one, and an important value. Leisure in my opinion is the guideline needed for any decision relating to the quality of life.

Let us now turn to some of the more technical aspects of investigating the quality of life. First, let us consider a potential source of confusion.

Approach and Mode

We shall distinguish two approaches (the objective and the subjective) and two modes (a quantitative and a qualitative one). Let us look at the following concepts.

> *Quantity:* some amount or frequency;
> *Quality:* a peculiar and essential character of something or someone, its nature; or a distinguishing attribute;
> *Objective:* (for our purposes) existing outside and independent of the mind; not influenced by personal feelings or biases; publicly observable;
> *Subjective:* (for our purposes) relating to or arising within one's mind, in contrast to what is outside; personal; not directly observable.

Most people are familiar with these terms. What may and often does lead to confusion, however, is their relationships to each other. We sometimes assume that objective means quantitative, and subjective qualitative. To some degree there is justification for this, since this is how we frequently behave. When we think of an objective approach, we think of amounts and numbers; when we consider a subjective method, we become concerned with qualitative aspects. I have listed this very point as one of the implications of switching to a subjective definition of leisure. One reason for our having adopted this way of thinking is that not until recently have we succeeded in quantifying subjective phenomena. It was only in the 1930s that psychologists like Thurstone and others began to solve the problems inherent in such quantifications (Thurstone, 1928; Thurstone and Chave, 1929).[3]

The problem is important enough to suggest the paradigm shown in Table 4.1. The difference between the objective and subjective approach, using either a quantitative or qualitative mode, is highlighted in terms of targets studied. In the objective approach one deals with people, things, or events—objects or happenings that one can see or touch. In the subjective approach the phenomena of concern are not *publicly* observable. I can observe—in the sense of becoming aware of or feeling—my own experiences; but I cannot observe those of others. At best I can observe the manifestations of their experiences. Regardless of approach, however, I may choose either a quantitative or a qualitative mode (or both) to study the phenomenon in question. When working in the quantitative mode, we tend to use terms like number, amount, and duration, for the objective approach (A); in the subjective approach (C), we are more likely to speak of in-

Table 4.1. *Targets of the Objective and Subjective Approach in the Quantitative and Qualitative Mode*

		Mode	
		Quantitative	Qualitative
Approach			
	Objective	Number, (A) amount, or duration of: people, things, or events	Type, (B) or nature of: people, things, or events
	Subjective	Intensity, (C) direction, or stability of: cognitions, feelings, attitudes	Type, (D) or nature of: cognitions, feelings, attitudes

tensity, direction, or stability, although number, amount, or duration are still relevant. When working in the qualitative mode, we are primarily concerned with analyzing the type or nature of either the object (B) or experience (D) in question.

Unfortunately, the term *quality of life* is in itself somewhat misleading. While it is intended to emphasize the qualitative aspects of life (in response to a feeling of dissatisfaction with our cultural values that overemphasize the importance and value of quantity), quantitative aspects are intrinsic to any qualitative experience.

SOCIAL INDICATORS

The term *social indicators* has emerged quite suddenly as a major focus of both public and professional interest, to the degree that several authors have referred to a social indicator "movement" (for example, Wilcox et al., 1972; Andrews and Withey, 1976). We shall consider the philosophical and social reasons for this development in later chapters. At this point we shall restrict ourselves to methodological issues, but briefly touch on the history of this movement.

A Historical Perspective

The recognition for the need and possibility of the quantification and measurement of social conditions has been traced back to the early seventeenth century (Lazarsfeld, 1961). Both ethical and pragmatic concerns contributed to these developments. The rise of national states and the concurrent industrialization of society created the need for information about the state of society to an extent never before demanded. The necessary tools to acquire this knowledge began to be developed. For example, many statistical techniques owe their origin to this period.

In the United States, interest in social indicators was stimulated first in 1929, when President Hoover commissioned a group of scientists to study the feasibility of a national survey of social trends. This work resulted in a report that attempted to monitor such social phenomena as changing social attitudes and interests, rural life, the family, recreation and leisure-time activities, crime and punishment, health and medical practices, and others. Two general insights were gained: (1) an interdisciplinary approach is essential for any such undertaking, and (2) trend analyses are required to become aware of where a society is moving to. That is, one needs longitudinal research—surveys carried out over time, for consecutive periods or points in time. One outcome of these efforts was the creation of the National Council of Economic Advisers.

The 1940s and 1950s still emphasized economic indicators, although studies related to social phenomena were carried out, notably some relating to the mental health of Americans (e.g., Faris and Dunham, 1939; Goldhammer and Marshall, 1953; Hollingshead and Redlich, 1958; Srole et al., 1962).

The next crucial impetus came, strangely enough, from outer space. Some people were wondering where our space technology was taking us, particularly in regard to social events and developments on this earth. It was also discovered that we had hardly any means of evaluating whether certain national goals for Americans had been achieved, that had previously been set by a presidential commission under President Eisenhower. President Johnson finally commissioned a project that was to produce social indicators designed to measure progress toward societal goals and assess the well-being of Americans. The last few years have seen any number of organizations engaged in work and research in this area, and the literature on the topic is rapidly growing. The goal is to perfect an annual social report of the president, just as we now have an annual economic report. Let it be emphasized that this development is by no means an American phenomenon only; it flourishes in all industrial countries.

Definition and Functions

Let us now look a bit closer at what a social indicator actually is. How does it differ, for example, from census data? Or may it be considered one kind of such information? Following are a number of early definitions of social indicators that will throw light on these questions.

> [Social indicators are] measurements of social phenomena whose movements indicate whether a particular problem is getting better or worse relative to some goal (Katzman, 1968, p. 86).

> [A social indicator is] a framework for evaluating social policies and programs in terms of their effectiveness in achieving these goals (Holleb, 1968, p. 83).

> [A social indicator is] a statistic of direct normative interest measuring some state of welfare and if it changes in the "right" direction, can be interpreted as "things have gotten better, or people are better off" (U.S. Dept. of H.E.W., 1969, p. 97).

Two aspects are essential in these definitions. (1) They all imply a longitudinal approach, that is, a concern with changes over time. (2) The variables dealt with must be socially relevant. Campbell and Converse (1972, pp. 2, 3) express these points as follows:

> . . . At least two distinctive emphases ought to be associated with the definition of social indicators and provide it with unique connotations.
>
> First, the term is intended to convey a stress on descriptive measurement which is much more "dynamic" than most social science research has been to date. . . . Any strong causal inference requires longitudinal measurement, or continued "monitoring" of a system over time.
>
> Second, . . . a heavy stress on policy relevance. . . . Among the myriads of possible social variables that might be measured, high priority should be given to those that seem on the one hand most central in any assessment of the evolving quality of American social life and, on the other, that are amenable to manipulation through policy change.

These statements certainly clarify the nature of social indicators, but leave the question unanswered as to how to select those variables that, indeed, are the socially relevant ones. This is a task in which social indicators may play a crucial role, but which clearly transcends their purpose. Setting goals is a matter of social values, and means must not be confused with ends.[4]

Problems and Issues

Anyone who has ever attempted to master some craft—such as carpentry, jewelry making, or pottery—knows the importance of having the right tool for the given task, and using it the right way. Social indicators represent research tools, designed for specific tasks and requiring appropriate methods of use for optimal results. Like every methodology, this one has its set of problems and we shall briefly look at some of these.[5]

Selection and Criterion Choice. One problem, just mentioned, is the selection of indicators. What is to be included? A related issue is the following. An indicator is supposed to indicate "when things are getting better, or worse." But who is to decide what is better and what is worse? This question seems easy when dealing with such matters as health or income. In either case, "more" can readily be accepted as better. But how are we to judge such data as divorce rates, abortion rates, crowding, and so on. There is much disagreement here on what is desirable (e.g., Proshansky et al., 1972; Zlutnick and Altman, 1972). Perhaps the critical issue is not the direction of preferred change but the importance of the issue itself.

Objective versus Subjective Indicators. We have already discussed general issues related to objective versus subjective measurements. There is agreement that both types of indicators are needed. We not only want to know how many hospitals there are in a given area, but how well satisfied the population of that area is with the health services received from these hospitals. There is the recognition, however, that obtaining valid data about the latter type of information represents much greater problems than does the former. The majority of social indicators, for this reason as well as others, are therefore still objective measures.

Distributive versus Collective Measures. Should indicators emphasize individual and/or family-oriented information (distributive measures)? or rather institutional or governmental data (collective measures)? Arguments can be raised for either, and the ideal solution would be to cover each area both ways. For example, in education we would want to have information about individuals, such as years of schooling completed, degrees obtained, and so on. But we also need to know changes in the number of educational institutions, fluctuations in expenditures by government and private institutions, and similar matters. Individual well-being and institutional well-being are not necessarily perfectly correlated.

Economic versus Noneconomic Aspects. Social indicators arose out of the need to measure the noneconomic aspects—"the 'quality' of life and not merely the magnitude of market activity" (Duncan, 1974, p. 16).

> The very idea of social indicators was predicated on the judgment that there is a mind-set which is destroying the social fabric, both in regard to its ability to perform economic functions and with respect to the maintenance of culture. It is the spirit of hedonism and materialism, the insistence that a means-ends calculus be applied to everything. The public senses that this is happening; they feel that society is going to hell while everyone is getting richer. (Duncan, 1974, p. 18.)

This paragraph speaks for itself. It underscores the fact that one's approach to research is very much determined by one's belief about human nature.

Two other issues, related to all statistical data, are relevant. One, statistics can be misused, or even if the misuse is not intentional, they can be misleading. Improper or inappropriate use of techniques can lead to false conclusions. Thus, expertise both in the analyses of data and in their presentation to the public, and particularly the policymakers, is essential. The second issue is the common tendency to interpret correlations as causative. If social indicators, for example, covary consistently with certain background variables, such as sex, age, or race, these may then be viewed as the causative agents of these relationships. Presentations of social-indicator data should clearly warn the reader of the inappropriateness of such interpretations.

We want to finish this section by reporting some data on the actual use of social indicators. For example, one study examined the degree to which federal executives utilized *Social Indicators, 1973* (1973) in actual policymaking decisions (Caplan and Barton, 1976). Findings indicate that

> not many of the executives had heard of SI73 [*Social Indicators, 1973*]. Of those who had, few reported that they found it useful. Those who found it useful used it for such things as speechwriting, and not for policy decisions. If SI73 was intended as a tool for policymakers, something seemed to have gone wrong. (*Social Indicators Newsletters*, 1977, p. 9.)

The authors offer several reasons for this outcome: SI73 did not offer a clear statement of national goals; it lacked subjective data; the range of topics was limited; and the data were old. There was no attempt to interpret the data. Caplan and Barton (1976) state that before social indicator reports can be expected to be used in policymaking, there must be (a) the deliberate setting of national goals; (b) the institutionalization of commitment to those goals throughout government; (c) agreement to the use of specific social indicators for the purpose of evaluating progress to achieving goal objectives; and (d) the establishment of bureaucratic arrangements with the capacity for legitimizing the importance of the informational value of the social indicators produced.

It certainly would not be fair to judge the value of social indicators by this one study. If anything, it makes evident the need to publicize the availability of such data and to promote a recognition of their value.

LEISURE

Leisure and recreation have traditionally been studied as one of the topics relevant to the quality of life. Such investigations have typically been carried out within the framework of an objective or residual conceptualization of leisure. No doubt that will continue for some time to come. Thus, the emphasis is on amount of free time available, activities people engage in, and expenditures connected with these activities. With the increasing emphasis on subjective indicators, leisure as a state of mind is bound to receive its fair share of attention in the not so distant future. (Once the role of leisure as *the* criterion for the quality of life is recognized, a whole new chapter of leisure research will emerge; this recognition, however, seems still quite a distance away.)

First, an encouraging word. Research on leisure and leisure-related topics is becoming more popular. Only a few years ago, Rabel J. Burdge (1974), the then editor of the *Journal of Leisure Research,* in describing the state of leisure research, reflected quite a pessimistic view:

> Only persons who wish to avoid promotions would consider doing research on such interdisciplinary topics as pollution, natural resources development, the energy crisis, let alone leisure and recreation.

I believe that the climate is changing, an indication of which is the appearance of any number of leisure studies departments at universities in the United States and Canada (Ibrahim, 1975), as well as the greater involvement of traditional departments in leisure research. Another indication is the recent publication of yet another scholarly and interdisciplinary journal on leisure research, namely *Leisure Sciences* (1977).

Meanwhile, the task of keeping track of leisure research and publications has become a nightmare. As in all the other sciences, the task has outgrown any one individual's capacity, and several institutional efforts to provide such information have been initiated.[6]

What constitutes leisure research? A frequently quoted classification is that of Meyersohn (1969), who has grouped leisure research as follows: activities, expenditures of time and money, and meanings. Neulinger and Breit (1969) have suggested that a fourth category be added, namely research into leisure attitudes. A survey of leisure researchers has provided a three way categorization of current research interests, namely "conceptual-historical, sociology of leisure, and sports" (Crandall and Lewko, 1976). Most commonly reported future research directions in this work were "antecedents and consequences of leisure behavior, planning and service delivery, and the development of measurement methodologies."

Yet another three-way classification of leisure research is that by Gray (1973), who lists the following: "Recreation studies, 'how people use their time' studies, or sociology." Recreation studies are said to involve planning issues, and ask the question, What facilities are necessary to meet users' current needs and demands? Time-budget studies provide descriptive information on people's activities throughout the day. The third category is sociological research that has been carried out in the domain of leisure without being called leisure research. Thus, studies of the family, of participation in formal voluntary organizations, and of interaction in informal networks are listed as examples.

The above listings are intended to give the reader some idea of what research is actually being carried out in this area. We shall now consider a number of specific topics in which an objective approach prevails. The purpose of this and the following chapter is not to teach the readers how to conduct research, but to make them aware of the problems and issues involved and become a more discriminating and demanding consumer of leisure research.

Time-Budget Studies

Time-budget studies, as the name implies, involve an investigation of how time is spent. A time diary, the instrument used in such research, has been defined as "a log . . . of the sequence and duration of activities engaged in by an individual over a specific period, most typically the 24 hour day" (Converse, 1968).

It is easy to see how this approach blends in with, or might even instigate, a residual view of leisure as time left over. Szalai, in the introduction to *The Use of Time* (1972a)—a work we shall consider next

—points out that time-budget research has turned into a branch of survey research. This development has been beneficial to time-budget studies because greatly improved techniques have been introduced, but it also

> hindered the adequate development of a field of great potential interest to psychological research: the analysis of personality traits expressing themselves in the individual's "treatment" of time, in this "time husbandry." (P. 7.)

One might add to this that the popularization of the residual definition of leisure, much promoted by these studies, did far greater damage by keeping psychological considerations in general out of these surveys until very recently (e.g., Levy, 1975).

Szalai states that

> the bulk of time-budget studies published before World War II originated in Great Britain, the Soviet Union and the United States, quite a few in France and Germany; other countries were only sporadically represented. (P. 6.) [7]

Classical time-budget studies in the United States (e.g., Lundberg et al., 1934; Sorokin and Berger, 1939) have been reviewed by Robinson and Converse (1972) and summarized by others (e.g., Neulinger, 1974a; Levy, 1975). The scope of time-budget studies, given computer technology, has taken on truly monumental dimensions. Szalai (1972a), for example, reports on a time-budget survey based on "170,000 systematically conducted, technically refined and well controlled 'yesterday interviews' carried out in 1960–1961 by the Japanese Radio and Television Culture Research Institute" (p. 8). He further states that "between 1959 and 1965 alone time-budget surveys involving well over 100,000 man-days of recorded human activities were carried out by the Institute for Economics of the Soviet Academy of Sciences in Novosibirsk and by some related research organizations . . ." (p. 8). And *The Use of Time,* a cross-cultural research project carried out under the leadership of Alexander Szalai, is perhaps the best example of such a gigantic undertaking.

Of particular interest to us as leisure professionals is of course the fact that "leisure, or the lack of it, is the central theme of an incredible number of time-budget studies carried out since World War II in practically all countries where social research has reached a certain stage of development" (Szalai, 1972a, p. 8). As I said before, there is cause for optimism.

We shall organize our discussion of problems and issues of time-budget studies around Alexander Szalai's text, *The use of time: daily* activities of urban and suburban populations in twelve countries (1972b).[8] This volume was edited by Szalai in collaboration with Philip E. Converse, Pierre Feldheim, Erwin K. Scheuch, and Philip J. Stone, and reflects the work of dozens if not hundreds of researchers across twelve countries. What follows is not in any way a summary of the book. The reader may obtain that from a very useful review of it in the Journal of Leisure Research (Dunn, 1974). Rather, to illustrate certain issues or problems, we shall use what has been said in the book about the research.

Parallel Activities. Time-budgets resemble financial budgets, the accounting of income and expenditures. However, as Szalai (1972a, p. 1) points out: "Time can only be spent, not 'earned'. Therefore time-budgets have no income side." This statement, besides reminding us of our mortality and the fact that our days are, indeed, counted, also alerts us to the fact that the real subject of time-budget studies is not time per se, but the use people make of their time—thus the title of that study! The fact that everyone starts out with exactly twenty-four hours, or to be more precise 1440 minutes per day, seems to give these studies a certain elegance of design, a common baseline for every subject. Unfortunately, even this simplicity is an illusion. Since we are interested in activities rather than time, we soon discover what we all know: that people engage in more than one activity at a time. Somebody, either the respondent or the investigator, must decide which of two or more activities is the primary one, an act that clearly introduces subjectivity into this objective procedure. One can, of course, record secondary or even tertiary activities, or try to resolve the issue in some other manner. But,

> any time-budget study which does not grapple in some way with the problem of recording secondary or parallel activities is essentially unable to give a balanced account of the great variety of activities which fill up everyday life. (P. 3.)

There is evidence and theorizing that parallel activities are on the increase. Pretests for the Szalai study indicated "the more a person is part of an industrial society with a very high density of communication, and the more educated a person, the more likely he is to do a number of activities simultaneously" (p. 77). Scheuch coined the term time-deepening as an analogy to capital deepening, to describe this phenomenon: "If a person develops the ability to do several things simultaneously, he can crowd a greater number of activities into the same 24 hours" (Szalai, 1972b, p. 77). Godbey (1976) made this term the basis of a most insightful article, referring among others to Linder's (1970) analysis of our perception of scarcity of time, and Meyersohn's (1968) concept of "the more, the more," implying that under conditions of appropriate motivation, the more people do, the more they want to do, and vice versa. Godbey points out that this time deepening may well be related to tremendous psychological stress, accounting, in part, for our society's rather shocking state of mental and physical health. One is reminded also of Toffler's (1970) analysis of the way in which modern society attempts to cope with that "peculiarly superindustrial dilemma: overchoice" (p. 264). Let me end this aside with the following quote:

> A more basic and radical method of raising the yield on time used in consumption is to increase the amount of consumer goods to be enjoyed per time unit. Just as working time becomes more productive when combined with more capital, so consumption time can give a higher yield when combined with more consumer goods. (Linder, 1970, p. 4.)

Attributes Studied. Back to Szalai's work. The attributes of activities studied in this project were four temporal variables: *duration*, how much time is spent on a certain activity; *frequency*, how often that activity is undertaken during the day; *timing*, when that activity is undertaken during the day; and *sequential order*, what activity came before and what follows. Although this last variable has some obvious theoretical as well as practical implications, Szalai reports that he found not "a single published study which attempted to look deeper into the sequential structure of people's daily agenda" (1972a, p. 4). A spatial variable covered *location*, where the activity was carried out; and finally, a social variable covered the person or persons *with whom* the activity was undertaken. In short, the study considered "Who does what (and what else simultaneously) during the day, for how long, how often, at what time, in what order, where, and with whom" (p. 5). It was the first time that a study had considered all of these aspects simultaneously.

Much can be learned from the chapter on "Design specifications for the surveys" (written by Szalai) and the difficulties encountered in carrying out these specifications, as described in a following chapter, "The implementation of survey design" (written by Converse).

Sampling and Generalizability. A problem of any study, be it experimental or survey, is the question of generalizability, and within that context lies the more specific question: What is the population to which the findings apply? The designers of this study chose to use specific survey sites within each country, rather than attempt to obtain national samples. The decision was to know in depth more about a certain type of human environment, namely cities with between

30,000 to 280,000 inhabitants, and to make this, rather than a national population, the one to generalize to. Of course, attempts were made to keep these sites as comparable as possible in all twelve countries studied. And while "all participants have been meticulously aware of the inability to generalize results from a specific city to urban dwellers of the country as a whole, . . . it becomes a stylistic convenience to refer to things like 'Polish data' and 'Poland' even though no more than the Torun materials are involved" (p. 51). As Dunn (1974) points out, the limitations of generalizability do need to be emphasized most strongly, particularly in a study of this nature.

In this context one particular aspect of survey research deserves mention. Gallup (1977) carried out a global survey on human needs and satisfactions that sampled two-thirds of the world's population, 95 percent of the 2.6 billion people living in nations that would allow surveys of this type without governmental interference. In reporting on this material to a Senate Foreign Relations Committee Hearing, Dr. George Gallup (1976) made the following important point:

> In the case of almost every survey employing sampling procedures, the layman's first question has to do with the *number* of persons included in the survey. A common, but false assumption, is that the size of the universe (in this case the 2.6 billion persons residing in the free world) dictates the size of the sample.
>
> The laws of probability, however, operate in quite a different manner. Beyond a certain point, the number of cases that must be taken to assure a high level of accuracy bears little relation to the size of the universe to be sampled.

Gallup then illustrated further how a sample, correctly drawn, of between 1000 to 2000 respondents is quite adequate for national surveys of the United States or even larger populations. Given that sample size, the results are likely to be within two to three percentage points of the correct figure, so an increase in sample size would not substantially improve the quality of the results. (The sample size for the global survey was about 2000 for each continent!) Does this sound unbelievable? Well, there is one important catch. Sample size does impose limitations on the generalizability of the results, in relation to possible breakdowns. If one is interested only in results that apply to the population as a whole, everything is fine. But if one wants to look at subpopulations—males versus females, smaller geographic sections, age groups, etc.—then the respective sample sizes do pose problems. Thus, in this global study few breakdowns by individual nations were possible; results had to be reported for continents as a whole. This again shows that a researcher must be clear about goals when designing a study; a choice has to be made between broadness of generalizability versus specificity to a well-defined population.

In the Szalai project, specificity was the choice. The sample size was set at approximately 2000 interviews at each site, and the characteristics of both sites and the respondents at each site were precisely delineated. A random sampling procedure was recommended, consisting of a two-step method of probability sampling which took the household (or dwelling) as the sample unit, with the choice of a single individual from each household (p. 36).

Classification and Coding. A major problem of any survey of activities is that of classification and coding. In the present study it was decided to let respondents choose their own colloquial terms to describe their activities. These were later coded by research teams into one of ninety-six activity categories, using a two-digit system.

> The first digit divided activities into ten main groups: work (0), housework (1), child care (2), shopping (3), personal needs (4), education (5), organizational activity (6), entertainment (7), active leisure (8) and passive leisure (9). A third activity digit describing further facets of the activity, such as type of books read or means of transport used for travel, was constructed, but its use was made optional for project participants. (P. 561.)

Few project participants used a third digit potential, and no cross-national analyses were thus performed using third digits.

The ninety-six activity categories were further reduced to thirty-seven activities, which can be further collapsed into nine exhaustive subtotals, and two further (partially overlapping) subtotals, defined as total "free time" activities and total travel (see Table 4.2).

As mentioned previously, the distinction between main or *primary,* and accompanying or *secondary,* activity, was a relatively subjective one and depended on how the respondents described their behavior. "There was no other satisfactory way to decide, for example, whether a person is watching TV while eating, or eating while watching TV, except by this method" (p. 561). The more detailed a system of activity classification, the less serious is the problem of which categories to designate as leisure. If another researcher disagrees with the system used, the option is at least available of regrouping the data. Note that the categories as used are incompatible with a subjective approach to leisure, and that they help to reify the work-leisure dichotomy. I shall suggest a way of incorporating subjective dimensions into a time-budget approach in chapter 9. It has also been done by Levy (1975).

The planners of this study did make a distinction between "total leisure," and "total free time." It might be an interesting exercise to examine how this classification fits in with the various leisure cate-

Table 4.2. *Correspondence between the Original 96 Activity Categories and the Reduced 37 Activity Categories*

Reduced 37 categories, with subtotals	Original 96 categories
1. Main job	00 Regular work
	01 Work at home
	02 Overtime
	03 Travel for job
	04 Waiting, delays
2. Second job	05 Second job
3. At work, other	07 At work, other
	08 Work breaks
4. Travel to job	09 Travel to job
Total work	00–05, 07–09
5. Cooking	10 Prepare food
6. Home chores	11 Meal cleanup
	12 Clean house
	13 Outdoor chores
7. Laundry	14 Laundry, ironing
	15 Clothes upkeep
8. Marketing	30 Marketing
Total housework	10–15, 30
9. Garden, animal care	17 Gardening, animal care
10. Errands, shopping	31 Shopping
	34 Administrative service
	35 Repair service
	36 Waiting in line
	37 Other service
11. Other house	16 Other upkeep
	18 Heat, water
	19 Other duties
	42 Care to adults
Other household obligations	16–19, 31, 34–37, 42
12. Child care	20 Baby care
	21 Child care
	26 Child health
13. Other child	22 Help on homework
	23 Talk to children
	24 Indoor playing
	25 Outdoor playing
	27 Other, babysit
Total child care	20–27

14. Personal care	32 Personal care
	33 Medical care
	40 Personal hygiene
	41 Personal medical
	48 Private, other
15. Eating	06 Meals at work
	43 Meals, snacks
	44 Restaurant meals
16. Sleep	45 Night sleep
	46 Daytime sleep
Total personal needs	06, 32–33, 40–41, 43–46, 48
17. Personal travel	29 Travel with child
	39 Travel, service
	49 Travel, personal
18. Leisure travel	59 Travel, study
	69 Travel, organization
	79 Travel, social
	89 Travel, pastime
	99 Travel, leisure
Total non-work travel	29, 39, 49, 59, 69, 79, 89, 99
19. Study	50 Attend school
	51 Other classes
	52 Special lecture
	53 Political courses
	54 Homework
	55 Read to learn
	56 Other study
20. Religion	64 Religious organizations
	65 Religious practice
21. Organization	60 Union, politics
	61 Work as officer
	62 Other participation
	63 Civic activities
	66 Factory council
	67 Misc. organization
	68 Other organization
Study and participation	50–56, 60–68
22. Radio	90 Radio
23. TV (home)	91 TV (when location code 0 or 2)
24. TV (away)	91 TV (with other location codes)
25. Read paper	95 Read paper
26. Read magazine	94 Read magazine
27. Read books	93 Read book
28. Movies	72 Movies
Total mass media	72, 90–91, 93–95

Table 4.2. (Continued)

29. Social (home)	75 Visiting with friends	(when location
	76 Party, meals	code 0 or 2)
	87 Parlor games	
30. Social (away)	75 Visiting with friends	
	76 Party, meals	(with other
	77 Cafe, pubs	location codes)
	78 Other social	
	87 Parlor games	
31. Conversation	96 Conversation	
32. Active sports	90 Active sports	
33. Outdoors	81 Fishing, hiking	
	82 Taking a walk	
34. Entertainment	70 Sports events	
	71 Mass culture	
35. Cultural events	73 Theatre	
	74 Museums	
36. Resting	47 Resting	
	98 Relax, think	
37. Other leisure	83 Hobbies	
	84 Ladies' hobbies	
	85 Art work	
	86 Making music	
	88 Other pastime	
	92 Play records	
	97 Letters, private	
Total leisure	47, 70–71, 73–78, 80–88, 92, 96–98	

ADDITIONAL SUBTOTALS:	
Total free time	47, 50–56, 59, 60–69, 70–79, 80–89,
(Categories 18–37)	90–99

Total travel	03, 09, 29, 39, 49, 59, 69, 79, 89, 99

Source: "Statistical appendix," ed. Susan Ferge, with Claude Javeau and Annerose Schneider. In Alexander Szalai (ed.), *The use of time: Daily activities of urban and suburban populations in twelve countries* (The Hague: Mouton, 1972), pp. 564–566.

gorizations and conceptualizations described in chapter 2 of this book. The distinction is, of course, further confirmation of the generally accepted recognition that leisure and free time are not synonymous; unfortunately it avoids coming to grips with the real issue (see chapter 3, section entitled "The Free Time–Leisure Distinction").

One of the reasons for presenting Table 4.2 is to give the reader the concrete opportunity of examining at least one such system of classification (and obviously a very thoroughly worked-on and thought-through one). Ponder the degree of relative arbitrariness involved in any such system, plus the degree to which any given activity category spans a nearly infinite number of possible motivations and meanings. And then there is, of course, the glaring omission of the unmentionable: "Time-budget interviews do not, for example, mention such activities as sexual behavior" (p. 72). It might have been interesting to know, at least, how many people would have listed such an activity as a *secondary* one!

Data Collection. A final problem we shall consider briefly is that of collecting

> answers that correspond to reality with at least some degree of accuracy. Representing the expenditure of time is one of those subject matters where the reliability and validity of data are extremely sensitive to details in the manner of data collection. (P. 69.)

Scheuch, who wrote the chapter on "The time-budget interview," lists five types of data collection: self-reports via mail questionnaires; self-reports using a diary with personal instructions; interviews without instruments to aid recall; interviews with recall aids, such as checklists; and standard personal interviews with structured questionnaires. In addition, the researcher has to decide what time span to investigate (the most frequent being a whole week or a single day), and whether to ask for a chronological report, or whether to let the respondent list activities as they come to mind and then probe the memory. All in all, this would represent about twenty types of techniques (p. 70). Each of these has advantages and disadvantages which cannot be considered here, nor can the issue whether recall questionnaires might have produced equivalent results. This latter question has been investigated by Bishop et al. (1975), who describe a recall questionnaire as one that

> asks the respondent to estimate (by recall) how often he or she has participated in each activity or the total time that he or she devoted to it over a long period, during which many activities have been interspersed (e.g., "How often do you go bowling?" or "How many hours do you watch TV during a typical week?").

By contrast, the time diary, as the authors point out, asks the respondent to record the duration of each occurrence of the activity as—or immediately after—it occurs. The authors conclude that "the use of time diaries might be an unnecessary expense and effort in some studies that are aimed at the collection of *summary* information about activity participation."

Clearly a valid choice will have to be based on the purpose of any particular study. The researchers in the Szalai project decided to use so-called yesterday interviews, which shrink "the time between behavior and its recall in an interview to a minimum," and increase "accuracy in remembering the length of time spent for certain activities, and also lead to a more complete reporting of incidental behavior" (p. 73). An elaborate procedure of data collection was used, involving visits to the respondent both the day before and the day after the one to which the collected data referred. In addition, for every tenth respondent the interviewer had to carry out another "yesterday interview," referring to the day prior to first contact.

Perhaps a rather naive way of concluding this section is to state that collecting valid survey data does not consist of dreaming up some nebulous questions, and then having them answered in some haphazard fashion by anyone who happens to be available. It requires much expertise and solid work, but carried out appropriately can result in meaningful and often very much needed information.

Recreation Studies

"Recreation research is an open field" (Meyer et al., 1969, p. 78). It is open in terms of theory and philosophy, and in terms of techniques or methodologies; and there is a wide choice of areas to investigate, from recreation planning, through administration and action, to policy. The reader may wish to refer back to our listing of classifications of leisure research given at the beginning of this section on "Leisure," for example that by Gray (1973), to gain a feeling for what kind of research has actually been done.

Recreation research had been a neglected area for quite some time, but the need for such work has now become obvious and recognized. Martin (1974) reports the anecdote that when talking about recreation research to professionals, the first comment he tends to get is "What research?" Of course, Martin had the answer. His own research, providing computer based information about therapeutic recreation research, gave partial evidence of a considerable amount of work, 210 studies between 1965 and 1973, the years searched (Martin, 1974). About half of these were of the survey type, which remains the predominant methodology in this area. Another effort of making recreation research easily available is the "1974 Catalogue of Ontario Recreation and Leisure Research," which listed 115 projects in 1973 and 268 in 1974 (Martin and Bigness, 1974).[9] As was pointed out before, there are now an increasing number of such sources of information available.

With all these studies undertaken, one might well ask, "Why has the field of the sociology of leisure seen so little cumulative research?"

(Bull, 1973). This question, indeed, was asked in 1972 of participants in two panel discussions concerned with the future of the sociology of leisure. In his comments, Neil Bull sees the lack of a unifying theory "as the main stumbling block to productive leisure research." Other reasons listed by Bull were "second, the heavy emphasis on description; third, the lack of sociologists who have leisure as their main focus of study and fourth, the lack of funding for leisure research."

From Activities to Motivation and Choice. Recreation research is undergoing changes which reflect current trends in the philosophy of the recreation profession, which in turn are reflected in, or perhaps are an outcome of, the changing view of leisure. We see a greater emphasis on the human aspects of recreation and recreation related issues. For example, Gray and Greben (1973) state the following in regard to program planning:

> Critics argue that much planning is anti-human and in many cases they are right. It is easy to lose social, cultural, and psychological values in the overwhelming desire to maximize economic efficiency.

People, rather than institutions or structures, are to be the focus of the planning process. The emphasis shifts from one of activities planning as such to motivation, attitudes, and personal choice. This orientation has led to an increased demand by sociologists for inclusion of motivational (i.e., psychological information) measures among leisure surveys.

Cherry (1976), addressing himself to trends of leisure and recreation studies, reports similar observations. Speaking about research in Britain (and the same held true for the United States, e.g., see Berger, 1963), he asserts that the predominant approach has been to relate recreation participation to certain key variables, like age, sex, marital status, and so on. The result? "We now know there are particular groups of participants with pronounced activity relationships." It is time to move on. Repeating a much-sounded criticism, Cherry states that "these surveys shed little light on *why* individuals engage in the activities they do, or on such matters as the quality of the individual experience."

He suggests that research focus on the importance of personal preferences and choices and the social network of constraint and opportunity. He specifically singles out motivation and choice as the areas of increased interest. In fact, he states that "research should move into 'leisure' and away from 'recreation.'" Not surprisingly, he complains about confusion in the conceptual domain of leisure, specifically the area of definitions.

It becomes evident that the recreation field is going through an overall shift from the traditional objective view of leisure to one of a subjective nature. I included recreation studies in this chapter because until relatively recently the emphasis had been on objectively oriented survey studies. There is little doubt that had this book been written at a future date, a major proportion of recreation studies would belong in the next chapter.

Recreation research, then, has the task of providing the knowledge base for intelligent planning, administration, and policy decisions. This knowledge, however, is not in itself a guarantee of success; it still needs to be applied appropriately and effectively. How do we know whether these tasks are being carried out successfully? This question leads to yet another area of recreation research, one that deserves special and independent treatment.

Evaluation Research. It is relatively easy to design and carry out research on what people do with their time, how many recreation facilities exist, or even what people's needs or leisure attitudes are. It is also relatively easy to come up with suggestions and programs based on such research to bring about desirable and desired changes. This is particularly easy if nobody ever checks whether such programs produce the changes they were designed to achieve. This checking process has come to be known as evaluation research, and is a most difficult task.

The need for such research has long been recognized. For example, Sherwood (1967) stated

> . . . More and better evaluation studies of social action programs are needed if our society is going to be able to make increasingly more rational allocations of resources to the solution of social problems.

The increase in public spending on social action programs, particularly in the 1960s, has led to an ever increasing demand for accountability. What are we getting for our money? is the question asked. In some instances this pressure has led to unfortunate results and has become another political weapon. Changes in social conditions may be the result of a tremendous amount of factors. To demonstrate unambiguously that any one program either has or has not "worked," and to do this in one single evaluation study (usually quickly designed after the fact and carried out with great haste) is practically an impossible task.

Yet the pressure for evaluation in the 1960s had its good effects. It led to the recognition that any serious program must have such an evaluation component built into its design from the very beginning. It forced a coming to grips with the most important issue of any evaluation, namely a clear understanding of what the criterion is. Just what is to be accomplished and what will constitute success, must be spelled out in unambiguous terms, something rarely if ever done in an area that is so much controlled by political factors. Finally, our sophistication in evaluation research has increased considerably over the past decade as a result of these efforts and much work has been accomplished (e.g., Caro, 1971; Gutentag and Streuning, 1975; Mullen and Dumpson, 1972; Rossi and Williams, 1972; Suchman, 1967; Weiss, 1972a, 1972b).[10]

Have I exhausted the topics in recreation research? My feeling is that I have not even scratched the surface. However, this outline should suffice as a sampling of the exciting and challenging issues confronting the recreation researcher, and might stimulate some enough to want to get personally involved in this area.

SUMMARY

This and the following chapter look at the nature of, and means and ways of, evaluating the quality of life. Our orientation is toward method rather than content. We elaborated on the distinction between an objective and a subjective approach, and the present chapter restricted itself to the former. The fact was stressed that both the objective and the subjective approach involve quantitative as well as qualitative modes of investigation.

We placed leisure research within the larger context of the quality of life for two reasons: (1) leisure is a most important component of that quality, and (2) it may in fact be considered *the* guideline for any decision relating to the quality of life. Social indicators, the monitoring tools of social progress, were viewed from a historical perspective and their definition, functions, and problems were discussed. Their development was seen, by necessity, to be heavily influenced by political and value judgments.

Leisure research was seen to be on the increase and finally gaining respectability. This is also reflected in the increase of leisure studies departments across this country and Canada. Keeping track of information gathered in this area is becoming a nearly impossible task. A number of categorizations of leisure research were listed, and two areas were considered in detail: time-budget studies and recreation research. Discussion of the former was centered around Szalai's twelve-nation research, a monumental work attesting to scholarly professionalism as well as to the political skill in getting such a task accomplished. The emphasis in our discussions was on problems and issues of technique. The potentials of a well-conceived survey are truly mind-boggling, as shown by a recent Gallup research effort containing information from about two-thirds of the world's population.

Recreation research studies are becoming recognized as an essential condition for rational policy decisions in this area. The emphasis both in research and policy is shifting toward motivation, choice, or more generally the human aspects of recreation. Finally, the importance of evaluation research was recognized. Good intentions and even good actions are not enough unless they can be shown to have good results.

ENDNOTES

[1] Suggested readings are Kerlinger (1973) and Welkowitz et al. (1976).

[2] The topics listed, plus leisure, comprise the eight chapters of *Social Indicators, 1973* (1973).

[3] Unfortunately, some critics of the scientific method seem not at all aware of the progress made in this area, and still act as if subjective phenomena were not quantifiable. They also confuse the measurement of a phenomenon with the full comprehension or experience of that phenomenon. These two are *obviously* not the same. This negative bias toward the researcher's necessary and healthy fascination with the measurement process has no place in any endeavor that tries to disentangle nature's most complex and surprisingly orderly structure.

[4] Examples of choices of variables may be found in the following works: Sheldon and Moore (1968); *Social Indicators, 1973* (1973); *Social Indicators, 1976* (1977).

[5] This list of issues is derived primarily from Van Dusen (1974), particularly the article by Otis D. Duncan (1974).

[6] An example of such a listing of information resources is given below. It is taken from "Guide to information resources programing for persons with handicapping conditions through physical education, recreation, and related disciplines," appendix in Donald A. Pelegrino (ed.), *What recreation research says to the recreation practitioner* (Washington, D.C.: American Alliance for Health, Physical Education, and Recreation, 1975), pp. 44–72.

> Computer Assisted Planning, Communications Center
> Professional Studies Research and Development Complex
> State University College at Buffalo
> 1300 Elmwood Avenue
> Buffalo, NY 14222

> Council for Exceptional Children Information Center (CEC)
> The Council for Exceptional Children
> Suite 900
> 411 South Jefferson Davis Highway
> Arlington, VA 22202

> National Institute of Education
> Dissemination Task Force

Code 401
Washington, DC 20202

Medical Literature Analysis Retrieval System (MEDLARS)
National Library of Medicine
8600 Rockville Pike
Bethesda, MD 20014

Microform Publications
School of Health, Physical Education and Recreation
University of Oregon
Eugene, OR 97403

National Clearing House for Mental Health Information
National Institute of Mental Health
5600 Fishers Lane
Rockville MD 20852

Psychological Abstract Information Service
American Psychological Association
1200 Seventeenth Street, N.W.
Washington, D.C. 20036

Science Information Exchange
209 Madison National Bank Building
1730 M Street, N.W.
Washington, DC 20036

Select–Ed, Inc.
P.O. Box 323
117 North Chester
Olathe, KS 66061

CLOSER LOOK
Box 1492
Washington, DC 20013

Special Education Instructional Materials Centers
Regional Media Centers Network (SEIM/RMC)
14 Centers listed.

Therapeutic Recreation Information Center
Department of Recreation and Leisure Studies
University of Waterloo
Ontario, Canada

University Microfilms
300 North Zeeb Road
Ann Arbor, MI 48106

and others

For each of these centers, relevant information is listed in the "Guide."

[7] For a more detailed review of the origins and the history of time-budget research, Szalai suggests reading two of his essays, both entitled "Trends in contemporary time-budget research" (1966 and 1968).

The volume *The Use of Time* (Szalai, 1972b) contains an extensive bibliography of the Multinational Comparative Time-Budget Research Project, as well as a twenty-eight-page bibliography of selected time-budget literature, listed by country.

[8] Unless otherwise indicated, quotes throughout the remainder of the section on "Problems and Issues" are taken from *The Use of Time* (Szalai, 1972b).

[9] Also see Fain and Hitzhusen (1977).

[10] Take note also of the journal *Evaluation and Program Planning,* published by Pergamon Press, Maxwell House, Fairview Park, Elmsford, NY 10523, starting in 1978.

5

Research—
the quality of life:
subjective approaches

We are now turning to research that deals primarily with the subjective aspects of the quality of life and leisure. Quality involves a subjective component. The Romans expressed this in the phrase: *de gustibus non est disputandum* (there is no disputing about tastes). Philosophers have pondered whether the falling tree makes any noise when there is no one to hear. In the final analysis, all that exists, exists as a perception in the mind of the perceiver. This position leads to solipsism, a view that maintains that the individual self is the whole of reality and that the external world has no independent existence. This is a fascinating philosophical view, but not a practical one for investigating the quality of life.

When we speak of the subjective aspects of the quality of life, we take cognizance of the following facts and their implications. The perceived and experienced characteristics of an object or event are not only a function of that object or event, but also of the perceiver. The very process of perception as well as that of cognition is subject to this interaction. The perceiver's physical and equally, if not more so, mental makeup are involved, including such items as personality, values, attitudes, habits, or whatever labels one prefers to use in describing these phenomena. In all respects, we are moving deeply into the psychological domain.[1]

Let me illustrate the practical implications of what we are talking about. For example, when collecting data about community centers or playgrounds we inquire not only about their frequency, size, type, or number of visitors, but we obtain information on their *perceived* usefulness, the neighborhood's *awareness* of their existence, *perceived* safety conditions, and so on. Our dissatisfaction with the Gross National Product (GNP) as the prime indicator of the quality of life reflects the same shift of emphasis from the object to the perception of the object.

The recognition of the importance of the perceiver in any judgment process has led to the tendency to include measures of mental states into the study of the quality of life. A most direct approach is to ask the respondents about their state of happiness or satisfaction with life in general, a method that is becoming more and more frequent (e.g., Gurin et al., 1960; Bradburn and Caplovitz, 1965; Cantril, 1965; Campbell et al., 1976; Gallup, 1977). However, measures will also concern themselves with respondents' values and attitudes, which, in turn, may include their attitudes toward leisure and the quality of life itself.

It seems hardly necessary to document further the need for a psychological approach in the leisure field; it has been widely recognized. But let me give one more example from the area of recreation research that illustrates the spreading awareness of what is required, but at the same time shows hesitancy in pursuing the necessary implications. In *A Program for Outdoor Recreation Research* (1969, p. 2) one of the illustrative research problems is listed as "Demand for and supply of outdoor recreation." It is recognized that knowing who participates in what, is not sufficient as a basis for the prediction of future recreation behavior; we must also consider *latent demand*. "One must also have knowledge of the people who would *potentially* have chosen to participate in such activities, but for some reasons did not." Two means are given for discovering this demand potential: (1) surveying people's values, the activities in which they engage, and their preferences (mostly psychological dimensions), and (2) "testing a user survey in some sort of system-simulation model that includes latent-demand pressure by implication." The authors show bias in favor of method 2, allegedly because method 1 is "inordinately expensive and time-consuming," and because "by observing *what people actually do,* one avoids the problem . . . of trusting what *they say they will do."* Thus, while on the one hand, the authors stress that "latent-demand pressures, and not just measures of consumption, be taken into account"—an argument eloquently put forth by Kaplan (1975, p. 404) and discussed later in this volume in the chapter on policy—their distrust of subjective phenomena makes them revert back to an objective base of "what people actually do." [2] There is no doubt that there are great and special problems involved in the investigation of subjective phenomena. The difficulty of approach, however, should not deter us from attempting to resolve the problems; on the contrary, it only makes it more challenging (as any mountain climber will tell you). In this spirit let us turn to a consideration of subjective approaches in the study of the quality of life.

ISSUES IN PSYCHOLOGICAL RESEARCH

The above heading is, of course, too ambitious. To cover what this title implies would require volumes. For our purposes I shall restrict myself to three broadly conceived areas: mental dispositions, the person, and the environment. This categorization is arbitrary and does not even have mutually exclusive classes; mental dispositions obviously are part of the person. However, it will allow me to address issues that are particularly relevant to leisure research and the quality of life in general.

Mental Dispositions: Attitude [3]

We shall center our discussion around the concept of attitude. As the heading above indicates, this section also has relevance to related concepts such as values. A value is usually conceived as being a broader concept than attitude and as not referring to any specific object (Rokeach, 1973). Attitude research has been an integral part of social psychology since its inception (e.g., Thomas and Znaniecki, 1918; Allport, 1968). One can distinguish two broad areas of attitude research: attitude measurement and attitude change. Both of these areas are becoming more and more relevant to leisure, the first through the increased emphasis on subjective aspects in leisure planning and policy decisions, and the second through the new field of leisure education, which I have referred to elsewhere as "an issue of attitude change."

Much has been written, often in very critical terms, about the frequently low correlation between attitudes and behavior (e.g., Chein, 1949; Wicker, 1969). It is indeed a fact that very often what one would like to do (according to one's attitude) is not what one ends up doing. Does that imply that one has no attitude, or that attitudes do not exist, or that one should not even bother to try to find out what people's attitudes are? Certainly not. One might even argue that it is precisely because of these low correlations that one should increase one's concern with attitude measurement. Why are people not more often able to act according to their attitudes? This, after all, is a question that policymakers should be concerned with. Anyone denying the concept of attitude is adopting the viewpoint that the person is an automaton, a reactive rather than active agent. Such a viewpoint is obviously incompatible with a philosophy of leisure as expressed here. There have been a number of articles recently that have defended the usefulness of the concept of attitude and that have demonstrated that the low correlations tend to be due to methodological problems (Heberlein and Black, 1976; Kelman, 1974; P. E. Murphy, 1975; Weigel and Newman, 1976). Whatever the reason, let us just say that one's attitude is bound to determine one's actions in this respect!

The following discussion of issues in attitude measurement research is based on an outline for the description and measurement of attitudes devised by Isidor Chein.[4] The purpose of this outline is to make the reader aware of the many and complex aspects one needs to consider when trying to answer the simple question, What is your attitude about this or that?

I have defined a person's attitude toward leisure as one's particular way of thinking about, feeling about, and acting toward or in regard to, leisure. This definition refers to the three generally accepted components of attitude—the cognitive, the affective, and the policy orientation—as well as to the object of an attitude, in this instance leisure.

Cognitive Orientation. This refers to the perceptions, beliefs, and expectations concerning attributes of the object of the attitude. For example, my attitude toward spinach might be based on the fact that I consider spinach to be a green vegetable containing iron, that is healthy and relatively inexpensive. My attitude toward leisure may reflect my thinking of it as free time, or on the other hand as a state of mind. It is easy to see that the perceptions I have of an object will affect my overall attitude toward that object. It should also be clear that such differences in perception represent a major obstacle in attitude measurement.

Affective Orientation. This refers to one's positive, neutral, or negative affect toward the object; one's liking or disliking of it. It also refers to other feelings related to the object: for example, it might make me feel anxious, sad, or joyful.

Policy Orientation. This refers to the action contemplated or carried out in regard to the object. We may distinguish here as follows: (a) a general principle: what should be done? (b) a personal prediction: what would *I* do if . . . ? (c) a personal commitment: what should or must *I* do if . . . ? Note that there is a wide range of possible answers to each of these questions and that a person's attitude may well contain some very inconsistent aspects.

The three orientations listed are the basic components of any attitude. A full exploration and the successful measurement of an attitude requires, however, the consideration of the following further dimensions.

Certainty, Intensity, or Conviction. Each of the three components of attitude can be experienced with varying degrees of these dimensions. This needs little elaboration, although the implications are obviously considerable.

Overtness or Covertness. This refers to the degree of readiness of the person to express the attitude, and has obvious implications for measurement.

Consistency or Inconsistency. This concerns the degree to which a person may experience ambivalence in any of the previously mentioned areas, and in fact may be and act inconsistent. This obviously complicates measurement, but if we want to include people in our "prediction equations" we must take them as they are and not as we would like them to be.

The Salience of the Object. This involves the degree of prominence the object has in the person's life—a frequently overlooked factor in survey questionnaires. Persons who have hardly any contact with the attitude object still give responses, and these are accepted as meaningful.

Consciousness or Unconsciousness. Not everyone has accepted the existence of unconscious attitudes or motivation. But even of those who have, how many are paying only lip service to this belief? It is a very threatening realization that a rational being, *Homo sapiens,* meaning you and me, may be driven by factors we are not aware of and have no control over. Again, implications for measurement and the understanding of behavior in general are weighty.

Tenacity. This refers to the resistance to change of the attitude in general, or of any of its dimensions.

Isolation or Interdependence. The meaning of this dimension is clear: attitudes may exist relatively isolated in the person's mind, or they may be anchored to other attitudes, like a tree that has spread its roots widely and is intertwined with those of many others. The most obvious implication relates to the just-mentioned dimension, namely tenacity.

Let us now once more go over some of these points and consider their implications for the measurement of attitudes in general and of those toward leisure in particular. To begin there is the problem of whether to define the object of the to-be-measured attitude. This often poses an unresolvable dilemma. Should you spell out what *you* mean by leisure, or should you leave that decision up to the respondent? Given the purpose of the particular study, your approach must be determined by weighing the pros and cons present, and frequently by consulting your intuition. Asking after the fact what the person meant by leisure, and then sorting answers accordingly, is one approach to coping with this problem. Another is to deal with certain aspects of leisure rather than with the concept itself. This was our approach to developing an instrument to measure leisure attitudes.

Numerous studies have shown that the affective component of an attitude tends to be the most powerful one and to color everything else. This holds equally for such situations as evaluations, ratings, and admission and hiring procedures. It has also been demonstrated that people change their cognitions so as to bring them in line with their affective positions, just as inconsistency among cognitions themselves is said to have motivational force (Festinger, 1957). This has implications for attitude change processes and thus leisure education. The literature on attitude change is vast and cannot be touched on here.[5]

I am sure we all have experienced inconsistencies in our policy orientations, for example, between what I should do, and what I would or will do. Similarly, we have all experienced positive policy orientations toward certain objects and activities, that is, we might have wanted them, but did not act in line with our attitude because of external restraints, such as lack of money. I might very much like to travel all over the world, go skiing in Switzerland, cruise on a yacht, and play tennis at the local country club, but my behavior does not indicate this at all. It needs to be repeated: such lack of correlation between attitude and behavior does not make the attitude less real or important.

Much work has been done devising methods designed to overcome the person's reluctance to state his or her "true" attitude. This problem is particularly relevant in the area of measuring prejudice, but also applies to other instances where people respond in terms of what they perceive as the "desired" answer. The issue has been appropriately referred to as the problem of social desirability. All we can do here is alert the reader to the problem; suggestions on how to deal with it may be found in most books on the methodology of social psychology.

Similarly, many techniques have been developed to get at the person's unconscious attitudes, ranging from physiological measures to the well-known projective techniques. One of the major problems of these techniques is their validity: Are they really measuring what they purport to measure? Again, all we can do is suggest that the reader consult works in these special areas, when the need arises. The important point is to be aware that such problems do exist.

The Person

There are several reasons for picking this heading. One is the increasing emphasis paid by leisure and recreation professionals to the humanistic or person aspects of leisure. Another is the trend toward a holistic rather than atomistic view of the person in psychology in general. In line with this is a typological rather than trait-oriented approach that leads to a concern with person types rather than individual attributes of people. The question that concerns us is how best to take into account an individual's specific characteristics and requirements in dealing with issues of leisure or the quality of life. We shall emphasize one major issue in our discussion, that of a person's needs, but shall at least point to other topics as well.

"Taking the person into account" is quite a task. How is one to proceed? Inquiring about people's attitudes is a step in that direction, but it is not getting at the core of the person. Attitudes may have motivating force, especially if their intensity is strong enough; but we tend to think of them as channeling action rather than originating it. We use terms like *motivation, drive, instinct, need,* and so on, when referring to the forces within us that make us do the things we do. These forces are more basic, although they also develop within the context of the interaction of person and environment, and some may even be totally environmentally determined and learned. For example, some people have developed a force that drives them to achieve—in different areas, in different ways, but achieve they must. While the origin of this drive may be of great theoretical interest and the respective contributions of "nature versus nurture" may have long-range implications, our interest lies in the identification of the drive and its implications for leisure.

We need a theoretical framework that allows us to include these forces in the design of our investigations. In short, we need a personality theory. A great many such theories have been advanced and several are well-suited to serve our task. We shall be eclectic and pick aspects of those that are particularly useful for our purposes.

The Concept of Needs. Our task requires a theory that spells out individuals' requirements as determined by their personality, in specific and measurable ways. A dynamic theory such as that of Freud, which is based primarily on the struggle of intrapsychic forces, may be the answer to our eventual understanding of human nature; but it is as yet too abstract and nonquantitative to be suitable for our purposes. A more appropriate theory, which is rooted in a psychoanalytic background but has evolved very specific means of identifying and measuring personality demands, is that of Henry A. Murray (1938).

Murray is a person with a diverse background. He was born in New York City in 1893, received an A.B. from Harvard College in 1915, with a major in history. In 1919 he graduated at the head of his class from the Columbia College of Physicians and Surgeons, obtained an M.A. in biology from Columbia University, became an instructor in physiology at Harvard University, and did a two-year surgical internship at Presbyterian Hospital in New York. After doing embryological research for two years at the Rockefeller Institute for Medical Research in New York City, he went on to earn a Ph.D. in biochemistry from Cambridge in 1927. It was during that period that he came to know and be strongly influenced by Carl Jung. In 1927 he accepted an invitation to go to Harvard University, where he soon become the leader of the Harvard Psychological Clinic. He was one of the charter members of the Boston Psychoanalytic Society, and completed his training in psychoanalysis in 1935. In 1943 he joined the Army Medical Corps, directing an assessment service for the Office of Strategic Services. In 1947 he returned to Harvard and continued his work in the Department of Social Relations. It should be mentioned in passing that Murray has also achieved a reputation as an expert on Herman Melville.

The reason for this rather lengthy biographic sketch is to indicate the depth of Murray's understanding and the broadness of his background. The theory of personality that he developed and for which he used the term "personology" (Murray, 1938) is an attempt to delineate individuals in all of their complexity. While his theory is anchored in psychoanalytic concepts, it has a number of features that make it quite unique. The reader is referred elsewhere for a full description of the many and complex aspects of the theory (Hall and Lindzey, 1970). We shall limit our discussion to the relevant usefulness of this theory as a tool for investigating leisure-related phenomena.

Murray's prime emphasis is on the investigation of the motivational aspects of behavior. There are two critical features in his approach. One is his stress on the importance of considering the environment when attempting to understand a person's behavior. "The organism and its milieu must be considered together. . . ." (Murray, 1938, p. 40). Murray used the concept *press* as the unit of analysis of the environment, and we shall elaborate on that term in a later section, entitled "The Environment." A second feature that makes Murray distinct from other psychoanalytically oriented theorists is his emphasis on measurement. He states as one of his basic aims the intention "to devise *techniques* for getting at some of the more important attributes of personality" (Murray, 1938, p. 4).

A central attribute of Murray's theory is the concept of *need*.

> A need is a construct (a convenient fiction or hypothetical concept) which stands for a force . . . in the brain region, a force which organizes perception, apperception, intellection, conation and action in such a way as to transform in a certain direction an existing, unsatisfying situation. A need is sometimes provoked directly by internal processes of a certain kind . . . but, more frequently . . . by the occurrence of one of a few commonly effective press (or by anticipatory images of such press). Thus, it manifests itself by leading the organism to search for or to avoid encountering or, when encountered, to attend and respond to certain kinds of press. . . . (Murray, 1938, pp. 123–124.)

Note the explicit emphasis on the need-press interaction in the very definition of the concept. In cooperation with a team of professional colleagues, Murray identified about twenty critical needs (such as abasement, achievement, affiliation, and so on), and also developed instruments and techniques for measuring these (e.g., the *Thematic Apperception Test,* Morgan and Murray, 1935, pp. 289–306).[6]

The theory further stresses that needs do not operate independently from one other; they interact. Each person must be viewed within the context of a dynamic hierarchy of needs. It is important to take this statement seriously, because it implies that the direction a given need will take is in fact partially determined by other needs. Thus the need for achievement may in one person express itself in the direction of affiliative behavior (if linked with a need for affiliation), while in another it may result in greater intellectual achievements (if linked with a need for understanding). It is this dynamic aspect of the theory that qualifies it to deal with the person as a whole rather than limiting it to a concern with needs taken individually. Murray's system is thus ideally suited to a typological approach to personality, and has in fact led to such work (for example, Stein, 1963; Stein and Neulinger, 1968; Neulinger, 1967; 1968; 1974a, pp. 60–65). In such an approach the unit of analysis is the person rather than a particular trait or activity of the person. It implies a multi-variable design and allows the complexity and individuality of the person to be expressed. The merit of the typological approach is a controversial one (e.g., Burt, 1946; Stephenson, 1953), but its advantages seem to have been recognized by a number of leisure researchers. For example, Ditton et al. (1975) state that "typologies enable the identification of activities and facilities which may complement or substitute for others in the type." They also lead to greater predictability of other behavior characteristics of the individuals in the type. The number of studies using a typological approach are numerous (e.g., Proctor, 1962; Bishop, 1970; Witt, 1971; Burton, 1971; McKechnie, 1974; Ditton et al., 1975; Ritchie, 1975). It should be stressed that not every typological approach is a person-type approach; in fact, most tend to be activity- or "variable"-oriented.[7] Similarities among activities rather than people form the basis of clustering.

Some researchers have used Murray's (1938) need system as the basis of their typologies (e.g., Tinsley, Barrett and Kass, 1977), but this particular choice is of course not essential. What is important is that a relatively large number of valid and hopefully uni-dimensional and independent measures form the basis of the analysis, and that these measures are relevant to the purpose of the research. One of the advantages of a typological approach is that one can make the types as general or as specific as one's task demands.

In summary, it is essential that leisure researchers, and in turn planners, confront the implications of individual differences as well as of similarities. Two issues are involved: (1) finding a valid method for probing and identifying an individual's need hierarchy; and (2) relating this individuality to behavior patterns, finding ways of maximizing need satisfaction, and channeling behavior into socially and individually beneficial directions. That final statement may cause some raised eyebrows, but it is only fair to make it explicit: the leisure professional cannot help but be involved with questions of values.

The Concept of Need Hierarchy. We have mentioned that Murray sees individual needs as interacting with each other, and forming hierarchical structures within the personality system. The nature of these hierarchies, however, is assumed to be very much a function of the unique individual and his or her history. A psychologist who has emphasized a certain universality in the rank order of such needs, and thus their hierarchical structure, is Maslow (1954) whose work is well recognized among leisure professionals. Maslow's humanistic approach, and his elaboration of broad categories of needs that require progressive satisfaction if one is to aspire to the final goal of self-actualization, make his work particularly suitable for issues related to the quality of life.

Maslow's view has been called holistic-dynamic and organismic (Hall and Lindzey, 1970). An organismic theory stresses the unity and integrity of the normal personality; its investigation starts from the "whole" and moves toward the parts, rather than the other way around. Its emphasis is on one sovereign drive: self-actualization or self-realization. It sees human nature as essentially positive and constructive rather than destructive.

Maslow's (1954) theory of human motivation aligns needs according to a hierarchy of priority or potency. Only when the needs with the greater potency are satisfied do those next on the hierarchy emerge and press for satisfaction. Five levels are described, in the following ascending order: (1) physiological needs, like hunger and thirst; (2) safety needs; (3) needs for belongingness and love; (4) esteem needs, like the need for approval or recognition; and (5) needs for self-actualization, consisting of cognitive needs (thirst for knowledge) and aesthetic needs (desire for beauty).

While Maslow's theory is "positive," it must be noted that this does not imply that his outlook is too optimistic. He sees growth toward self-actualization as happening rarely (less than 1 percent of the adult population); he is aware that such growth involves many intrinsic pains and not just rewards and pleasures; and he sees our society as being in a "value interregnum: nothing worth dying for" (Maslow, 1965, p. 312).

The relevance Maslow's need hierarchy has to the study of the quality of life is well demonstrated in an article by Campbell (1972), called "Aspiration, satisfaction, and fulfillment." Campbell elaborates on the psychological nature of satisfaction and deprivation—the fact that objectively equal or similar levels of living may still have different meanings to the person in question. He then goes on to document that, in actuality, levels of living when viewed in terms of Maslow's hierarchy are far from equal in the United States. For example, 19 percent of American children live in families that do not meet minimum food needs as established by the Department of Agriculture; 50 percent of black children live in such families! This is not the place to consider content, since we are primarily concerned with methodology, but this article is highly recommended as collateral reading with this section.

The implications of such a need hierarchy are twofold. One, they relate to the nature and potency of the individual's motivation. What will be salient, relevant, and pressing for any given individual will depend largely on where his or her place is on this ladder of need satisfaction. This is a consideration that should never be overlooked in trying to ascertain what people want, and it leads to the necessity of establishing a baseline for any given individual in such endeavors as leisure education or counseling.

The second equally important consideration is that freedom—that ultimate and essential characteristic of leisure—will obviously be very much a function of the person's position on this hierarchy. The Greeks who established contemplation and music as the highest goals of leisure were not the ones at the bottom of the ladder. Our hope is that modern technology will give the means to all or most of us to be in a position where we will have the freedom that the ancient philosophers enjoyed; no doubt, we have a long way to go.

The Concept of Developmental Stages. Some wise philosopher once pointed out that we cannot tell how two things are different unless we know in what way they are the same; and similarly, that we cannot discern a sameness unless we are aware of a difference. In the previous two sections we have been concerned with both individual differences and sameness, among people. We shall now turn to differences that exist within the individual over time. Broadly speaking, the task of developmental psychology is to explain or account for how a person remains the same person throughout the life span, and yet changes in many and often significant respects. That there are some very fundamental differences between childhood and adulthood has long been recognized, and been most convincingly demonstrated through the research of Piaget (e.g., 1926, 1928, 1930, 1955). Lately, however, it has become more and more accepted that quite substantial developmental changes take place even after adolescence, in fact, right up to the moment of death (e.g., Erikson, 1950; Kuebler-Ross, 1969). Furthermore, there is convincing evidence that these changes are quite universal, that is, they occur with regularity and in an orderly fashion in all people, although at different times and often in a somewhat overlapping or concurrent manner.

We shall not discuss the nature or content of these stages at this point; we merely want to stress the fact that they add yet another dimension to the already complicated picture. Thus, it is not enough to realize that there are quite obvious differences between the person who is just beginning a career, is in the middle phase of it, or just about to retire. We have to realize that such differences are tied in with stages of character development that permeate the person's total outlook on life, the professional as well as the social, and that persons at different stages of their lives are coping with problems unique to that period. The implications are that both the requirements and the goals of what constitutes the good life will vary a great deal throughout the life cycle.

Let us conclude our discussion of the person. We have suggested three lines of approach. The first was to obtain as clear as possible a delineation of the person's need structure. While science cannot touch what is unique in the person, it can help to highlight it. This often overlooked fact becomes comprehensible through the following frequently quoted phrase:

> Every man is in certain respects (a) like all other men, (b) like some other men, (c) like no other man. (Kluckhohn and Murray, 1962, p. 53.)

Science deals with the a and b aspects, but in doing so actually brings to light the c characteristics of people as well.[8] It is the b aspect that suggests a typological approach.

The second line of approach suggested placing the person on a scale of need satisfaction, in other words, within a framework of a need hierarchy. For this task, which brings us into close contact with societal and environmental issues, Maslow's work was seen as most suitable.

The third approach may be called a life-stage approach. Researchers have become cognizant of the fact that people face quite different problems at certain stages of their life, and that the very characterological makeup of the person changes as a function of attempts to cope with these issues. The implications of such differences are most clearly and directly reflected in the changing meaning of the quality of life throughout the life cycle.

The Environment

There are obviously many ways in which the environment is relevant to the quality of life. For example, there are such issues as the way we deplete our natural resources, destroy the very air we breathe, and so on. These, however, shall not be our concern here; we shall address ourselves to more basic matters. We want to alert the reader to the problem of the perception and interpretation of the environment—the way the person becomes aware of, interacts with, is influenced by and in turn influences the environment. We want to point to the fact that an object is not the same to everyone, and that these differences in meaning (and in utility, desirability, value, etc.) are a function of the interaction of the person and the object.

An old barn may have been a decrepit, useless, and forgotten appendix of a farm in which the farmer stored equally useless, outdated, and broken-down equipment. To the city dweller who just acquired it, it may represent the dream come true of rustic housing for the planned artist's workshop. We are all aware of this phenomenon. It holds not only for the perception of objects but for that of events and people as well. Spending an evening with the neighbors may be a delight for one, a drag for another, and a threat to a third. And we are talking about the same neighbors, of course!

There are several reasons why it is important to come to grips with this issue. One is a theoretical one. Psychologists and social scientists in general have finally come to realize that the person can only be fully understood as a functioning unit within the larger environment, both physical and social. It is not enough to construct elaborate theories of personality, as if the person were living *in vacuo*. The environment must be included as an integral part of any theoretical system that wants to explain the complexities of life. The second reason for an increased interest in this issue is a practical one. Improving the quality of life (which may be assumed to be the goal of any progressive society) means, in part, to affect the environment in a desired direction. To accomplish this requires a definition of the particular environment, classifying it for purposes of action. But what are to be the criteria of classification? Should we define objects in terms of "what they are" (somehow "objectively" measured), or in terms of "what they mean" (measured "subjectively")? Mean to whom? Under what conditions? How stable is that meaning? Suddenly we find ourselves in a nightmare of confusion. But the problem is there, and it will not go away by our closing of eyes. (We have done this for too long.) Confronting this issue is another aspect of being serious about maintaining a humanistic orientation.

Fortunately the situation is not hopeless; there is order in the universe. And while people's perceptions vary a great deal, one might well paraphrase the statement quoted previously, as follows:

An object is perceived in certain respects (a) the same by all people, (b) in different yet similar ways by others, (c) in unique ways by still others.

Let us concretize what we have been talking about in terms of a specific example, a social environment: a summer camp for children from underprivileged parents. What are the characteristics of this summer camp? Anyone who has had even the slightest experience with such a phenomenon will tell you that there are probably as many different views of the camp as there are people who are in some way or other affected by it: the children and the staff (and there are obviously wide variations within these groups), the parents, the neighbors of the camp, the local authorities, and so on. We all know this, intuitively and vaguely. The question is, how can we become aware of these perceptions accurately and to the degree that such information is relevant for planning and policy decisions?

There are a number of personality theorists who have attempted to take this problem systematically into account. The most influential of these was Kurt Lewin, whose well-known formula—B = f(P,E) (behavior is a function of the person and the environment)—and concept of *life-space* made the subjective environment indeed an integral part of his conceptualization. Murray's *personology* (1938) also deals with the environment in a systematic fashion, and anyone who is already using the concept of *needs* in their conceptualization will find this approach particularly helpful.

Parallel to a system of needs, Murray conceived of a system of *press. Press* is the label he used to refer to the environment, in the following sense:

> The *press* of an object is what it can *do to the subject* or *for the subject,* the power that it has to affect the well-being of the subject in one way or another. (Murray, 1938, p. 121.)

Thus, by *press* is meant not the inert, neutral or just-existing environment, but the environment as it is perceived and experienced by the individual and as it is, at least potentially, interacting with the person.

This is not the place to elaborate on this system and its actual application. Let us just restate the issue. To deal with the environment (that is, to include it in our research designs, to develop and execute plans to affect it, to formulate policy about it) requires its classification in terms of its meaning to particular persons, if indeed we wish to pursue a person-oriented or humanistic approach. This task is necessitated by the fact that these meanings may differ greatly for different people.

We have touched here on one particular issue related to the environment. Environmental psychology has moved far beyond this particular problem and has become a separate branch of psychology, with its own agenda and carved-out subject matter (e.g., Proshansky et al., 1970; English and Mayfield, 1972). Leisure researchers are moving right along with this trend, as exemplified by the work of Driver (1972), Lime (1972), Marans (1972), Shafer and Mietz (1972), Veal (1973), Goodey (1974), and others.

In concluding this section, one point should be stressed. While the perception and other subjective aspects of the environment are within the particular domain of the psychologist, it is obvious that environmental research necessitates an interdisciplinary orientation. The subjective must be anchored in the objective, and the latter aspects require as much investigation as the former.

AREAS OF PSYCHOLOGICAL RESEARCH
OF PARTICULAR RELEVANCE TO LEISURE

We now want to turn the table around and look not at the way in which certain problems of leisure require a psychological approach, but at the ways in which certain problems investigated by psychologists are relevant to leisure (without most of the time being so recognized). For this purpose we are making the assumption that we are dealing with a subjective conceptualization of leisure. This section is primarily intended to alert psychologists to the relevance of their work to the domain of leisure, in the hope of increasing their involvement in this area of great social concern.[9] If nothing else, it might give the researcher an idea about an unthought-of source of funding for the next project planned!

Three areas of psychological research will be considered: the perception of causality, individual differences in the perception of freedom, and the nature and role of intrinsic versus extrinsic motivation.[10] Another area, that of mental health, will be discussed in a later chapter on leisure counseling (chapter 9).

The Perception of Causality

The study of causality, discussed by Fritz Heider (1944, 1958) quite some time ago, has only recently become a major topic of interest in psychology, particularly through the impetus of attribution theory (e.g., Kelley, 1967, 1973). Heider emphasized people's desire to know the causes of events and distinguished between internal (person-related) and external (environmental) causes. Person perception is further concerned with analyzing how we attribute such causes to either the person or the environment (e.g., Jones and Davis, 1965) and it is easy to see that the perception of causality as located in the person may lead to the perception of freedom. deCharms et al. (1965) originated the concept of *origin-pawn* in person perception. As deCharms states it (1968):

> when a person feels that he is an Origin, his behavior should be characteristically different from his behavior when he feels like a Pawn.

Our argument, of course, is that not only will his behavior be different, but so will his experience, and this very difference is what we have identified as leisure.

The study of causality through attribution theory, which includes a theory of self-perception or self-attribution (Bem, 1972), has mushroomed and seems to have displaced dissonance theory as the most popular theory in social psychology (see any 1970s issue of the *Journal of Personality and Social Psychology*). The issue of perceived freedom itself has also received considerable attention (e.g., Steiner, 1970; Lefcourt, 1973). Nowhere, however, is a link made to the issue of leisure.

Individual Differences in the Perception of Freedom

Attribution theorists tend to be concerned with determining causality for a specific behavior act in a given situation, from environmental and personal clues. Causality is then assigned either to the person or the environment and as a consequence a varying sense of perceived freedom is assigned to the person in question, or to oneself in the case of self-perception. A different approach is one of considering a sense of freedom or a feeling of responsibility for one's acts as a personality dimension, a lasting trait. One could easily make a case for suggesting that one's personal history could result in developing such a trait to a greater or lesser degree. Individual differences in the perception of freedom have been investigated under many different labels, for example, as the "internal-external control" dimension (Rotter, 1966), various alienation scales (Robinson and Shaver, 1972), or fatalism (Brim et al., 1969). There is convincing evidence that people indeed do differ very much in terms of assigning responsibility for their acts to either themselves or outside sources. A huge number of studies have applied these constructs to the investigation of problems ranging from political discontent to educational achievement level. The degree to which these dimensions may be related to the person's capacity or desire for leisure, or the perception of leisure as a threat, has not been systematically investigated.

Intrinsic Motivation

Two aspects of intrinsic motivation have been studied quite extensively. One is its very nature, the other its relationship to or interaction with extrinsic motivation.

The Nature of Intrinsic Motivation. A person is assumed to engage in intrinsically motivated behavior to the degree that no salient, unambiguous, and sufficient extrinsic contingencies can be detected (Lepper et al., 1973). What then is it that motivates? There is no longer any question that such motivation is real. Deci (1975, p. 1) states that "an enormous amount of research . . . establishes unequivocally that intrinsic motivation exists." His review of this research concludes that attempts to account for the fact that behavior is motivated by desires both to reduce and to induce stimulation have led to three approaches to understanding intrinsic motivation. As listed by Deci (1975, p. 59), with relevant references, these are

1. optimal arousal theories (e.g., Hebb, 1955; Leuba, 1955)

2. optimal incongruity theories (e.g., Hunt, 1965; Dember and Earl, 1957; Berlyne, 1973)

3. competence and self-determination theories (e.g., White, 1959; deCharms, 1968; Deci, 1972)

Deci shows a preference for the approach developed by White (1959), and defines intrinsically motivated behaviors as "behaviors which a person engages in to feel competent and self-determining" (p. 61).

A different but related approach is taken by Mihaly Csikszentmihalyi (1975), who divides the literature on the topic into three areas: (1) self-actualization and peak experiences, (2) play, and finally (3) intrinsic motivation. Through a number of fascinating studies he explores the nature of intrinsic motivation in what he calls the *flow experience*, and attempts to determine the conditions that are essential to bring it about.

The power and pervasiveness of intrinsic motivation is perhaps most startlingly revealed in a study by Bruner, mentioned in Erikson's (1977, p. 48) *Toys and Reasons:*

from the start of human infancy, a good visual stimulus, concentrically organized and sharply contoured, will have the effect of inhibiting sucking altogether, suggesting that the epistemic needs of the newborn organism are not completely swamped by the need for food and comfort (Bruner, 1968, p. 32).

Intrinsic and Extrinsic Motivation Combined. The role of intrinsic motivation and its effect on behavior that is already externally motivated have been investigated both for theoretical and practical implications (e.g., Lepper et al., 1973; Deci, 1971; Levine and Fasnacht, 1974; Neff, 1968; Macarov, 1970). Indications are that the two types of motivation, under certain conditions, are not additive but rather interact with each other such that an activity that was originally intrinsically motivating may cease to be so (e.g., Calder and Staw, 1975). There is still much controversy in this area of research (e.g., Ford and

Foster, 1976; Levine and Fasnacht, 1976). Whatever the final outcome, however, the implications will be potent for such areas as education, the job situation, and of course, leisure.

Of the three areas discussed, the research on intrinsic motivation is linked most closely to leisure, and the word *leisure* is actually mentioned (listed on ten pages in the index of Csikszentmihalyi, 1975, though not in the index of Deci, 1975), and even included as a dependent variable in a study by Calder and Staw (1975). An explicit recognition of the relationship of leisure to these areas of research could start a most fruitful line of investigations and resolve for psychologists at least partially the quest for relevance that has been an overriding issue of theirs for the past few years, particularly in the field of social psychology (for example, Gergen, 1973; Hebb, 1974; McGuire, 1973; Lipsey, 1974; Smith, 1973).

SUMMARY

This chapter addressed itself to a very basic issue: the world without meaning is a meaningless world. This translates into Plato's allegory of the cave which permits us to see the shadow of things, but never the things themselves. It refers to the saying that "beauty is in the eyes of the beholder." And it raises the questions of how meaning comes about and how we can deal with it in a scientific manner.

The dilemma can be expressed another way. A parks commissioner, as part of his or her daily routine and job role, may have to order park benches, swings for the playground, and trees for the promenade. All of these are very concrete and solid objects, clearly identified as per invoice and designated for specific purposes. Once out in the park, however, the situation changes. It is no longer the objects that count, but the perception of them that matters. And this perception, the perceived utility, beauty, desirability, adequacy, and so on, may vary from person to person. Taking this fact into account is, in part, what we mean by a humanistic approach in leisure research. This is also implied in saying that perception is the result of an interaction between the object and the person, and it is what we tried to cover in the section "Issues in Psychological Research" earlier in this chapter.

We first treated the issue of mental dispositions and attitude in particular. This concept has been thoroughly investigated in social psychology in recognition of its crucial role in understanding how people relate to objects (which include other people and events). Problems related to the conceptualization and measurement of attitudes were discussed in terms of an outline of attitude components and dimensions. This scheme alerts one to the complexity of the problem and makes obvious the need for thorough planning in attitude measurement.

Assuming an interaction approach [symbolized by $B = f(P,E)$] to be the only appropriate one, we turned next to the person. The need for a comprehensive yet detailed description of the person was recognized, and Murray's (1938) system of needs was suggested as one possible theory that could lend itself to the task. A typological approach was seen as useful and used in leisure research. Placing the person within a framework of the larger society, perhaps in terms of a need hierarchy as developed by Maslow (1954), was seen as another essential step in understanding leisure and the quality of life, as it relates to a given individual. A final factor taken into account is the person's place in the life cycle. Specific issues and problems are associated with different stages in one's life, an obvious but frequently overlooked fact in dealing with questions of leisure.

The environment, the second factor in our basic formula, was then analyzed. Environmental psychology has only recently come of age and methodologies for dealing with psychological aspects of the environment are still few. One such system, Murray's (1938) personology, was pointed to as being particularly useful for the task of relating the person meaningfully to the environment.

A final section of this chapter was designed to alert psychologists working in certain areas of research to the realization that what they were doing is very relevant to leisure. Areas discussed were (1) the perception of causality, (2) individual differences in the perception of freedom, and (3) intrinsic motivation. Research was cited to give the reader the chance to look further into areas of particular interest, and perhaps to reach the cited researchers themselves to encourage them to get involved in the study of leisure. Social psychology in particular has been sounding the call for relevance for many years now, while at the same time totally neglecting this area of most relevant and socially significant research opportunity.

ENDNOTES

[1] This is the reason why I have used at times the term *psychological definition* when referring to the *subjective definition* of leisure.

[2] The authors also miss the point that "saying something" is also behavior, i.e., verbal behavior is an objectively observable phenomenon.

[3] For additional material, the reader is referred to "Measuring Leisure Attitudes" (pp. 52–60) and "The Formation of Leisure Attitudes" (pp. 115–130), the first a section and the second a chapter in *The Psychology of Leisure* (Neulinger, 1974a).

[4] This outline is based on notes from a course at New York University with Professor Chein, whose penetrating thought has much influenced my own, and to whom I owe much more than just this particular though most valuable guide. See also Chein, 1951, pp. 381–390.

[5] The interested reader might look at such works as Insko (1967); Cohen (1964); McGuire (1969); and Kiesler et al. (1969).

[6] A number of instruments have been developed to measure Murray's need concepts, for example, *The Edwards Personal Preference Schedule* (Edwards, 1953), The *Stein Self-Description Questionnaire* (Stein, 1963).

[7] This topic is sometimes treated as *R* versus *Q* factor analysis. Issues involved are complex and beyond the scope of this book.

[8] It is the artist who is primarily concerned with the c characteristics; to the scientist, c represents "error variance."

[9] If the reader doubts that leisure has been neglected by psychologists, consider the following: the *Annual Review of Psychology* contains one entry under leisure for its period of publication (1950–1979), two paragraphs on *leisure time* in a chapter on mass communication (vol. 22, 1971). The five-volume *Handbook of Social Psychology* (Lindzey and Aronson, 1968) does not even list leisure in its 147-page subject index, and neither does the *Handbook of clinical psychology* (Wolman, 1965) nor the *Handbook of personality theory and research* (Borgatta and Lambert, 1968). On the other hand, let us also observe a positive development, the publication of two volumes that are bound to stimulate interaction between psychologists and leisure professionals, namely *Social psychological perspective on leisure and recreation* (Iso-Ahola, 1980) and *The social psychology of leisure and recreation* (Iso-Ahola, *in press*).

[10] Also see Neulinger (1976a).

6

Leisure during non-free time

Each of the following chapters deals with leisure as it is experienced in certain areas of life. The thought occurred of grouping these chapters under the heading "Applied Aspects of Leisure." In some ways that would have expressed what we hope to achieve in this portion of the book: increase the awareness of how leisure comes about and illuminate the conditions that allow it to manifest itself. In that respect we are dealing with applied aspects of the discipline of leisure. But in a more precise sense, the suggested heading would be wrong. Let us once again use the analogy to health. There is applied medicine, but it does not make sense to speak of applied health. One uses medical knowledge to make health more prevalent or to increase the level of existing health, and it is in this sense that we wish to apply our knowledge about the conditions for leisure in order to promote its prevalence.

It is inappropriate to speak of applied aspects of leisure because this implies an incongruency. Leisure is its own end and thus needs not, nor can it, be applied for a purpose. Is this statement, then, in contradiction to the condition we have labeled *Leisure-job* (chapter 2, Table 2.2, cell 3)? Does this cell not represent an activity carried out freely, but with a purpose? Yes it does, but the essential and *primary* condition for leisure is that of freedom. I choose to do the activity because I want to do it, at this moment and in this place. I enjoy it; it gives me pleasure; it makes me aware of myself; it helps me assert myself; and so on. As a by-product the activity may have payoffs, important ones, such as improving my health. But those are not my prime reasons for engaging in the activity.

The matter deserves another example. When spending the summer in the country, I obtained a bicycle. There are winding country roads, grazing cows in the meadows, and there is the need to exercise (especially after writing all day). Onto the bike, the first day! A wonderful experience, in spite of dogs chasing after me: conquering the hills, feeling the wind, viewing the scenery, escaping danger (dog bites), the pleasant sense of aching muscles at the day's end, and all along a feeling of doing something healthy. Certainly a leisure experience the first day, the second day, . . . the fourth day. And the fifth? The eighth? The dogs are becoming more menacing, the hills loom larger, and the time never seems right. But the health aspect is still there, taking on larger and larger proportions. Guilt appears: I didn't ride today. The activity has changed its character. It has become a duty, it has lost its freedom. Not necessarily forever; it may return at any time. But only when that freedom is there can the experience be called leisure. The health aspect—that is, the applied aspect—is there all the time. But it is not what makes or breaks the case for leisure.[1]

The reader might wonder whether it really matters that much what we call things. Aren't we making too much out of this? I have answered that question before, and it needs repeating. Yes, it does matter. If we want to understand what leisure is, what the conditions are that bring it about, we must be able to identify it. This may be difficult and at times even impossible. But we must keep it as our goal if we wish to pursue the study of leisure.

As the first area of leisure to discuss we have picked that of non-free time. In a sense this is a challenge. We have staked our position on the assumption that leisure is not the same as free time, or as de Grazia (1962, p. 5) phrases it, "leisure and free time live in two different worlds." An implication of this is that non-free time is also not necessarily nonleisure. To put it differently, leisure may well arise during non-free time.[2] Does that sound incongruous? Only if we consider freedom a characteristic or function of time. At the risk of sounding redundant, let us state it this way: freedom and free time also live in two different worlds. Free time, that concept which emerged during the eighteenth and nineteenth centuries (Nahrstedt, 1972), may have had freedom associated with it at one time (see chapter 3). But it has never been identical with it, nor is it by its very definition capable of approaching the complexities involved in the conditions for freedom. Perceived freedom certainly can arise at the same time that we are under objective, and even subjective, obligations. Unless we can accept this, the chances for leisure are extremely dim as there are hardly any conditions when we are not under some obligation to someone or some representation of someone, such as a norm of some kind.

Since in this and the following chapters we are moving into "the real world," we must be willing to transgress the limits of abstract paradigms and realize that we are now in a gray zone, an area of shades: degrees of perceived freedom and degrees of intrinsic and extrinsic motivation (cells 2 and 5, Table 2.1). As philosophers we may remain in the realm of essences; as social innovators we must move into the world of existence.

"WORK" OR THE JOB

Work, as it is most commonly used, refers to paid employment or self-employment. One works in order to make a living; one holds a job or one is one's own boss. At regular intervals one gets paid for one's activity, either at the end of the day, the week, two weeks, a month, or at some other usually prearranged point in time. If one is self-employed, one draws money out of the business or from one's intake at certain, usually regular, intervals. In either case that money is used for living expenses and is the prime reason for holding a job, though not necessarily the one presently engaged in. It is this concept of work that is put in opposite leisure when we employ the residual definition.

It is my contention that leisure can occur in the so-called work situation, that is, during paid employment (including self-employment). To clarify this position, let us look once more at leisure and then at some conditions of work.

Leisure is not an all-or-nothing experience; it may vary both in intensity and in quality (*timbre*). Changes in these characteristics may occur frequently or, on the other hand, the experience of leisure may be of a more steady and even nature. We may also shift from leisure to nonleisure states (from cell 2 to cell 5, Table 2.2) in seconds, minutes, or perhaps sometimes not for hours. Furthermore, since we are conceptualizing the leisure-nonleisure experience as a continuum, we face the problem of placing a dividing point on that continuum. People are sure to differ in that respect, since there are individual differences both in the perception of freedom and in intrinsic motivation.

The work situation or the job,[3] like any other social setting or institution, may lead to a leisure experience or not, depending on certain factors. We shall discuss three of those: the nature of the job, job conditions, and the job's role in the person's life.

The Nature of the Job

The term *work* tends to be used indiscriminately to describe activities carried out in the most diverse jobs. The president of the United States works in his Oval Office, the plumber works under the kitchen sink, the dentist works on your teeth, the secretary works from nine to five, the teenager works at the supermarket, the comedian works at the nightclub, the artist works on a new creation, and so on. On some level we are made to believe that what all these people are doing is equally significant (everyone is carrying out their calling!); the only thing that really matters is that the person works. As long as the answer to the question, "Do you work?" is yes, everything is fine. We might not actually sigh with relief, but we certainly feel more at ease with such a person. There are exceptions, of course: children, the elderly, the sick and feeble, and to some, the housewife. But for the rest of us, we had better work if we want to be accepted as worthy fellow human beings. And it does not matter what it is we do, as long as it is a job! That is our society's norm.

Of course, we also know that it does matter. The nature of one's job carries many different implications that are solidly embedded in our societal norms also. And it is precisely these contradictions in norms that may lead to neurotic personalities (Horney, 1937) and a divided society (Slater, 1968).

An example of the importance of one's job is the relative social standing it guarantees the job holder. "By and large, status in the work organization has determined status in the surrounding society" (Gardell, 1973, p. 2). A by-now-classical study investigated this issue in the United States for the period 1925 to 1963 (Hodge et al., 1964). The authors obtained status ratings for a large number of occupations and their conclusions were that "the structure of occupational prestige is remarkably stable through time as well as space." For example, the 1963 replication of a 1947 study not only repeated top rankings accorded to U.S. Supreme Court justice and to physician and the bottom rankings to garbage collector, street sweeper, and shoe shiner, but showed a correlation of .99 between prestige scores in the 1963 and 1947 studies of the total of ninety occupations investigated.

Status, however, is only one of the many important dimensions along which jobs differ. Similar to pay received, it has an extrinsic nature. It is a consequence of the job, and the satisfactions derived from this payoff are not necessarily the same as those obtained from the activities of the job itself. To examine the job's relevance to leisure we suggest a categorization that is related more directly to job performance: (a) how much freedom a person is allowed to experience in the pursuit of the job, and (b) how much opportunity for intrinsically motivating activities the job offers. Examples at the extreme ends of these two continua are the creative artist who makes freedom in his work the very condition for accepting a job and who, one assumes, gets satisfaction out of creating, and the assembly-line worker whose every movement is prescribed and for whom the product worked on has very little meaning. Could one rank-order jobs along these dimensions? Are these dimensions distinct and salient enough to permit reliable and valid measurements? We do not have answers to these questions at present; however, some of my colleagues, my students, and I are in the process of investigating these very issues.

Let us look at some research that has been done in regard to desired characteristics or qualities of a job. One of the most frequently investigated issues is job satisfaction. Our own rather pessimistic view is in line with the predictions of many others who suggest that jobs are bound to have less and less potential for such satisfaction in the presently developing post-industrial societies. As Gardell (1973, p. 4) expresses it:

> The psychological rewards of work, in the form of fellowship and self-realization achieved through the present industrial order,

can be considered satisfactory for no more than a minority of people.

And later, referring to the "limits of work re-design," Gardell (p. 11) states:

> For how many people can we hope that work will take on a meaning deep enough to foster their personality development and self-realization? . . . Work is going to lose its dominant importance to the individual for his self-esteem and security. . . .

When we look at empirical measures and data of "job satisfaction" we are confronted with all of the problems discussed in the chapters on social indicators (chapters 4 and 5). What are we to accept as a measure of job satisfaction? Objective measures, such as productivity, reduction in turnover or absenteeism, or even such factors as alcohol and drug abuse, sabotage, and theft? Intuitively, one would expect a relationship between these variables and job satisfaction; empirically, findings are rather unclear. Data for productivity run from positive, through nonsignificant, to negative correlations (U.S. Department of Labor, 1974, p. 2; Vroom, 1964; Brayfield and Crockett, 1955; Herzberg et al., 1957; Yadov and Kissel, 1977). There is some evidence that points to a relationship between the other variables listed and job satisfaction, but it would be stretching the point to accept such correlations as actual measures of job satisfaction.[4]

Subjective measures, that is, the workers' responses to actual questions about job satisfaction, tend to be the common way of measuring this variable. According to a report by the U.S. Department of Labor (1974, p. 1), the results of studies based on such data indicate that

> in spite of public speculation to the contrary, there is no conclusive evidence of a widespread, dramatic decline in job satisfaction. Reanalysis of 15 national surveys conducted since 1958 indicates that there has not been any significant decrease in overall levels of job satisfaction over the last decade.

Reported results of these national surveys show percentages of "satisfied" workers ranging between 81 percent to 92 percent (when "don't know" answers were excluded from the percentage bases).

On the surface that sounds pretty good. One of the many problems with this type of data is that it is based on single-question measures of overall job satisfaction. Different questions lead to very different results, and as the report points out,

> the two most frequently used subjective measures of job satisfaction, "All in all, would you say you are satisfied or dissatisfied

> with your job?", and its variant, "On the whole would you say
> you are satisfied or dissatisfied with the work you do?" produce
> the highest estimate of satisfied workers. (P. 51.)

Workers may become quite defensive about admitting dissatisfaction
with their jobs. In addition, there may be a dissonance phenomenon
(Festinger, 1957) at work: remaining at a job that is unsatisfactory is
not something one likes to see oneself doing; one way of reducing the
resulting dissonance is to heighten one's expressed and perhaps even
felt satisfaction with the job. The conclusions of the authors of the
U.S. Department of Labor report were that it is very difficult to determine absolute levels of job satisfaction.

Perhaps we should look at the more specific aspects of jobs.
What, in particular, makes a job satisfying or desirable? What is important on the job? Unfortunately, the data here are not much better.
For example, a review by Herzberg and his colleagues (Herzberg et al.,
1957) of sixteen studies of importance ratings of job facets carried out
prior to 1957 led to results that, in many ways, were the reverse of
those reached by Lawler in a review of forty-nine similar (and in some
cases identical) studies (Lawler, 1971). For example, while the Herzberg
et al. study placed *pay* relatively low in importance (sixth place), the
Lawler review puts it closer to third rank, with about one quarter of
the studies ranking it first in importance. The range for pay goes all the
way from a rank of one to a rank of nine.

The previously referred to U.S. Department of Labor report (1974)
summarizes data from a 1969–1970 survey of working conditions, in
which importance ratings were grouped through a factor-analysis procedure into the following categories: [5]

> having adequate resources to do one's work
> financial rewards
> challenge
> relations with co-workers
> comfort

Overall findings were again ambiguous; workers were seen as being

> highly concerned both with the economic and noneconomic as-
> pects of their jobs. Their noneconomic concerns, however, were
> less with avoiding interesting, challenging employment than with
> securing it. (P. 17.)

The only clear conclusion seems to be that neither the pure "economic
man" nor a "self-actualizing being" tradition is supported. Reality
seems to lie somewhere in between.

There are a number of studies that deal more directly with variables closely related to those of greatest interest to us, namely perceived freedom and intrinsic motivation. For example, studies by Kornhauser (1965) and Gardell (1971) both show that jobs with low degrees of autonomy (perceived freedom) and skill (intrinsic motivation, by inference) have low "needs-satisfying value" for the individual. Gardell (1975, p. 2) describes as follows the two aspects of job content that he sees as critical for the satisfaction of basic human needs at work:

> —the degree of discretion given to the individual to determine the work layout, working methods, pace and social interaction; to perform a task in various ways, improve his performance and further develop any aptitudes he may have;
> —the level of skill that the task requires of the individual: his know-how, initiative, independence and ability to initiate contacts—in short, all the creative talents needed to do a satisfactory job.

One might nearly say, in short, that these two aspects are equivalent to perceived freedom and intrinsic motivation. Gardell's results indicate that feelings of monotony, mental strain, and social isolation are more widespread and intense among workers whose jobs are severely limited in terms of the above variables. He also points to large individual differences among workers in the perception of the two types of job content, as described above. In line with this latter finding is Gardell's (1973) suggestion that any policy planning take into account not only the total work environment, but also the total life setting of the person.

Let us mention one more example of a classification of work motivation that is relevant to our purposes, and that is that of Ossowski (1967). His system has been described by Kulpinska (1977, p. 36) as follows:

> *autotelic,* when work brings about the feeling of having achieved something, gives satisfaction due to the tasks and creativity inherent in it;
> *instrumental,* when work is considered to be the means of achieving other goals—economic or social, such as income, power, or prestige.
> *pressure,* which may be of a direct character, i.e., physical coercion, or indirect, i.e., economic, or social.

The first two categories clearly relate to our dimension of intrinsic-extrinsic motivation, and the third to that of perceived freedom. The author sees the autotelic character of work as a social ideal, and the main obstacles to bringing it about to be the character of division of labor, technical means, and organizational procedures.

It is quite safe to assume then that different jobs and/or job environments will result in variations in the perception of freedom and the potential for intrinsic motivation. It follows that people engaged in these various job settings will, indeed, experience various degrees of leisure. In Murray's (1938) terms, jobs differ in *press-leisure*.

What we have been exploring here is, of course, known to all of us. We know that jobs differ in these characteristics, and we know that we are very much affected by them. There is a difference, however, between being vaguely aware of these factors, and clearly identifying and relating them explicitly to leisure. Given the changing nature of jobs in our society and our changing demands on the job, it is essential that we have a clear picture of what can be expected from a given occupation. Such knowledge has implications not only for work satisfaction, but for job selection (and thus life counseling) and a host of related issues.

In this section we have argued that the nature of the job sets limits on the degree to which we experience leisure during one kind of non-free time, namely paid employment. We move next to variations within a given job that may further affect the likelihood of the experience of leisure.

Job Conditions [6]

The experience of leisure, to stress again, is very much a function of social and societal conditions. Since our time is characterized by truly revolutionary changes in all areas of life, we must be ready to abandon old beliefs and open to viewing life as it exists now. For example, the statement "a job is a job," may have been valid at some point in time, and may still be valid for some people in our society and for many in the rest of the world. But for the majority in a post-industrial society this statement is simply no longer true, even as a generality. As we have just discussed, this is reflected in people being more selective about the type of job they choose, but it also shows in the greater demands that are placed on conditions prevailing within a given job.

A job may fulfill any number of functions in a person's life. In late nineteenth- and early twentieth-century industrial society, working conditions were such that most people had to be content to find a job at all, and for many, one job was indeed as good as any other. The main function of the job, under such conditions, is to provide the person with funds to secure subsistence needs. As conditions changed, through the efforts of unions and political action, workers slowly became able to pass the point where both their time and energy were totally taken up by matters of survival. Entrepreneurs, on the other hand, started to recognize, though slowly, that paying heed to some of their employees' "higher needs" might even improve production. Industrial psychologists took note of these developments in the late 1920s (e.g., the classical "Hawthorne" study by Mayo and his colleagues, as reported in Homans, 1965), and their views came to be known as the human relations school, in contrast to the classic theories of organizations. Social factors, such as recognition (i.e., esteem needs) were recognized as having more effect on worker output than physical factors, such as the colors of the walls or even the length of the work day. Recent years have seen a further shift from emphasis on social interaction to one on active participation in decision making and increases in intrinsically motivated activities (e.g., Likert, 1967). In part this shift was due to the realization that under certain conditions people welcome work and value self-direction, self-control, and responsibility (e.g., McGregor, 1960).

It is evident that the factors that are being singled out for attention are the very ones that are conducive to leisure, namely perceived freedom and intrinsic motivation. To state it more explicitly, job conditions are being changed by progressive management in such a way as to increase the potential for leisure. A look at a couple of concrete examples will illustrate this point.

A.T.&.T. (American Telephone and Telegraph) introduced the concept of *job enrichment* in 1973. This meant changing tasks wherever possible to give employees more responsibility and a feeling of accomplishment. The results included better employee attitudes, improved productivity and a reduction in the number of employees by eliminating menial jobs (Ford, 1975).

Many firms have instituted *management-by-objectives* (MBO) programs in which employers and employees jointly set goals to be achieved. The participation and involvement of employees creates a situation which is highly motivating and contributes to worker satisfaction (Tosi and Carroll, 1975).

The *Scanlon Plan* is another illustration of employee participation. Employees are encouraged to make suggestions about improving management and/or production procedures. Profits derived from such implemented suggestions are shared by all employees (Siegel and Lane, 1974).

The use of T-groups or sensitivity training for management development has been widespread in industry and government agencies during the last decade. While these methods are designed primarily toward a better understanding of interpersonal relationships and group processes, their end results are bound to lead to an increased perception of freedom in people exposed to managers successfully trained in this manner. Being listened to by a sensitized supervisor will lead to the perception of being an active agent rather than a powerless pawn.

Another significant way in which job conditions can be affected is through changes in work schedules or patterns. The emphasis in these efforts is either on giving the worker some degree of freedom in choosing the beginning and finishing time of daily work periods, or on shortening the total work period and thus providing freedom through increased free time. Some of the methods used are flexitime, staggered work hours, permanent part-time employment, and job sharing (Robinson, 1976). Flexitime has been defined to mean "that the working day is composed of core time, during which all employees must be present, and flexible time" (Fiss, 1976). This flexible time can be either at the beginning and at the end of the working period, or it may include a third flexible portion around lunch time.

Staggered hours implies a work schedule other than the normal nine-to-five routine. It is usually designed to alleviate traffic problems. Part-time employment means working fewer hours per day than would constitute a full shift. Job sharing, on the other hand, implies dividing a full-time job in two, a procedure that is currently still quite rare.

Last, but certainly not least in importance, is the spreading of the four-day work week. This phenomenon has been around for quite a while in some industries. For example, fuel oil and gasoline delivery trucks have tended to have worked a four-day week for the past forty years (Poor, 1970). But as a "movement," this trend really started only in the late 1960s. According to a recent *New York Times* article, at present "roughly 750,000 workers are already members of the Thank-God-It's-Thursday Club" (Raskin, 1978). Most importantly, however, is the change in the reasons why the four-day work week is sought after. In the early 1970s, this schedule tended to be introduced by management rather than labor, primarily for the sake of increasing productivity or increasing production efficiency. The general rule was that the number of hours worked per week (forty) remained the same, but were compressed into four rather than five days (Poor, 1970; Wilson and Byham, 1973). Recently, however, much broader social-political issues have become involved. Conservationists see the four-day work week as helping to conserve energy by reducing the need for heating industrial plants an extra day and by cutting down on travel to and from work. Those concerned with unemployment see it as a device to spread available work among all employees. For example, deceased AFL-CIO president George Meany came out in favor of a shortened work week as part of a national effort to check unemployment and ward off a depression (Asher, 1975). In conjunction with such an attitude, unions are now pushing for a thirty-two-hour, four-day work week with the same pay as the previous forty-hour one.

At present, some of the main obstacles to achieving the goal of a reduced work week are federal legislation pertaining to overtime rules and related issues, inertia, and probably in many an inability to, or a fear of being unable to handle the implications of such changes.

Nevertheless, the feeling is that a shorter work week is definitely in sight during the near future, and as the president of the United Automobile Workers Union Douglas A. Fraser puts it, "the only thing uncertain about general adoption of the four day work week in factory and office is 'how fast we get there' " (Raskin, 1978).

The Job's Function

We have pointed to the fact that a majority in our society have reached a living standard that allows them to ask more of their job than the mere satisfaction of subsistence needs. Yet the need for a job, some way of earning a living, is still very much a reality even for that group. Besides the majority, there are two minorities: one at the lower end and one at the upper end of the scale. People who struggle with problems of daily survival are not in a position to put many demands on their jobs. Neither are they likely to get the chance to bid for those that might offer the potential for leisure. This minority, in fact, is the most leisure-deprived one in our society, as it has always been in any society. At this point, however, we want to consider the other minority, those that do not have to worry at all about earning a living, or providing for daily subsistence needs.

The first and most striking fact about such people is that most seem to want a job, even though they do not need it from a financial viewpoint. This becomes evident when we consider the number of relatively rich people in this country who nevertheless hold jobs, and it becomes equally obvious when we meet "retired" people (relatively well-off) who either have already found another job after retirement or are desperately looking for one. We shall deal with this latter phenomenon in the chapter on leisure and the life cycle.

At this point we are not so much concerned with what motive drives people of this group to seek jobs, than with the rather obvious fact that the job does not need to fulfill for them one of work's primary functions, namely the opportunity to earn a living. This fact carries two major implications: (1) Such people hold their jobs by choice; they have alternatives. (2) They are likely to have chosen a job that will satisfy their particular needs, whatever they may be. They are likely to engage in an activity that they find interesting, if not exciting. It follows that this group is very likely to experience leisure on the job. One might even say that their job, in fact, is their primary source of leisure experience.

It is hardly necessary to give examples of this situation. Everyone knows of such people, either through personal experience or from the public record. What is important is to recognize such a case when confronted with it, and to realize that such a person's job performance is likely to be very different from that of a person who does not enjoy this degree of freedom. The reader is referred back to p. 41 to a quote by Leo Perlis who describes the very same phenomenon. Unfortunately, this difference in the perception of work (and a lack of understanding for that difference) may also be part of the outlook of a large number of our political, business, and industrial—and even scientific and professional—leaders. The U.S. Senate is often referred to as a millionaires' club; the income of corporate executives may run beyond what most people only dream of making; and the scientific and professional elite whose work may contain some routineness, are nevertheless removed from the drudgery of a routine job. This difference in the perception of work may, to a large degree, account for the persistence of the work ethic and its exhortation by such leaders.

One might well argue that it is this last group, the working "independent rich," who have the least free time, that is, time away from their jobs, but who enjoy more leisure than any other group on their job. Some very important questions should be raised here, even though some of the answers may seem obvious. Why do most of these people still insist on drawing salaries? Why do they not offer their services as volunteers? Does the value of a job really have to be measured in the amount of money paid for it? What other confirmations of worth might we introduce instead of money? Would we be better off if we could accept a limit to wealth deemed necessary for happiness? Are our social mores changing in that direction? Should we aim for such a change? We shall let the readers arrive at their own answers.

In concluding this section, let us look once more at the three factors discussed with an eye toward the promotion of leisure. We have seen that some jobs by their nature are less likely to bring forth a leisure experience than others. The simplest procedure, then, would be to eliminate or at least reduce in quantity those jobs at the lower end of the continuum. This is hardly something an individual would or could set out to do. Changes in job patterns are the result of societal changes: new technologies, resources, consumer demands, and so on. Changing job patterns in the light of their leisure potential ought to be included in periodic quality-of-life surveys, that is, as social indicators. Such information would be invaluable both for societal planning and individual counseling.

Job conditions tend to change through intentional planning, introduced by the employer usually for the sake of improving production or services. Since worker morale is seen as related to productivity, innovations may also be introduced to change working conditions per se. It is a confirmation of the importance of leisure that changes advocated by management and labor tend to be made in the direction of increasing the job's potential for leisure.

The third factor, the job's function, is very much related to the individual's stage in life and position in society. The degree to which a job has leisure potentials in turn is bound up with these aspects as well. One social innovation that might radically improve the chances for leisure within this context is the introduction of a guaranteed income. Such a guarantee might finally provide the minority on the lower end of the income scale with at least some of the freedom necessary to look for jobs that would offer them too the opportunity for leisure.

OTHER NON-FREE TIME

It is generally recognized that obligations other than the job limit one's free time. For example, Dumazedier (1974a, p. 67) lists two additional categories: family obligations and sociospiritual obligations. One could obviously formulate other categorizations; but as long as these refer to social or societal obligations, their relevance to or effect on leisure will be a matter of the individual's perception. Dumazedier recognizes this in his "definition no. 1" (1974a, p. 68), and for that reason rejects the usefulness of a psychologcal definition of leisure. This of course is a matter of choice and preference.

I find it quite acceptable to consider the possibility of experiencing leisure while, for example, playing with one's children. Clearly, playing with one's children is a social obligation. But equally clearly it does not have to be and hopefully is not experienced primarily as such. To the degree that it is, and when it is, such an experience naturally is not leisure. On the other hand, to exclude playing with your children as even a potential activity leading to leisure seems quite out of line with everyday experience.

A parallel situation prevails in the domain of sociospiritual obligations, whether one engages in political, religious, or any other such activities. The emergence of leisure will depend on the degree to which a societal obligation *is felt to be the reason* for one's participation in the particular activity.

The issue relates to the difference between an obligation and a compulsion. One can choose to honor an obligation, or one can choose to ignore it. A compulsion is irresistible; it does not permit that freedom. If I act in accordance with an obligation that is in line with what my intentions were in the first place, I may not be aware of the act as an obligation. If I choose to act in accordance with an obligation that may interfere with some alternate preferred activity, I still may experience a degree of freedom. I have chosen "to play the game." The ultimate question, in terms of perceived freedom, may be, Can I afford *not* to play the game?

On the other hand, there is very little that is free about a compulsion, as the very word implies. A social obligation may have been internalized to such a degree that one has lost control over when or when not to follow its demands. In that event, it has in fact turned into a compulsion and ruled out the experience of leisure. This way of losing freedom is not restricted to compulsions derived from social norms only; obviously, it extends to compulsions of any kind.

Perhaps it is most appropriate to end this section by asking the following question: Is it possible to experience leisure in prison or in any other institution that severely limits your physical freedom? Is it possible that Ivan Denisovich Shukhov experienced leisure while he continued to work on his brick wall, in a slave labor camp, even after the "whistle" was blown? He chose to stay behind, and did he not seem to be totally intrinsically motivated (Solzhenitsyn, 1963)? At the risk of sounding like a philosopher or even worse, a mystic, I emphatically say yes, it is possible. I would add that in affirming this potential I am simply pointing to one of the ways in which humanity has learned to accept and overcome the human condition. The development of consciousness—and thereby awareness of our limitations, vulnerability, and inevitable and final demise—needs to be accompanied by the ability to suppress or even repress such consciousness, to make life livable.

SUMMARY

This was the first of a number of chapters dealing with issues of leisure in a specific context. We chose non-free time as the first area of discussion to emphasize the fact that leisure is not restricted to so-called free time only. Since "work," understood as paid employment (i.e., the job), is usually taken to be the prime delimiter of free time, we have centered our explorations on that topic.

If we view leisure as a state of mind, then it is just that: an experience that one has at a given moment; that may be short or last for quite a while; that may vary in intensity and in quality (timbre). Just like a tone, the basic leisure experience acquires a different character depending on the resonant overtones of accompanying motivations.

Three aspects of the job were examined as crucial in determining the potential for leisure. Keeping in mind the essential conditions for leisure, namely perceived freedom and intrinsic motivation, it is evident that some jobs by their nature are more likely to provide a positive *press-leisure*. There is evidence that people have an awareness of this characteristic of the job, but at present the public and even most professionals do not yet view these issues as lying within the domain of leisure.

We are still a work-oriented society and we still feel the need to identify with our jobs. Yet the majority of us have risen to a level of existence that allows us to look beyond mere survival needs. The job is thus ascribed a number of functions for which it is often ill-suited. Job conditions, however, are changing as a result of these demands and many of these changes introduced are increasing the job's leisure potential. Examples of such "job improvements" were given and a number of other methods of positively affecting job conditions were discussed, such as flexitime, staggered work hours, part-time employment and job sharing, and the four-day work week.

Within the context of the job's function we explored that minority of our society who are in a position not to concern themselves with "making a living." If such people nevertheless hold a job, it has, indeed, much potential for leisure. An important consequence of this is that one's perception of the job is likely to be positive. This should be kept in mind when such people are praising work, and the question might be asked: are they talking about a job or are they talking about meaningful activity carried out under self-chosen conditions?

The chapter concluded with a brief discussion of other non-free–time areas than work. What holds for the job situation holds equally for these other areas of obligation. As long as activities are perceived as obligations and carried out for that reason, they will not lead to a leisure experience. However, an obligation does not necessarily eliminate the possibility of a leisure experience. It all depends on how the person perceives the situation and the degree to which the obligation is in line with the person's intentions. This is an important way in which a psychological definition of leisure differs from a sociological one. As was pointed out much earlier, the definition one prefers to use will depend on one's purpose and personal orientation.

ENDNOTES

[1] One might raise yet another argument. Could leisure not be viewed as a final end in the sense of Rokeach's (1973) terminal values, but not as the only one? And if so, could there not be a hierarchy of such final ends, such that leisure may yet come to serve another end? Assume that health is viewed as the ultimate end, and that one knows that the person who has learned to leisure is also the healthy person. The person may be concerned with leisure as an ultimate goal, but society at large may wish to promote leisure as an instrumental goal for the sake of health. Note, however, that we are shifting here from a personal (psychological) to a societal (sociological) viewpoint, and thus have left the context of the psychological paradigm of leisure.

[2] This position is an amendment of an opinion expressed previously: "No matter what leisure conceptualization one adopts, free time is always a

necessary, although not necessarily sufficient, condition for leisure" (Neulinger, 1974a, p. 67).

[3] I prefer to use the term *job* for paid employment, giving the term *work* a broader meaning and implying meaningful activity.

[4] According to Wray Herbert (1977), absenteeism, turnover, alcoholism, drug misuse, sabotage, and union militancy have all been on the rise in recent years.

[5] The factor analysis and data pertinent to its replicability are available in Quinn and Cobb (1971).

[6] The reader interested in theoretical issues is referred to a most illuminating article by William Notz (1975). This article considers the intricate relationship between intrinsic and extrinsic rewards and reviews relevant literature. The issues are too complex for inclusion in this volume, but should be considered by those who are in any way involved in a job-enrichment program.

7

Leisure during free time

In the last chapter we faced the problem of having to clarify what we mean by non-free time. We resolved the issue by accepting, for purposes of the chapter, the traditional work–free time distinction, and concentrating mostly on the job situation as the most significant non-free time component of life. We did make reference to other non-free time conditions, such as those determined by family and sociospiritual obligations. Now that we wish to talk about leisure during free time, we are confronting the same problem all over again. What is free time and how shall we delimit it?

We have traced the development of the modern concept of *free time* in chapter 3, in terms of Nahrstedt's (1972) incisive analysis. There are, however, new difficulties arising specific to the second half of the twentieth century that promise to become even more salient as we shall move into the next century. I am referring to the breakdown of the traditional work-nonwork distinction, which in turn makes obvious the inappropriateness of a work-leisure dichotomy and confirms the need for a psychological conceptualization of leisure.

The recognition that the difference between work and nonwork is decreasing and that this distinction is becoming outdated is widespread. For example, Kaplan (1975, p. 102) states that "by the last two decades of the century, distinctions between work and nonwork may be quite diminished." We have already quoted Dumazedier's (1974a, p. 209) conviction that the labor-leisure dichotomy is becoming nonfunctional. To add one more voice, Bolgov and Kalkei (1974), in an article on spare time under socialism, express the following view: "The structures of working and spare time will become more and more similar." Thus there is little doubt about the direction this trend is taking.

Additional problems, however, are raised by the fact that there are different ways in which one might become "separated" from work: temporarily or permanently, voluntarily or involuntarily, and others. And within these categories we may make still further differentiations, each of which may affect the way free time is experienced.

Dumazedier (1974a, pp. 14–15) recognizes this issue when he states:

> In contemporary pre-industrial societies, many workers are deprived of jobs or reduced to irregular short-term employment by

technological underdevelopment. I shall not call this free time,
let alone leisure, but idle time.

Similar considerations obviously apply to industrial and post-industrial society.

One way of organizing our approach to free time must be, then, a separation of groups according to the nature of their free-time status. To put it differently, the conditions for leisure will vary as a function of persons' means of having gained their free time. We shall treat this matter under the label *free-time groups.*

Other issues are interwoven with the above considerations, but deserve special attention. One is the issue of organized versus non-organized free time. Another is changes in free time that the individual might experience, where such changes were brought about by societal factors rather than individual choice.

Throughout this chapter the reader will be aware that we are not trying to cover the traditional material on free-time activities: the whole area of recreation. This does not reflect a discounting of the importance of that domain, but rather a realization that it has been well covered already, in its traditional ways, in many excellent works.

FREE-TIME GROUPS

We shall now look at different groups of people who share one common element: they have free time. These groups will differ in terms of the origin of their free time; the reasons for their having "time on their hands" or being without obligations (that is, certain obligations) will vary. Before we start, however, let us once more look at the expression "having free time."

Free time is, indeed, something one can have. One can possess it; one can be given it. The boss may decide to let everyone take the afternoon off! One can accumulate free time; instead of taking one week of vacation now, and one later, one might combine the two or even carry them over to the next year. One can earn free time. One might work overtime one week in order to have some free days the next. One can use one's free time as one can use most of one's possessions. Thus one can squander one's free time, or one can use it "productively." One can even give it away. One can offer to take somebody else's job for a day, so that that person may have free time.

Why am I belaboring this point? Because it makes explicit more than anything else the distinction between free time and leisure. None of what was stated about free time applies to leisure. The distinction reflects the difference between *having* and *being,* which Fromm (1976) elaborated so insightfully in his work *To Have or to Be?* He goes so far as to call it the most crucial problem of existence.

> . . . having and being are two fundamental modes of experience, the respective strength of which determine the differences between the characters of individuals and various types of social character. (P. 16.)

Leisure is not something one has, but something one experiences. One is in a state of leisure. When we use the term *having leisure,* we follow contemporary usage, as in such expressions as "*I have* a problem" (instead of "*I am* troubled"), or "*I have* a happy marriage" (instead of "*I am* happily married"). Fromm uses these examples to point to our attempts of eliminating subjective experiences and replacing feelings with something one possesses. In this manner one may succeed in turning one's very self into an object from which one is alienated, but which one can deal with without emotion.

One of the critical implications of either the having or being mode of experience is its correspondence to alienated or nonalienated activities.

> In alienated activity I do not experience myself as the acting subject of my activity; rather, I experience the *outcome* of my activity. . . .
>
> In alienated activity *I* do not really act; I am *acted upon* by external or internal forces. . . .
>
> In nonalienated activity, I experience *myself* as the *subject* of my activity. Nonalienated activity is a process of giving birth to something, of producing something and remaining related to what I produce. (Fromm, 1976, pp. 90–91.)

Fromm calls this nonalienated activity *productive activity,* corresponding to what he previously called *spontaneous activity* (in Fromm, 1941). There is little doubt that this is the type of activity that forms the basis of the leisure experience.

Let us restate it: one cannot possess leisure; one cannot accumulate it, earn it, use it, or fill it up with activities. But one can have free time. We shall now turn to people who have such free time, to consider how they may experience leisure in their particular circumstances.

Traditional Free-Timers (and Leisure-relevant Factors)

Let us begin with the following group: members have a steady five-days-a-week job, working from nine to five, or eight to four, or some such regular hours. When they walk out of the factory gate or office door, they do not take work home with them; nor does the nature of their work require that they even think about their job during non-working hours. The job's task is not a salient feature of their thoughts or concerns while away from the job. There is a clear-cut separation between work time and nonwork time; one's obligations to the job are limited to the time spent at the job, and once away from there one has free time: total freedom from the obligations of the job.[1]

This group exists in our society. It requires a routine job, where the task performed has become a matter of course. There is no challenge, nor even a worry whether one might have difficulty in performing the task required. There is hardly a way in which one could improve the performance, even if one tried. The classical member of this group is the assembly-line worker. Whether this group as a whole is increasing or decreasing is hard to judge. The number of routine jobs, created by the progressive mechanization of production, is said to be increasing. On the other hand, the number of people working in service-related jobs has surpassed those working in production. And while many of these service-related jobs may be of the nine-to-five character, they are likely to involve some overflow into the nonwork time, at least in the domain of thoughts and concerns. Dealing with people is never entirely routine and is subject to complications that may linger on in the person's mind.

In any case, there is a group of people who have free time that is quite separate from job time, and we want to concern ourselves with them. We even make the further assumption that these people are relatively well off; that they are at least at a point where they do not have to worry about subsistence needs. Given these conditions, what are the factors, then, that will determine whether such people experience leisure during their free time or not? We have previously identified the two conditions that we consider crucial: perceived freedom and intrinsic motivation. Let us now consider some factors which may either interfere with or enhance the realization of these two conditions and thus affect the intensity or quality of the leisure experience. We shall merely list such factors at this point, and take up the issue of coping with them in the chapter on leisure education and counseling.

Other-than-Job Obligations. We discussed the issue of family, socio-spiritual, and other societal obligations in the last chapter. Such obligations interfere with the experience of leisure to the degree that one acts because of them, is painfully aware of them, or feels guilty if not complying with them. They do not, however, negate the possibility of leisure.

Compulsions. In the previous chapter we referred to compulsions as a serious impediment to leisure. This implication seems rather self-evident, but needs to be kept in mind when we observe the tremendous amount of driven behavior manifested during free time. It is difficult, for example, to draw a line between healthy striving in competition (including competition with one's own previous achievements) and the kind of unrelenting, even unrealistic pushing of oneself that knows no limits. But when "success" (winning) rather than joy in the activity has become the goal, we are obviously no longer dealing with leisure.

Leisure Attitudes. There is another force that may interfere with one's leisure, and that is that of guilt. We may call it a person's conscience, "inner voice," superego, "internalized Other," or something else; but we know that if we do not follow its commands we are likely to experience guilt. In our society, such guilt abounds in relation to leisure, and one of the ways this manifests itself is through one's leisure attitudes. We have identified a leisure-attitude dimension, *affinity for leisure,* that reflects the person's liking of leisure, but also one's guilt about having free time.

> It may identify the people who feel that leisure must be earned to be enjoyed, those who feel that people have an obligation to work, that while work is a moral deed, leisure is at best neutral and unimportant if not outright immoral. (Neulinger and Breit, 1969.)

A person with such an attitude may have considerable difficulties experiencing leisure during free time.

Other leisure attitudes, such as *self-definition through leisure or work* or *amount of leisure perceived* (see Neulinger, 1974a) may not actually prevent the emergence of a leisure experience, but may certainly influence its intensity and quality. For example, if one consciously recognizes that what one truly is, is better expressed during one's free time than while at the job, one may experience leisure during that time in greater depth and with more devotion than if one is not aware of the source of one's identity.

Anxiety and Boredom. There are different explanations of the genesis of anxiety, depending largely on the theoretical orientation used. It is generally recognized, however, that free time may be related to the onset or increase of anxiety. The psychiatrist Ferenczi is usually credited with having first described this problem. Martin (1967*b*) describes how analysis of Ferenczi's patients "revealed that certain nervous conditions developed on a certain day of the week and then recurred regularly on a day of rest, usually Sunday." Ferenczi (1950) referred to this phenomenon as *Sunday neurosis.* Another manifestation of this phenomenon may be seen in the fact that a study showed alcoholics to prefer those free-time activities which by their very nature limited the freedom permitted within the activity (Berg and Neulinger, 1976). Alcoholics ranked free-time activities reflecting *press-order*[2] in first or second place, compared to a *norm* group, who placed these activities in ninth place, the lowest possible rank.

Free time may also be associated with boredom or apathy rather than anxiety (as every activities director knows only too well). Boredom may be viewed as a psychopathological symptom, or it may be considered "normal" (Martin, 1967*b*). In the former case, the person is said to experience boredom because of an intrapersonal struggle between conscious and unconscious forces; alleviation of this kind of boredom may require psychotherapeutic intervention. In the latter case ("normal" boredom), situational factors are seen as the prime determinants, and the emphasis in dealing with boredom would vary accordingly.

An interesting link between boredom and anxiety is outlined in Csikszentmihalyi's (1975) book *Beyond Boredom and Anxiety,* in which he traces the emergence of either state as a function of action capabilities (skills) and action opportunities (challenges). More importantly, however, he shows that the very factors that can produce anxiety and boredom may also produce a *flow* experience, given an appropriate balance between them. By *flow* Csikszentmihalyi means an autotelic experience, "one of complete involvement of the actor with his activity" (p. 36). This concept overlaps in many ways with leisure.

Both anxiety and boredom are alien to leisure. Csikszentmihalyi's model delineates *flow* (leisure?) from the states of anxiety and boredom, by giving the conditions for respective arousals. Since anxiety and boredom are multi-determined by conditions likely to transcend Csikszentmihalyi's model, we can also look at them not only as end states but as causal agents themselves. In this sense, we would say that anxiety interferes with the emergence of leisure, while "the moment boredom enters, leisure leaves" (Neulinger, 1974a, p. 141). The opposite, of course, is also true: once leisure enters, boredom is inconceivable.

Knowledge, Skills, and Expectations. Our society may be characterized as an achievement-oriented one. We value success, winning, competition, striving, being first, and these values are reflected in the expectations we have about our own and others' behavior. Unfortunately, our knowledge and skills are not always in line with our expectations. Such a discrepancy might result in free-time behavior that could lead to anxiety (Csikszentmihalyi, 1975), or it might lead to our refraining from certain activities altogether. In either case the chance for leisure is lost.

The Capacity for Leisure. We have referred to the fact that the perception of freedom is an individual-differences variable (chapter 5) that may be related to the person's capacity for leisure. As I have pointed out previously (Neulinger, 1974a, p. 117), such a capacity may well be formed very early in life. To feel free requires "a sense of basic trust" (Erikson, 1950) that allows one to be unconcerned about matters of survival. Such basic trust is recognized as one of the most crucial variables in character development, and people vary greatly in the degree to which they have achieved it. This link between trust and leisure has significant implications for leisure counseling. In some instances, such counseling may have to deal with very basic personality issues and thus require a psychotherapeutic approach.

Environmental Factors. My emphasis so far on personality-related factors is a reflection of my orientation and not a measure of the relative importance of these versus environmental factors in the genesis of leisure. If what we have said about leisure and trust is valid, environmental factors are tremendously important in the development of the very capacity for leisure. But even in the immediate situation the environment may play a very decisive role in whether a person experiences leisure or not, and more importantly, any given environment may interact with any given personality in different ways.

For one, we must distinguish between different time settings of free time. Dumazedier (1974a, p. 72) speaks of four periods of leisure: "leisure at the end of the day, at the weekend, at the end of the year (holidays) and at the end of life (retirement)." It is most likely that the conditions for leisure (i.e., the potential for freedom and intrinsically motivating activities) will vary in these different time periods, in part as a function of environmental resources and in part as a function of the individual's predisposition.

Second, the environment as such will have an enormous impact on the person's chance for leisure. In chapter 5, we referred to the concept of *press* as descriptive of the situation's potential for satisfying certain needs. In chapter 6, we suggested that occupations or jobs may be classified in terms of *press-leisure,* that is, their potential for leading to a leisure experience. An equally challenging task might be to categorize free-time periods, situations, or activities in this manner. The results of such an effort would be of tremendous value for policy and planning decisions. We would certainly want to encourage anyone who wants to do this in the strongest possible manner.

This completes our consideration of factors that may either enhance or hinder the experience of leisure. We discussed these in the context of a group we labeled *traditional free-timers.* We now turn to other free-time *groups.* The factors discussed so far are equally relevant to the groups to be considered next; they represent basic issues that may need to be taken into account in any context. In addition, however, the following groups each have their idiosyncrasies that may need to be dealt with.

Ambiguous Free-Timers

Members of this group are also employed or self-employed; but while they work full time, they are not likely to have a nine-to-five job. Their work time probably consists of a combination of regularly scheduled periods during the week, plus other hours throughout the week, including evenings and weekends. Members of this group do take work home; as a matter of fact, some of them may spend a great deal of time working at home, perhaps in a specially designated room. Their work may require considerable travel. The job's task is very much a salient feature of their thoughts and concerns while away from the job. In fact, they are never really "away from the job." This involvement in the job is, in part, imposed by the nature of the work, but also by their interest in what they are doing. Their life, including their social activities, tends to center around their job and often involves people who work in related areas.

This group also exists in our society. Theirs is not a routine job, but one that offers challenge, opportunity for creative expression, and often considerable extrinsic rewards in addition to the intrinsic nature of the job. Representatives of this group are professionals or business executives and managers. While they may represent a relatively small proportion of the total population, their influence through economic and political power and as social and value trend setters makes them a very potent minority.

Much has been written about the diffuse boundaries between work and free time for this group, as a group. But there are obviously wide variations within the group, as in any other group that one tries to characterize simply by a profile of the average. Thus while there may be some for whom the term *free time* literally does not apply, there may be others who do set aside a period of time, perhaps once during the year, when they attempt very intentionally to cut off all ties with their regular activities.

A strange phenomenon may be taking place. Since these people are already doing on their job what they like best and are most interested in, they might prefer to avoid free time. On the other hand, we live in a society that adheres to a "fun morality" (Wolfenstein, 1951) and makes it obligatory for us to "have fun." However, since we perceive the job as a very serious matter, not one that one ought to get "pleasure" from, these perceptions may lead these people to feel guilt on the one hand about experiencing joy through their work, and on the other about presumably not getting their share of fun. And so they may feel obliged to carve out at least some free time from their busy schedule.

What, then, can we say about leisure during free time, to the degree that we can identify such a period for this group? As we mentioned before, all the factors discussed in the previous section apply here also. In addition, given this group's financial well-being, they have the resources and training to take full advantage of all that the good life offers. It is not surprising, then, that we find them well represented among many of the traditional free-time activities, such as skiing, boating, golfing, and so on. And when they ski down that slope, they probably enjoy it just as much as the traditional free-timer, if not more. Theirs may be a true leisure experience, except that when we take a closer look it may yet turn out that it was not leisure during free time, but on the job. The person on the slope next to them just happened to be a prospective client!

Farmers and Artists. Two subgroups of ambiguous free-timers deserve special attention. The first consists of traditional farmers, those who have not yet turned farming into an industrial enterprise, but for whom it is still a family affair. Free time does not exist for them or their families in the sense of clearly defined periods of time, occurring at regular intervals. Cyclic demands of farm work and conditions of nature are the prime factors in determining "free time," or the chance for engaging in activities that are not determined by necessity rather than one's fancy: chatting with a passerby, tinkering with some not-really-essential activity, playing with one's children, or sitting extendedly over one's meal. Such periods of time are probably not consciously perceived as "free time." Others may include the time one takes off to go to town to participate in a local committee meeting, or to visit the fair. How much leisure do farmers experience? A lot probably depends on their success with their farm, but the prime factor must revolve around the question of whether or not they enjoy being farmers. If they do, then they will experience leisure both during work and during those unscheduled but frequently enough occurring interplays of work and nonwork periods. If they do not, I would not want to make a prediction without knowing more about individual cases, but I would have strong doubts about their being in a frame of mind for leisure at any time.

A second group for whom the traditional concept of free time does not fit consists of artists—writers, painters, composers, and so on; people who are not employed as commercial artists in an industrial enterprise, but who are more or less self-supporting in terms of their art. It is possible that such people will have periods of time that they set aside, quite consciously, as "free time." These may be occasions in which they remove themselves from their chosen professional activities; and the length, frequency and regularity of such periods will obviously depend on the individual. It is also possible that such periods of non-involvement in work activity will not consciously be perceived as free time. Most importantly, however, such periods will tend to be self-imposed, just as the work carried out is freely chosen and desired. These two factors are, of course, the ones that make artists a special case in any consideration of leisure.

No Free-Timers

If we continue the prevalent custom of defining free time in opposition to work (i.e., the job), and if we wish to be consistent, it follows that there are several groups in our society for whom free time is not a meaningful concept. These are groups whose members do not hold a regular job or who are not otherwise gainfully employed. Let us list some of these: children, students, housewives, the unemployed, the institutionalized (in hospitals, prisons, nursing homes, etc.), the sick and disabled at home, the rich who are not holding a job, the poor who are not holding a job (e.g., hoboes, bohemians, hippies), the retired, and other groups.

A number of factors may strike us as noteworthy as we look at these groups. First, nobody would doubt that some of these people, at one time or another, do experience leisure. This is obvious, but once again reminds us of the inadequacy of the traditional residual definition of leisure.

Another factor is the heterogeneity of this grouping. This very diversity makes it clearer than anything else, that we will have to develop quite distinct approaches to leisure depending on the groups of people we are dealing with. At this point, let us look at some of them in more detail.

Children. The number of questions that need to be asked, and answered here, is overwhelming. What is the meaning of leisure to children? At what point in their development does that concept become meaningful? That is to say, at what point does it make sense to use the term *nonleisure* in respect to children? How does leisure relate to play? How does the capacity for leisure develop? Can it be fostered? There are many more such questions. Some of these have already been investigated in a different context (for example, see Neulinger, 1979a). Others will require original research. It is clear that this is an area that will demand unique approaches, but which also promises to shed much light on leisure-related behavior and attitudes in later life.

Students. We might speak of students having free time if we substitute in our definition of free time *school* for *the job*. We can then treat students as any other *free-timers,* except that there are a number of additional considerations to be taken into account. The majority of students tend to be adolescents or early adults and either completely or partially dependent on support by others. This usually implies additional obligations, which may further limit their free-time options. Furthermore, if they are adolescents or early adults, they are in the process of coping with certain developmental "crises" (Erikson, 1950) that will inevitably affect the chances for leisure in very specific ways (see chapter 8).

Housewives. The classification of housewives as nonworkers has always been somewhat embarrassing for social scientists. It obviously has also been wrong, brought about by the equation of *work* with *paid employment*. Does the housewife have free time? Does she experience leisure? The readers will be able to answer these questions on their own, by now. To the degree that a housewife accepts certain role obligations (which can be considered the equivalent of a job), it is meaningful to define some periods of her day as free time in relation to those obligations. Whether she experiences leisure during her free time, or during any other period of the day, must be decided on the basis of her perception of any given activity. It would be most interesting to investigate, as we have suggested for occupations, the *press-leisure* of housewifery. It is my feeling that one would find large individual differences in the rating of this variable, that is, that housewives would have quite varying *beta press* for housewifery. One might even question whether it is at all possible to speak of or establish in this instance an *alpha press*.[3]

The Unemployed. We are using the term to refer to those who want a job, are able and in a position to hold a job, but for one reason or another cannot obtain one. *Free time* is a pretty meaningless term for such people, and so, unfortunately, may be *leisure*. If such unemployment is prolonged or frequent, the very conditions for leisure are reduced to a minimum. On the other hand, their need for leisure may be felt more strongly than by any other group, because they are deprived of the opportunity to be active agents within the context our society has sanctioned as the most appropriate one for that purpose. The outcome may be a very strong feeling of frustration. Since the individual cannot change the norms of society, he or she may attempt to escape this frustration through alienation, that is, by becoming separated from the values of society.

The Institutionalized. Anyone who has ever been in a hospital, nursing home, or prison, knows that the problem of free time looms large in such institutions. Aside from health issues, it may well represent the major problem of many institutions. Except perhaps in prison, there are no job boundaries here to free time either. And particularly in prison, the term *free time* is a contradiction in terms. But even in other institutions, there are always certain obligations that prevail twenty-four hours a day and are thus superimposed on any so-called free time.

Can there be leisure in an institutionalized setting? The answer is certainly yes, although the chances depend very much on the kind of institution, the conditions prevailing, and the nature of the individual involved. As we pointed out earlier, the perception of freedom may be an illusion and yet have real consequences (Lefcourt, 1973). It is possible to have at least moments of a leisure experience, even under the most adverse conditions. To take the most extreme example, leisure may be the difference between the person who dies peacefully accepting his or her fate, and one who struggles to the very end. Perhaps part of the art of increasing one's perceived freedom is the ability to recognize and accept incontrovertible limits.

Individual differences will determine to a large degree whether the institutionalized will experience leisure, but perhaps even more, the conditions in the institution will contribute their share. It is of the utmost importance for institutions to be aware of the conditions for leisure (i.e., perceived freedom and intrinsic motivation) and to see that the potential for those conditions is maximized.

The "Idle" Rich. Referring to the affluent who are not holding a job or are not otherwise gainfully employed as the "idle" rich, reflects once again the belief in our society that the only really worthwhile activity is carried out on the job. There is no doubt that the rich have the greatest potential for leisure. This is not to say that being rich guarantees that one will have the capacity for leisure or even experience leisure more frequently than one who is not rich. But who would plant a flower in poor soil, when rich soil is available? Who would expect the flower to bloom more fully in poor than in rich soil? Leisure, after all, is the result of the interaction of personal and environmental factors, and *ceteris paribus,* the rich can assure themselves of having the conditions most likely to be conducive to leisure.

Is the perhaps unconscious recognition of that fact the reason why money has become such an ultimate goal in our society? Is it the belief that freedom can be bought, possession by possession? Why are the rich so hesitant to praise and commend the life of leisure? Why is it that they either pretend or actually believe that what makes them happy is holding a job? Are there exceptions? Who are they? How and why do they manage to be different? Here lies another fascinating study, and perhaps a best seller that could make you rich and force you to confront these issues yourself!

The "Idle" Poor. There is a group in our society that we think of even less than the idle rich, and that is the "idle" poor. The fact that we have a negative attitude toward the poor has been well established

(Macarov, 1970). The reason for this may well be a partly conscious and partly unconscious realization that they dare to strive for a freedom which for most of us can only exist as a dream. And they attempt to do this in clear and open disregard of the norms of our society. The fact that our negative attitude is accentuated when the poor refuse to hold regular jobs, hardly needs to be substantiated. Hoboes and hippies (and I am not speaking of the "hippie" supported by rich parents) are seldom made into heroes in our society or models we want our children to imitate. The true hobo is probably a thing of the past, and our society is the poorer for that. Let me not be misunderstood; I am not romanticizing poverty. Far from it. Involuntary poverty is unpleasant, undesirable, and ought to be eliminated. The group considered here is one that has chosen poverty as a lifestyle, in recognition that there are values other than wealth that can make life meaningful. It is only through a real belief in that fact that this group can achieve leisure, in spite of their relatively low existence and subsistence levels. It requires a self-sufficiency and ability to disregard norms that few of us are capable of achieving.

The Retired. Finally, there is the group of retired people. Their case alone more than justifies and necessitates an approach to leisure that frees it from its dependence on the job as a definitional reference point. The retired are much too large a group to be considered as a homogeneous entity. But they do share many common experiences and problems, and free time—or perhaps more appropriately, time on their hands–has become a major issue for a large proportion of them. In some ways, the situation is ironic: that section of our population that in many instances has achieved the necessary subsistence level that could provide the conditions for "a life of leisure" seems to have the greatest trouble living it. We shall return to these issues in the following chapters on the life cycle and on leisure education and counseling.

CHANGING FREE-TIME CONDITIONS

In the previous section we looked at various groups in terms of the nature of their free time. We stressed that the origin of one's free time will have implications for the potential for leisure. We shall now turn to a consideration of environmental conditions for free time. We have made reference to the general importance of *environmental factors* in our discussion of the various groups, and it is clear that each of these requires specific optimal conditions. At this point, we shall address ourselves to three issues: changing work schedules, changing resources conditions, and changing norms.

Changing Work Schedules

We have already discussed changing work schedules as they affect the job situation (chapter 6). We now want to look at the same phenomena as they relate to off-the-job conditions.

The Four-Day Work Week. The most obvious and direct consequence of the four-day work week is that it potentially adds another whole day to the worker's free-time period. There are two distinct aspects to this phenomenon. One is the fact that the worker (and perhaps his or her family) has now three instead of two consecutive days to plan for and "enjoy." This extension of time widens considerably the range and nature of potential activities. The second aspect refers to the fact that the worker may now be out of step both with the family and with the larger social and societal circle. If the spouse works on a five-day week, there will be a discrepancy in schedules; children go to school for five days; friends may not be available to share the plans for the three-day weekend. Not all of these factors need be negative. Roads will be less crowded on Fridays, or even Thursday nights, if one plans a really long weekend. One might be able to obtain advantageous bookings at resorts, on airlines, or for cultural events. All of these factors come about because there still is only a small minority of the work force on the four-day work week. Once the phenomenon becomes the standard rather than the exception, much of this will change. Business and industry is bound to move quickly to accommodate the three-day weekender, and unfortunately, see to it that the level of consumption during those three days is kept to a maximum.

There is much contradictory information forthcoming about the "success" or "failure" of the four-day work week. Some reports indicate that both workers and management are enthusiastic about the shorter work week and all its implications. Others stress the shortcomings of one kind or another, and the fact that many companies return to a five-day work week after having experienced the four-day routine. I have two opinions on this matter: First, no matter how well designed evaluation research on the four-day work week may be, results at present cannot be very valid or useful for predictive purposes since the spreading of the very phenomenon being investigated is in the process of changing the conditions for its success. Second, the eventual spread of the four-day work week will not depend on a favorable evaluation, but will be brought about by the demands of our changing technology and the resulting societal structure.

From the viewpoint of contributing to the potential for leisure, what can be said in regard to the four-day work week? There is no doubt that one must take a positive view. It is a move that adds to the person's freedom, allowing more time for intrinsically motivated activities.

It is to be welcomed as just another step toward "the 3-day revolution to come: 3-day workweek, 4-day weekend" (Faught, 1970).

Flexitime. Flexitime and similar arrangements will have effects on the job situation, as previously pointed out. But these are likely to originate from changes these routines bring about during free time. By allowing the person greater flexibility in when to start work or when to quit, one is given more freedom in such matters as sleeping longer when the whim strikes, taking one's children to school when necessary or when one feels like it, handling that unexpected event, and doing any number of other things that otherwise might not be possible. All in all, the person is bound to get a feeling of being more in control of his or her life, which, of course, is the prime condition for leisure.

Changing Resources Conditions

In the previous section we looked at changing work schedules. It must have become evident that we viewed the changes taking place as positive: and the more the better. The reason for this was also quite clear; the changes were all in the direction of more free time and greater perceived freedom. When we consider changing resources conditions, we might assume a similar position. On the other hand, it is quite conceivable that in certain instances, more might lead to less as far as the experience of leisure is concerned. Let us explore this seeming contradiction in terms of three specific aspects: personal expenditures, free-time facilities, and the availability of greater choice.

Personal Expenditures. Personal income in the United States has been rising over the past decades. A large proportion of that increase is offset by a steady rate of inflation as well as by an increase in federal, state, and local taxes. Nevertheless, there is little doubt that the average American family spends ever more, and a larger proportion of their income, on goods and services that far exceed mere subsistence and existence requirements. Just consider the fact that tourism expenditures were the second ranking retail expenditures in the United States in 1972 (see chapter 1). On the surface, such evidence seems to indicate that we have not only reached a point where "a leisure society" is just around the corner, but that we have already turned that corner. We have made it clear throughout our discussion that the person must be free from the pressures of certain basic needs in order for leisure to manifest itself. A person with an empty stomach is neither free to do as he pleases nor in the frame of mind to pursue purely intrinsically rewarding activities.

Given our relative affluence, then, why is leisure not a much more common experience for at least the majority of people? Why the tremendous dissatisfaction with life that is so widespread? Why the rising demand for leisure education and leisure counseling, therapy and mental health services in general?

There is no single or easy answer to these questions, but one reason certainly has to do with the consumption habits that prevail in our society. I have previously referred to this phenomenon as the "frenzy of galloping consumption" (Neulinger, 1974a, p. 144). Philosophers have argued the point for centuries, and theoreticians and researchers always had trouble in defining just what existence and subsistence needs are. Psychologists speak of primary and secondary drives or needs. A *primary* drive is in its major form determined by the organism's heredity, is species-specific, and dependent on a physiological need. A *secondary* or acquired drive, on the other hand, is one aroused and/or satisfied in ways acquired by experience or learning (English and English, 1958). The problem is that secondary drives may become quite autonomous, that is, independent of the original primary drive and strongly determining forces of their own in the organism's behavior pattern. Whether we wish to view this matter within this or any other theoretical framework, the fact remains that all societies encourage the development of certain learned needs that reflect their current value system. There is little doubt that our society fosters the need to consume. To go shopping, to acquire possessions, to be able to spend money seems to have become an end in itself. It is this force that significantly counteracts the potential benefits of a steadily rising income. As long as our nonessential needs are artificially and by design kept always a step ahead of our capacity to fulfill them, the chances for leisure will be strongly undermined.

Free-Time Facilities. Again, there is little doubt that there has been a tremendous increase over the past years in the amount of free-time facilities and equipment that is available for both individual and group activities. The flourishing so-called leisure industry gives ample evidence for that fact. New devices are being developed daily, for every minute of our free time and every cent of our free-time budget. Consider the truly phenomenal advent of the snowmobile and its conquest of the northern territories; note the case of the Alpine Slide, a new sport that "gives ski slopes a piece of summer action" (Ball, 1977). Observe the spread of computer-type electronic games and television-linked contrivances. We all could readily add examples to this list.

The question that remains to be answered is the following: is this increase in our free-time resources paralleled by an increase in the rate, quality, and/or intensity of our leisure experiences? I shall not attempt to answer this question, but the reader probably has little doubt as to what the direction of my response would take. Let me state, however, that not all free-time resource planning is as negative as I may have painted the picture. There are some valiant and even powerful forces in our society who do care about the state of our nation, our environment, and our future. There are attempts by professional and government groups, conservationists, and individuals to institute relevant policies "as if people mattered" (Schumacher, 1973). Adventure playgrounds are an example of a development in free-time resources that is contrary to the common trend.[4] Encouraging and providing the opportunity for jogging is another; there are hardly any facilities required for that purpose.[5] Developments in the area of free-time facilities reveal most convincingly how important it is to get a clear conception of the nature of leisure if we wish to promote it.

Greater Choice. Choice is critical to the leisure experience, since it is an intrinsic component of freedom. You cannot conceive of freedom without the potential for choice. In my conceptualization of leisure I have tried, as much as possible, to avoid getting involved in a philosophical argument about the definition of freedom. *Perceived freedom* was defined as a state in which one feels that what one is doing, one does by choice. "Everybody knows the difference between doing something because one has to and doing something because one wants to" (Neulinger, 1974a, p. 15). Note that this definition has choice as an undefined variable. Under *ordinary* (again undefined!) conditions, this does not lead to a problem. We all understand the meaning of choice when confronted by it: would you like your drink on the rocks or straight? Should we walk or take a bus? Should I take history or geography next semester? Should I accept the job that offers more money, or stay with the one I have, because it has greater security? Should I marry this person or not? These are choice questions of varying importance, but all involve quite real and meaningful decisions and consequences.

When I pick a toothpaste out of an array of who-knows-how-many different brands; when I buy a household gadget without having the slightest idea of what makes it work or what even would constitute a better product; when I choose a lawyer, doctor, therapist, and politician without having any real knowledge of their qualifications—am I really exercising freedom? These are very difficult questions to answer. The range of possible behavior goes from completely random choice, through acting out a pattern of choices to which one has become culturally conditioned, to groping for a rational decision without the necessary information base. In some ways this problem has existed ever since people developed consciousness. It is, however, rapidly becoming an acute problem because of the tremendous number of alternatives and options we are faced with in modern life. As Toffler (1970) puts it, "Ironically, the people of the future may suffer not from an absence of choice, but from a paralyzing surfeit of it" (p. 264). Toffler calls this phenomenon *overchoice* and sees it as turning freedom into unfreedom.

The overabundance of alternatives represents one threat to the potential exercise of freedom. Another is "the manipulation of needs by vested interests" (Marcuse, 1964, p. 3). We referred to this issue already within the context of primary and secondary drives. Marcuse, in a similar though not identical manner, speaks about true and false needs. The former, in his words, represent the "vital ones—nourishment, clothing, lodging at the attainable level of culture" (p. 5). On the other hand,

> most of the prevailing needs to relax, to have fun, to behave and consume in accordance with the advertisements, to love and hate what others love and hate, belong to this category of false needs. (P. 5.)

To the degree that we adopt such manipulated needs as our own personal needs, we have become pawns in the hands of the manipulator. Yet promoting social norms as well as accepting and internalizing them cannot be viewed as necessarily bad. No society could exist without norms or a socialization process that makes us internalize these norms. The issue is one of values, a sifting out of "bad" and "good" norms. And what is needed is an ethic that will furnish us with the criteria of choice for that process.

Somehow this discussion has taken us a long way from playgrounds and similar free-time resources. Yet a consideration of the above issues is crucial when we come to make resource planning decisions. Perhaps something like this is meant when we speak of a humanistic approach in recreation.

Changing Norms

Norms are guidelines for our thoughts, feelings, and actions. They affect free time in two ways: (1) They contribute to our perception of what we consider to be free time, or what society allows us to view in this manner. Norms control certain obligations that may go beyond that of holding a job (see Dumazedier's leisure conceptualization in chapter 2). (2) Norms also determine very much what we do within our free time, whatever way defined. We shall consider this latter aspect of norms.

We have referred to the importance of internal restraints for the experience of leisure at several points before. Perceived freedom is a function not only of the number and nature of meaningful choices or the authenticity of needs, but obviously also of the nature of either initiatory or inhibitory forces, such as norms. The imperatives "you must" or "you must not," and "you ought to" or "you ought not to" play a major role in what our free-time behavior will look like, *and* whether we shall experience that behavior as leisure.

There is nothing particularly new about the fact that certain behaviors are considered appropriate under certain conditions. What is new is that the range of activities suddenly deemed appropriate for free-time activities is rapidly changing, and that the range of people for whom the activities are now permitted is steadily increasing. We see that in terms of age ranges, a breakdown in sex barriers, and a cross-cultural widening of the horizon.

We all could give examples of these phenomena. We have seen grandmothers whooshing down the ski slope, dance classes in the Hustle being offered in old-age homes, thirteen year olds going off on dates, and senior citizens taking college courses. We have seen women smoking cigars and riding motorcycles, and if we are lucky women may even pay our restaurant checks. Men now wear pocketbooks, colorful shirts and gowns, and expound their latest recipes. Our conception of what is feasible in terms of travel is, at the moment, only limited by the boundaries of the earth (and even that probably not for too long). We have an increased awareness of activities carried out in other cultures and have made many of these part of our free-time behavior repertoire.

What are the implications of all this for the leisure experience? Again the answer is not simple. A lifting of inhibitions and restrictions certainly can lead to an increase in perceived freedom. In this sense, the opportunity for greater choice has been extended and the person now has a nearly unlimited range of options. But this is also where problems may arise. The person is now confronted with the possibility of engaging in activities that might not even have entered the mind a few years ago. Consider the ready availability of legalized off-track betting, swing clubs, pornographic movies, or even face-lifting operations. And does not the mere fact that these options are now available make it obligatory, to some degree, that one engages in them? Are we not all supposed to have as much fun as possible? Are we not told through the media that everyone does it who really knows how to live? Are we not experiencing guilt now for *not* doing certain things rather than for doing them? Do we want all this freedom, all these choices?

As stated at the beginning of this section, norms are guidelines. Their relaxation in many instances may be most desirable; in others it may give us a feeling of being lost in a maze, wandering about without knowing where we are going or even where we want to go. The end result may be anxiety, a state that is not conducive to the experience of leisure.

SUMMARY

Traditional approaches tend to investigate free time in terms of the activities carried out during it, or in terms of the use made of it. We, on the other hand, looked at free time in terms of its origin, that is, how it comes about for a particular person. We grouped people according to this criterion into three major classes: traditional free-timers, ambiguous free-timers, and no-free-timers. Within each of these categories we then looked at certain subgroups and specific factors as they relate to leisure.

Before doing so, however, we stressed once more the crucial distinction between free time and leisure. One way of highlighting this difference is by becoming aware that free time may be appropriately thought of as something one can *have*. Leisure, on the other hand, is a process or a state of mind, appropriately expressed with the verbs *to be, to experience. I have* free time—but *I am* in a state of leisure, *I experience* leisure. Or, we may use the verb *to leisure* when referring to being engaged in an activity that brings about the state of leisure. Implications of this distinction between free time and leisure were elaborated on.

Traditional free-timers are those whose free time can be relatively well delineated by the limits of their job time. Factors that may enhance or inhibit a leisure experience for this group as well as all others, were discussed. These were other-than-job obligations, compulsions, leisure attitudes, anxiety and boredom, knowledge, skills, and expectations, the capacity for leisure, and environmental factors.

Ambiguous free-timers are also employed or self-employed, but in such a way as to make a clear distinction between job time and free time difficult. We find this type among professionals, executives, managers, and others. Many of these people are as likely to experience leisure on their job as during free time, or perhaps even more so. When they do experience leisure during their free time, we may find that this time might just as well be called job time, because it may turn out to be in fact job-functional. Two subgroups within this category were discussed further: farmers and artists.

No-free-timers are those who do not hold a regular job nor are otherwise gainfully employed. Obviously it does not make sense to define their free time in relation to a job. Equally obvious is the fact that such people may still experience leisure. This category is made up of very diverse groups, such as children, students, housewives, the unemployed, the institutionalized, the "idle" rich, the "idle" poor, and the retired. Within each of these groups the dynamics of leisure varies as a function of their specific context, and the main reason for listing these groups explicitly was to make that fact salient.

Turning from the person to environment factors, we next discussed changing free-time conditions in terms of work schedules, resource conditions, and norms. Implications of the four-day work week were discussed. It was predicted that this shorter work week would be common in the near future, primarily as a result of our changing technology and resulting societal pressures. The shorter work week, and work-schedule changes such as flexitime, were viewed as positive contributions to the potential for leisure.

Changing resource conditions were examined in terms of personal expenditures, free-time facilities, and the availability of choices or options. While there is a clear trend toward more of all of these resources it was argued that this development does not necessarily lead to more leisure. On the contrary, too many choices and the relaxation of norms may actually result in a lessening of perceived freedom and an increase in anxiety.

ENDNOTES

[1] This, of course, is not literally true. The worker still has obligations to the job, such as being in relatively good physical condition when returning to the job and scheduling free-time activities so they do not overlap with work time.

[2] The *press-order* activity was described as one that "gives you a chance to organize and arrange things. It demands precision and neatness. It requires a sense of planning, order and forethought."

[3] Murray (1938, p. 122) further distinguishes between
the alpha press, *which is the press that actually exists, as far as scientific inquiry can determine it; and . . . the* beta press, *which is the subject's own interpretation of the phenomena that he perceives.*
An understanding of the individual's behavior requires a knowledge of the *beta press;* an evaluation of the environment in the abstract would relate more closely to the *alpha press.*

[4] For a series of articles on Adventure Playgrounds, see the May 1974 issue of *Parks and Recreation* (1974), pp. 22–28. Also see William Crook (1974), pp. 45–49; and Arvid Bengtsson (1972).

[5] Even here, a whole industry has sprung up around this current fad: there are special shoes, socks, shorts, shirts, overalls—not to speak of foods and vitamins—that you are told to consume if you wish to be a successful runner.

8

Leisure throughout the life cycle

The material in the preceding two chapters was presented from the traditional view of the work versus nonwork dichotomy of life: chapter 6 dealt with life on the job, and chapter 7 with life off the job. The reason for organizing these chapters in this manner was that our life and our thinking are still very much in line with such a split. However, my philosophy of leisure is not, and I shall now attempt to escape this unfortunate habit of ours. This chapter will deal with leisure and life, or leisure and the person: the person as a whole. And rather than taking a horizontal slice of life, we shall view it from a vertical perspective. We shall follow the person from birth to death, that is, look at leisure and its manifestations and implications throughout the life cycle.

Our approach, then, will be very much like that of a developmental psychologist, except that most of what will be said will be speculative rather than based on empirical evidence. We shall refer to several classificatory systems of life or stages of life, as have been developed by various developmentalists (e.g., Bühler, 1968; Erikson, 1950, 1968; Piaget, 1950; Piaget and Inhelder, 1958). And we shall stay within a chronological framework of life. But rather than looking at stages of life, we shall focus on important positive or negative events, highlights or crises, that tend to be common to all or most people. We shall refer to such events as *milestones*, a term adopted from Kimmel (1974, p. 11), who views "the lifeline as a representation of a journey with a number of interesting places and crucial junctions along the way." Milestones or mileposts used to be placed along the road at appropriate distances to guide one's progress along the journey. If one strayed off in the wrong direction, they would also tell just how far off one had gone.

How many such milestones can we find in anyone's life? This in itself is a fascinating research question and depends very much on the individual's perception. What one person perceives as important, another may not. And which events a person does list as milestones may tell us quite a bit about that person. We shall suggest a brief exercise that plays around with that idea.

The milestones we chose to discuss are therefore only examples of a much wider range of events that could have been picked. They will serve, however, to illustrate the role of leisure in these events, which, after all, is the purpose of this chapter.

MILESTONES OF LIFE

In the following pages we shall first look at milestones within the framework of three age periods: childhood and adolescence, adolescence and adulthood, and adulthood and old age. We shall then take up milestones that are likely to occur at any age, and thus would not fit into that framework. We shall begin with a short exercise.

An Introductory Exercise

Appendix I consists of two forms designed for this exercise. We suggest that before reading on you complete these at this point, following the simple instructions given. We suggest further that you have some of your friends complete the forms as well, or perhaps that you do this in class with all your fellow students. Your responses will become much more meaningful when you compare them with those of others.

**TIME OUT FOR COMPLETING
APPENDIX 1**

We assume that you now have completed the two forms of appendix 1. Let us say a few words about this exercise. The information you gain is quite meaningful in its manifest content, and does not necessarily need clinical interpretation, although such may add considerable insights.

Where did you place yourself on your lifeline? Your response will take on much more meaning when you compare it to the responses of others, especially those your same age. You will notice that chronological age contributes to a relatively small part of where people place themselves. One reason of course is that before placing themselves on the lifeline everyone has to guess the age of his or her death in order to give a meaningful response, and obviously people will differ right there. Then again, people may not approach this task in such a systematic manner but rather may respond intuitively.[1] You might ponder such questions as, At what age does a person see half of one's life gone? What are the factors that account for differences? Are there sex differences? Differences related to religion, ethnic background, and so on?

What were the milestones in your life? What you did not put down is nearly as interesting as what you did. For example, did you consider your birth as a milestone? Some people do! What areas of life are your milestones in? Do they relate to the social sphere, the educational one, or are they mixed? How early in your life is your first milestone? How far removed is the last one mentioned from your present age? Again, all of these issues become more meaningful when you are able to compare your responses to those of others.

Similar questions can be considered in regard to your future life. Extremely few people indicate death as a milestone; it is probably too final to even think of. An interesting question to consider is whether future milestones lie in the domain of education and career or in the social sphere. Would one expect sex differences here? Would one expect these to change in the coming years?

I think we have asked enough questions. The purpose of this exercise was really twofold. First, to make you experience what is meant by a milestone. Second, we also hope to make you experience a bit of the excitement that one can obtain from doing research. What you have done here, collecting data, is of course only a beginning. But when you actually see data, when you see how people respond quite differently to even such a simple procedure as this, you wonder. It raises questions; it makes you want to understand. There is beauty in the search for truth!

Childhood and Adolescence

First a word about the headings of this and the following two sections. By overlapping the stages I am following a procedure adopted elsewhere. To quote myself there, "Since it is difficult and quite arbitrary to decide when childhood ends and adolescence begins or, for that matter, when adolescence ends and adulthood begins [and you may add, when adulthood ends and old age begins], we have included adolescence in both this and the next section" (Neulinger, 1974a, p. 116), and adulthood in both the next and final section.

Birth. We used to have a saying "in the old country": few of us are fortunate enough never to have been born. One might wonder whether this statement expresses a sense of pessimism or optimism, or just plain fatalism. But one thing is sure. Birth and death are the two milestones none of us can escape. We can deny their existence; we can live as if neither of them ever happened or will happen. But they are both there. The denial of death is a well-known phenomenon. Young children up to about the ages of nine or ten do not have the capacity to understand fully the meaning of death. Teenagers of course live forever. And the rest of us face the issue in varying degrees and denial is frequently quite a socially acceptable option.

What is perhaps not so widely recognized is the fact that most people also deny the fact of their birth. How many people want to consider that at one point they were nonexistent? Or that for a very long period after birth, they were totally dependent, weak, vulnerable —all things an adult is not supposed to be? But if they did think about this, they might even remember that once they knew what play was all about; what it meant to do things just for the sheer joy of doing them; what it meant to let oneself be totally dependent on somebody else, and enjoy it without guilt and shame.

Is birth an important milestone in relation to leisure? The answer is obvious. It is also obvious that we do not mean just the very fact of being born, but all the events and people involved during the early years of life. These are the years when the child must develop "a sense of basic trust" (Erikson, 1950). I have argued elsewhere that this time "may be of crucial importance in the development of a basic attitude of openness, optimism and confidence, that allows one fully to experience leisure" (Neulinger, 1974a, p. 117). The awareness of birth as a milestone, then, may be an indicator of the person's attitude toward and capacity for leisure.

School. The beginning of formal school is an important milestone in anybody's life who ever went to school. It carries many implications. The child has become a person with a partially developed and cognizant self. Hopefully an appropriate sense of autonomy has been achieved and a readiness to initiate one's own activities (Erikson, 1950). The child's horizon has been widened; beyond the immediate family there now are other significant others: peers, other adults, and now . . . the teacher.

> This is the period when the concept of work first enters into the child's life. He develops a "sense of industry." He is concerned with developing his skills, in perfecting himself, and he is on his way to develop habits which may later express themselves in his attitudes toward work and leisure. (Neulinger, 1974a, p. 119.) *

This is, unfortunately, the time when the child is taught the false dichotomy between work and leisure. Schoolwork and homework are things one must do; there seems little choice involved. Many, if not most of these, activities (except perhaps in the most progressive schools) are ones one would rather do without. And the child becomes aware of that precious period called "free time," often also referred to as "leisure time" or just plain "leisure." And so the pattern is set. Work

* Courtesy of Charles C Thomas, Publisher, Springfield, Illinois.

is done when one cannot escape it, in school and later on the job. Leisure one finds in one's free time, when one can do the things one really wants to do. But then something else happens. The child starts to become aware of, and slowly internalizes, a powerful norm. What one does in school is important, gets one praise, signs of approval and achievement. Furthermore, to get praise, signs of approval and achievement are important in themselves. What one does during one's free time (also referred to as leisure) is not really important; it may at best be of secondary significance especially if it is tied in with some school activity. One receives little extrinsic reward for one's free time activities, a clear indication that they are not considered essential.

The picture is exaggerated but true. Could it be otherwise? We shall return to this question in the next chapter which will deal with leisure education.

First Date. What a milestone! What an event! And then again, it may not even be remembered. I shall not attempt to dissect or analyze this milestone. It is too subjective a phenomenon and offers too many variations to allow generalizations. But of those for whom it does represent a salient event, one might ask certain questions. What really is the significant dimension that makes one remember it? Is it the fact that, for the first time, one really had to stand on one's own in a social situation? That one had to exercise choice, make decisions regarding another person? With nobody there to guide one, or limit one's freedom? Is it perhaps that one discovered how helpful or convenient it may become to be able to rely on internalized norms? Or was this the time when one found these most disturbing and interfering with one's "own" wishes?

And what is the role and relationship of sex to the first date? To what degree was it involved? What did it mean to you at that time? Do some people respond to this question in terms of their first sexual experience? How would you even begin to define the *first* sexual experience? [2]

And finally, what are the differences in the first dating experience in terms of a male-female distinction? Is this date still consistently initiated by the male? Is this pattern changing? Is the "first date" phenomenon actually going out of style?

I shall refrain from trying to guess how much of a leisure experience that first date might have been. All I wish to do is point to the relevant variables that are present, actually not only during that first date but any other date you might have had in later life. Did you really want that experience? Why did you want it? Because you enjoyed yourself while with that person and truly liked being with him or her? Or because having been with that person, having "had" that first date, provided you status and earned you points for doing the right and expected thing? Probably all of these factors and many more were involved. What matters, of course, is the proportion to which one or the other kind of motivation prevails, and that will determine the degree to which you will experience leisure in your social relations.

First Car. Much has been said and written about the function and meaning of a car beyond those that relate to it as a means of transportation. Its importance in terms of status, for example, has been stressed in Vance Packard's (1959) *The Status Seekers:* "They'll know you've *arrived* when you drive up in an Edsel" (p. 313, quoting from a two-page color advertisement). When it comes to your first car, especially if you are an adolescent boy, it probably does not matter what make it is. You have arrived! The big question is, where? One of my students (in response to Experience 2a, appendix 1) listed his first three cars as the three most important milestones in his life. As far as I could tell he was not trying to be facetious. Perhaps one might like to contrast the potential of the first date and the first car. We stressed that the significant potential of the date is that of a *being* experience. In the case of a car, the likely experience is one of *having:* I now possess, own, have an automobile. Both experiences have the potential for the opposite; as we mentioned, a date can be viewed as "having had" somebody or even something. Dates can serve to enrich one's picture-album collection. On the other hand, driving a car has the potential for excitement, exercising skills, and being a satisfying experience. But all in all, the likelihood is that the first car will take on its importance mostly for being a highly prized possession. Truly a crossroad in life. The car, after all, is a possession that can lead to all kinds of secondary satisfactions. And if it is true that this possession gains you all this happiness, is it not also true that the road to happiness is the acquisition of possessions, that is, *having?*

First Job. Let me state first what applies equally to the rest of the sections in this chapter; it is becoming more and more difficult to make meaningful generalizations about any event in our life. The rate of change that affects our society makes this task nearly impossible. The time and nature of one's first job experience may vary tremendously for people living in the United States, but similarly so for those in the rest of the world. And yet, when we look at the phenomenon from a larger perspective, we can distinguish certain universal aspects about it. Primarily, it is that point in one's life when one sets out systematically and quite consciously to earn money for services rendered or goods delivered. To be more precise—and this is very important—the realization must include the fact that one is specifically engaged in providing these services or goods *in order to* earn money. At that point one has learned the meaning of a job.

There is a similarity here to the school experience, where one does so many things *in order to* please the parents, get praise, or just get good grades. But the nature of the extrinsic reward is different. While for schoolwork, the extrinsic rewards relate primarily to self-image, esteem, and satisfaction, those obtained from a job also serve as a means to gain power: if necessary and needed, the power to provide for existence and subsistence needs; in the case of the affluent society and the middle and upper classes, the power to obtain and accumulate possessions. If the drive for possessions has become dominant, then the role and perception of the job (and possibly all future jobs) may indeed become fixed. It is something one does "in order to." The very thought of looking for a job that carries intrinsic satisfactions may not occur. These considerations have rather obvious and very serious implications for career or vocational counseling, and for leisure education and counseling in general.

Adolesence and Adulthood

We are moving along the life cycle; the person is entering a new phase and facing a different set of issues. Hopefully, one has by now gained a sense of identity (Erikson, 1950). To achieve this one had to work through and attain a balance along several dimensions. For example, one cannot always demand or obtain immediate action, nor should one always settle for complete inaction or becoming immobilized. One ought to be neither apathetic, nor overly involved; one must be confident of one's abilities and yet not conceited, be able to follow as well as lead. After a period of great fluctuations and uncertainties in these and other areas, one has achieved a feeling of who one is, where one is going, and what one is becoming. What still needs to be worked through is the acquisition of a sense of intimacy that will allow one to lead a life as a fully active member of society, and enjoy adult liberties as well as carry adult responsibilities (Erikson, 1950).

In Freud's terms, the two central spheres of life, to love and to work (*lieben und arbeiten*), must be confronted (Erikson, 1968, p. 136). In a narrow sense, this translates into finding an appropriate mate and an appropriate career. In a wider sense, this implies experiencing love not just for your spouse but also for yourself, for others, and for life itself; and becoming involved in meaningful activity (which may or may not be your job, or may far transcend the limits of any job).

Career Choice. The precise point in time when career choice takes place may be difficult to fix. For some, such a decision comes relatively easy and without much conflict; others may have arrived at that point in a roundabout manner and after much soul searching; and for yet others it may have all been a matter of coincidences. Whatever the approach used, let us concern ourselves with the person who is now holding the first job in a particular career line. Developmental psychologists agree that this is a crucial point in the person's life cycle. "Success and satisfaction in the occupation and family reaffirm the individual's sense of identity and also provide social recognition for that identity" (Kimmel, 1974, p. 243).

Few would argue with that statement. And yet, it is precisely with statements like this that we must take issue and emphasize an important distinction. Kimmel's statement reflects our predominant view, namely that we *must* find our identity primarily through our job (and the family). This orientation permeates most of the discussions dealing with achieving "a sense of identity" as well as a "sense of intimacy" (Erikson, 1950), and may be said to be valid for an industrial society. However, as we move into the post-industrial era, this norm is becoming dysfunctional and impossible to comply with for an ever larger proportion of our population.

The already much-discussed distinction between *work* and *job* becomes critical here. If by occupation (or work) we mean meaningful activity, in a broader sense, then we have no argument with Kimmel's statement. If occupation, however, is meant to refer to the activity by which one earns a living (a job), his statement is quite outdated and, what is more important, quite damaging to more and more people in our society.

There is no need to improve on Freud's statement, as Kimmel (1974, p. 271) suggests.[8] To fulfill the functions Freud ascribed to love and work, they both must be carried out *as leisure*, freely and for intrinsic satisfaction. If these conditions are not met, the two activities turn into prostitution and slave labor, hardly what one would expect a normal person to be able to do well or strive for.

What then is the implication of the milestone *career choice?* It is important that the person become aware of the nature of the choice made. It is possible that the particular occupation chosen does provide the potential for identity formation through the intrinsic satisfactions derived therefrom. But it is also possible, and ever more likely, that this is not the case. Then a realistic appraisal of the situation is necessary, and an alternative route to self-development may be indicated. This is where the role of free-time activities (i.e., non-earning-related activities) is becoming more and more important. The view expressed here is not new; work theoreticians, particularly those concerned with issues of alienation, have propounded it for years. But it has not really penetrated our thinking, much less our feeling. In no way have we accepted the tremendous implications of this state of affairs. One of the prime tasks of leisure education will be dealing with these issues.

First Marriage. This is the other side of the coin, or the first sphere in Freud's statement about love and work. There is again little doubt that love, or in a wider sense, the art of establishing meaningful social relationships, is crucial to a person's development. And the first marriage (and in modern society, this no longer need be a formally and legally recognized marriage, but may be just a long-term relationship based on personal commitment) is a critical test of having achieved that capacity. As Erikson (1961, p. 158) phrases it so beautifully, marriage provides the opportunity ". . . for the mutual verification through an experience of finding oneself, as one loses oneself, in another." One develops a sense of *shared identity*.

Let us look at two aspects of marriage, sexual love and that shared identity. It is very difficult, and perhaps impossible, not to become normative or prescriptive when speaking of "perfect" or "ideal" sexual love. Within the context of the values of our society, however, we may agree that perceived freedom is a critical aspect of such an activity. After all, rape or being raped is placed on the extreme negative end of such a continuum. Similarly, we frown on receiving or handing out extrinsic rewards for this activity. Indeed, the conditions for a leisure experience become quite explicit for the sexual act.

To enjoy a sense of freedom under the intimate conditions of mutual sexual activities requires a tremendous amount of trust. It presupposes an attitude of total surrender and dependence which cannot develop if one is concerned whether or when the other is going to "stick a knife into one's back." Hence the emphasis on the importance of basic trust in the experience of leisure. In no activity does this become clearer than in sexual love.

Let us turn to the concept of shared identity. This is a good time for raising an important issue. Several of my students have argued as follows: If we define leisure as a state of mind that comes about when I am engaged in activity that *I* want to do, that is *my* choice, and that gives *me* satisfaction, is this not a very selfish—nay immoral—way of looking at leisure? If we promote such a "leisure ethic," will this not lead to an extremely egoistic society, where "doing one's thing" is the ultimate rule with no concern for others?

The answer to this question and the rejection of this notion require a look at certain basic assumptions about the nature of people. If in fact people were basically self-sufficient, asocial, and destructive of others, no way of defining leisure would change this. If, on the other hand, one accepts the fact that people do depend on others, are "social animals," and capable of altruistic acts, then such a definition of leisure does not at all lead to such negative consequences. It may simply lead one to recognize *quasi*-selfish motivations in altruistic behavior. And one of the prime ways of developing such behavior may be through shared identity. By including the other within the realm of one's self, selfish acts in fact may turn into social and possibly altruistic ones. In the marriage relationship, this extension of the self is limited to one other. In the person who has achieved a "sense of generativity" (Erikson, 1950), it has expanded to a much wider circle, including the next generation. Such an expansion of one's self provides a tremendous increase in the potential for leisure. A whole new range of activities—such as giving birth, parenting, voluntary social service and political activism—may now fall under the category of intrinsically motivated behaviors. There is little doubt that acts carried out with that type of motivation will be perceived by the recipients quite differently from and more positively than the same acts performed out of a sense of duty.

First Child. It may need restating here that we are examining these milestones only in terms of their relationship to leisure. There are obviously many more issues related to each of them, one of them always being whether or not a person even lists the particular event as a milestone. In the case of the arrival of the first child, such an omission may have all kinds of implications; but we shall not make these our concern.

The first consequence that comes to mind in respect to leisure and the first child is one of loss of freedom. Or to put it a different way: the first thought is one of an increase in obligations. There are those who will strongly disagree with this statement. They will argue that the satisfactions derived from the experience of being a parent are qualitatively unique and exceed in value any potential loss of freedom to engage in other activities. That may well be true for some; perhaps even for many. But all other things being equal, a child will add additional burdens to existence and subsistence needs, particularly in our present-day, work-oriented society. The degree of burden may be very strongly and negatively related to amount of family income.

One of the most dramatic and often traumatic historical changes in our society is the fact that the motivation for having children has shifted from extrinsic to intrinsic reasons, or at least to less obvious extrinsic ones. In preindustrial, agricultural society, children were a great economic asset, a *sine qua non*. Today, children tend to be a tremendous financial burden. The cost of the educational expense alone (at least in this country) has risen to astronomical figures. Caring for children in a typical *nuclear family* (consisting only of the mother, father, and child), where both parents might work, has become a truly demanding task. There is less and less help available from the *extended family* (grandparents, aunts, uncles, etc.), either by reason of physical distance or just changed norms. As a result of all this, the most serious and devastating consequences may occur when the act of wanting and having a child is based on the illusion of leisure rather than on leisure itself. If the parent has the capacity and motivation to gain intrinsic satisfaction from the process of having and bringing up a child, then this experience may indeed be unique and totally rewarding. If, however, the motivation for having the child is primarily extrinsic, the likelihood of such satisfactions being realized and continuing for any length of time is exceedingly low.

One of the most promising prospects of a future leisure society is the assumption that people will then be in a better position to enjoy the intrinsically satisfying aspects of child rearing. And who knows, perhaps we shall be able to narrow the generation gap, not by accelerating the younger generation's growth, but by decelerating the aging process and by bringing us all closer to childhood again.

Acts of Separation: Divorce and Widowhood. We shall now consider a number of milestones all of which share one characteristic: they represent an act of separation. They may take place in early adulthood or in later life. We shall discuss two of these in this section and a number of others in the following.

Divorce [4] and widowhood both lead to separation from one's spouse. There are some obvious and crucial differences between the two events. Divorce involves a decision of choice for at least one of the partners; in the case of widowhood this is rarely the case. Divorce has some form of disagreement between the partners at its roots and is bound to lead to some if not necessarily a lot of negative feelings. Widowhood may involve anger as a clinical syndrome, but is more likely to center around feelings of sadness. Financial burdens may result from either act and many other issues may arise, particularly if the couple have children. However, we shall constrain ourselves to looking at questions related to leisure only.

Both events, divorce and widowhood, imply a lessening of obligations. The person with whom one had an intimate and binding relationship is suddenly no longer present. The person with whom one shared one's identity (the degree of this depending on the type of relationship that existed), is gone. There are two distinct implications here for leisure. (1) We should expect an increase in perceived freedom. (2) The loss of shared identity may decrease the potential for intrinsically motivating activities. Let us look at these points a bit more closely.

The release from obligations ought to increase one's sense of perceived freedom. Is this likely to happen? In the case of divorce it may, particularly if there were no children and no major financial burdens involved. And we all have heard the tale of "the merry widow." However, experience seems to indicate the contrary, especially in the case of widowhood. At least two rather obvious factors may account for that. One is grief and suffering, combined with potential economic and other complications. The other may have to do with the fact that the obligations of marriage may not have been experienced as restrictions, but were totally in line with one's desires and intentions. It was for that reason that we did not consider family, or any other social obligations, to be *necessarily* detrimental to the leisure experience.

The loss of shared identity may lead to a decrease in the meaning of many of one's activities and, depending on the degree of former intimacy, to a loss of the very meaning of one's life. Preparing a meal that one would share with one's spouse may have been a source of much intrinsic satisfaction; it has now turned into a task that one does in order to survive. Much extrinsic motivation is lost too. Many of the activities one used to engage in in order to be with one's partner no longer seem worth doing. Why try to make that trip to Europe possible if one can no longer share it? Why take that walk if there is no one to enjoy it with? Why even get out of bed?

Leisure counseling may be indicated for many individuals who have problems coping with acts of separation. Loss of identity and loneliness are associated with such events, and perceived freedom and intrinsic motivation are issues that are crucial in the resolution of these problems.

Adulthood and Old Age

We are moving further along the life cycle. We already have touched on one of the basic issues of this stage: acquiring a sense of generativity and avoiding self-absorption or stagnation (Erikson, 1950). To do this involves expanding one's horizon and concerns from the self to the immediate and extended family, and to the family of humanity in a broader sense, both in terms of its present and future generations. The vehicles for this growing process tend to be seen as parenthood and occupational achievements, and we once again want to stress the need for a rephrasing of the latter term.

The second major task one needs to confront when nearing the end of the life cycle is to acquire a sense of integrity and avoid a sense of despair (Erikson, 1950). One needs to gain the feeling that one's life was worth living; that given one's unique circumstances one did what could and needed to be done. Not everyone, of course, will be able to gain this sense of integrity and may thus experience regret, bitterness, or even despair.

Within this larger context we shall consider two topics. The first will relate to career issues and the second will consist of more acts of separation.

Positive Career Milestones. Life is not all bad, and some of the good events do take place in one's career. There are advancements, promotions, and other professional achievements, such as winning prestigious awards, achieving breakthroughs in technology or science, producing a piece of art, or even having one's book published. Can one relate these events to leisure? Perhaps not readily, but there are at least two generalizations that are appropriate. First, each of these events is likely to result in some degree of economic improvement for the person. And as we have pointed out before, all other things being equal, the more money people have, the greater their chances for experiencing leisure.

The second factor that ties these events to leisure is the likelihood that they all involve a considerable degree of intrinsically motivated activity. While it is possible to succeed in a given activity without intrinsic satisfaction, it is safe to assume that people who enjoy their job or occupation will put in more energy, care, and devotion. The events referred to may then be taken by inference as indications that the people involved experience a considerable degree of leisure in their job.

Any further comments on leisure and positive career milestones would require a more detailed knowledge of the particular event.

Negative Career Milestones. Examples of such events are temporary layoffs, career changes involving considerable retraining, being forced into accepting lower-paying positions or more unpleasant working conditions, and perhaps finally, realizing the limits of one's career potential. Generalizations here are equally difficult to make. In contrast to the positive career milestones, these negative ones may decrease the potential for one's chances for leisure, either temporarily or permanently.

Career changes, of course, may have long-range positive results. A person may be forced into a change due to external circumstances or to the realization that one's job does not offer the potential for leisure. As our society becomes more affluent, people more secure and less afraid of starvation, the latter reason for a mid-career change becomes more frequent. We hear of Wall Street brokers turning farmers, insurance agents becoming antique dealers, and advertising executives changing into school teachers. In these instances, the career changes are designed to increase one's leisure potential primarily on the job.

As in the previous section, we shall refrain from extensive generalizations about these events. The uniqueness of most individual circumstances would make such generalizations quite invalid. Instead we shall now turn to a number of further milestones which represent acts of separation.

Retirement. This is probably the milestone the meaning of which has changed most radically in recent years, and which is changing even more. As a matter of fact, the very label *retirement* is an unfortunate one, and quite outdated. There was a time when retirement really meant just that—you retired from your job, and for all practical purposes from life. Furthermore, not too much of life was left. Life expectancy, however, has risen and the elderly population (sixty-five years and above) in the United States has increased from about 3 million in 1900, to more than 22 million in 1975. This gain is much greater than that of the general population for the same period, which went from about 76 million to 215 million. It will take a number of years before we fully realize that "the increased longevity in years has been more than a postponement of death" (Kaplan, 1979, p. 243).

Retirement is still generally viewed as a very negative event. "Gerontologists consider that retirement—along with the death of a mate—are the two most shattering, traumatic events of later life" (Puner, 1977). It can represent a separation not only from your job, but from your friends, accustomed life patterns, accustomed physical environment, and from the very factors that gave meaning and identity to your life. It can mean all that, but it does not have to. As a matter of fact, both management and labor report a shift in attitudes toward retirement. In part, this may be brought about by the mere fact that there are so many more retirees these days. You are no longer alone; you are not the only one on the block; and you can observe that some of these retirees, at least, seem to have a very good time of it.

We still have a long way to go before everyone is going to look forward to retirement as perhaps the best years of one's life, or as I prefer to phrase it more simply, the years of *your* life. Years in which for the first time in most people's lives, their days can be their own. The trend is here, but there are major obstacles ahead. A recent political-economic issue demonstrated this well. I am referring to the political maneuvers used to push mandatory retirement age from sixty-five to seventy years. Rather than acknowledge that this step might be economically desirable to maintain the fluidity of the Social Security system, issues were discussed in terms of people's "right to work," "freedom for a meaningful life," and "deprivation of rights." Nowhere did we hear about the "right to leisure"; no one questioned whether the job was really the best means of obtaining meaning in later life. And no one seemed to see how pathetic it was that the country calling itself the richest in the world could only think of paid employment to give meaning to its elderly. The tremendous opportunities for voluntary service to others, to the less-developed countries, the chances for education and enrichment in cultural values, the chances for building a better world—all the many exciting things one could do in retirement (given the necessary subsistence income)—none of these was even mentioned.

The recognition of leisure as the criterion of the quality of life

could truly make a difference here. Instead of pushing mandatory retirement up, we should work towards lowering it consistently and pro-
gressively. At the moment this may be economically unattainable. But
we shall never even attempt to achieve it unless we make it our goal,
which we shall do only if and when we recognize the true nature of
leisure.

The "Empty Nest" Phenomenon. This label refers to the mother's lot
when all the children have left home. Depending of course on the degree of her involvement with her children and on other factors, this
event can be quite upsetting, and may be compared to the retirement
phenomenon for men. With her children gone, much of the mother's
daily routine has now changed or become meaningless. The focus of
her interest and concern has disappeared. She suddenly finds herself
with a lot of free time on her hands, and may make desperate attempts
"to fill up that time." This may lead to her taking a job, starting a new
career, or involving herself in more extended free-time activities. Like
the retired person, the "empty nest" mother may feel at a loss about
what to do with her life and how to bring meaning into it once more.
Both may be well advised to seek leisure counseling.

Death. This is the final separation. Death is an awesome word; as we
already pointed out, most of us tend to suppress or repress the thought
of it altogether. There is no way for us to know death. It is not just
technically unknowable, as the far side of the moon used to be; it is
the opposite of existence and thus not accessible to us in the living
dimension. There is, however, the process of dying, and that event
is very much a part of life. Our attitudes and behavior in regard to
dying are undergoing significant changes. Just as we speak of a humanistic approach to park management, so do we now refer to a humanistic approach to dying. Probably the most radical and outstanding example of this approach is the establishment of the so-called hospices,
places specifically designed to provide optimal conditions during the
process of dying. They are modeled after St. Christopher's Hospice,
founded in London in 1967 by Dr. Cicely Saunders. The prime emphasis
is on increasing the quality and not the quantity of the last days of
one's life. This is not the place to describe these institutions in detail.[5]
Suffice it to say that all is done to provide the patient with the potential for a leisure experience to the very last minute of life. Drugs are
used, if needed, to eliminate pain and to provide the necessary conditions for experiencing peace of mind in an often physically deterio-
rated body. The patient is given the dignity of freedom and choice in
regard to every possible action during the last days of life, including
the choice of death over life.

"Any Time" Milestones

Our previous discussion of milestones followed more or less the person's life cycle; there is a likelihood that these would be experienced at given stages of life. We are now turning to events that can happen at any time. This is not to say that when the actual event takes place, it will not interact with the age of the person. For example, a crippling accident at ten years of age will have totally different consequences and meaning than the same event at age seventy. What we are stressing is the fact that the events do not necessarily or even typically occur at certain stages of life. In many ways that may make them the most significant in any individual's life experience.

Health-Related Events. Any severe and/or permanently disabling disease or accident may constitute a critical milestone in a person's life. The actual consequences will depend very much on the severity of the injury and the period in life when they were obtained. In any case, it is safe to say that the results will mean a decrease in the potential for leisure. Any reduction in physical and/or mental capacity limits one's freedom and choice in many significant areas. To what degree a person actually loses that freedom depends very much on one's capacity and will power, the situation one finds oneself in, and the degree to which help is available. It is generally recognized that most people do not operate in their daily lives at maximal degrees of functioning. It is truly amazing how often handicapped people can develop a level of functioning that approaches and sometimes surpasses that of the so-called normal person. Much significant work has and continues to be done in this area (e.g., Overs et al., 1974).

Loss of Significant Others. We have already referred to widowhood as a milestone, and discussed it in terms of a problem of separation. The death of someone one cares for or who is important in one's life can of course occur at any time in life. Each such event is a unique experience, yet each relates to leisure in at least two significant ways. One is the loss of meaning; a whole range of activities previously directed toward the deceased is no longer available or purposeful. Second, to the degree that one has experienced a "shared identity" with the deceased, part of one's identity is now gone. Both of these factors are bound to lead to a feeling of emptiness and a search for a substitute. Problems of separation are clearly an important area of leisure counseling, as previously indicated.

Events beyond the Person's Control. The United States has been called the land of opportunity; the myth that success depends primarily on personal effort dies hard. The myth may even have been true for some

—though more so in the past than the present, and more so in this country than in most. But there are events in life (and people in Europe and the rest of the world may be more aware of this than Americans are) which are clearly beyond the individual's control: wars, revolutions, oppressive governments, natural and societal disasters, and others. These events may totally change the direction and quality of a person's life, and the individual may have minimal or no power to influence them. Developmental psychologists speak of *historical* (rather than *developmental*) factors in referring to such events, but in general, they tend to be much neglected in our case histories of individuals. This is likely to change in the future, because of an increased emphasis on environmental factors in general, and because the effects of external factors on the individual's life are becoming more and more obvious, even in the United States. The ecological crisis, the imminence of atomic warfare, the increasing obviousness of the power of the industrial giants and the military complex, and the concomitant loss of voice of the individual citizen—all of these factors and more lead inevitably to a realization of this state of affairs.

Perhaps therein lies the greatest threat to leisure. Leisure implies freedom, and any curtailment of freedom in any area is bound to have negative consequences in regard to the potential for leisure. The issues involved go far beyond the confines of this book. The challenge itself is reflective of the new kinds of problems of the post-industrial age: no longer the conquering of nature, but of social forces.

> . . . The goal is not control over nature but control over technique and over irrational social forces and institutions that threaten the survival of Western society, if not of the human race. (Fromm, 1976, p. 175.)

Is there hope? Is there anything that can be done? I shall refer the reader to Erich Fromm's (1976) final chapter for a list of suggestions. The message that comes through in all of these suggestions is that our only chance for survival lies in a change that comes from within us, a change of our attitudes and values. Indeed, as I like to express it, a change toward a new and positive leisure ethic.

SUMMARY

In this chapter we have looked at the implications for and of leisure throughout the life cycle. We did this by considering a sampling of milestones of life, that is, events that stand out in the person's life history. We started with an exercise that was intended to familiarize the reader with the concept of milestone, and also give a taste of the potential excitement of empirical research. It seems that it is the questions raised rather than the answers obtained that make such research so fascinating.

We shall not go through a listing of all the milestones discussed in this chapter; this can be gleaned from quickly reviewing the chapter subheadings. Our discussion of each milestone was rather brief in the text, so a further summary of the points made would be redundant. Let us just state that we considered each of the milestones from the viewpoint of leisure, that is, the degree to which the variables *perceived freedom* and *intrinsic motivation* are relevant.

Each milestone may have in some ways either inhibited or contributed to the potential for leisure. The concern here was with the degree to which leisure was experienced as the consequence or result of the conditions prevailing at that particular milestone. We might say that leisure was treated here as the *dependent* variable.

On the other hand, we also considered what the consequences may have been of the experience of leisure at a given milestone. We recognized that these experiences may have important effects on the person's later behavior and mental state. Here, we treat leisure as the *independent* variable.

At several points it became quite clear that leisure is intrinsically related to the general well-being of the person. We made frequent reference to the need for and appropriateness of leisure counseling in respect to many of these milestones.

Once again, we linked leisure to the more general topic of the quality of life. And we have reemphasized what we see as the role of leisure in post-industrial society: nothing less than the criterion for the quality of life.

ENDNOTES

[1] Did you actually count the number of dots on the "lifeline"? There are a hundred. There are some people who approach this task in this manner, although relatively few. It still does not get you out of the problem of having to guess the age of your death, and unless you happen to set it at one hundred, you will then get involved in all kinds of mathematical calculations. Which of course may help you forget thinking about death!

[2] It is primarily for this reason—namely, the difficulty of defining what the first sexual experience is—that I have not included sex as a milestone for discussion. Whatever the person defines as his or her first such experience is obviously of tremendous importance—too important, in fact, to discuss in a brief paragraph or two. Perhaps another day, a special volume devoted to that topic!

[3] "Perhaps Freud's answer to the question of what a normal person should be able to do well may need to be extended slightly today: the normal

person should be able *to love, to work,* and *to leisure"* (Kimmel, 1974, p. 271). The main problem with this statement is that it excludes the possibility of the experience of leisure from the activities of love and work, which indeed, would be a sad state of affairs.

[4] Separation may be substituted here for divorce.

[5] For information on hospices, see Stoddard (1978).

9

Roads to leisure

Let us open this chapter by restating some of our assumptions and facts as we see them. (1) We consider leisure to be an essential aspect of life, equaled in importance perhaps only by health. (2) Leisure is a highly personal experience. Nevertheless, its coming about is strongly interrelated with and dependent on the person's immediate environment as well as on societal conditions in general. Any discipline dealing with leisure must therefore concern itself with all three aspects: the person, the person's immediate environment, and society at large. (3) The chances that any given individual will experience leisure are limited in many ways; any number of obstacles and problems may interfere with the person's attainment of that state. Consequently, there exists a great need for leisure education and counseling. This need is widely recognized.

PREPARING FOR LEISURE

We find an early warning in such expressions as de Grazia's (1962, p. 4) well-known statement that "peace and prosperity are dangerous if a country doesn't know what to do with leisure," or Brightbill's (1960) statement: "The future will belong not only to the educated man but to the man who is educated to use his leisure wisely." More recent support for this position can readily be found, and the momentum of the movement toward such education is certainly gaining in strength.

G. W. Albee (1973), a recent president of the American Psychological Association, proposed that "universities should consider revising curricula to include the psychological study of leisure. . . ." B. F. Skinner (1971) devotes considerable attention to issues of leisure in *Beyond Freedom and Dignity*. He recognizes that "a sensitive test of the extent to which a culture promotes its own future is its treatment of leisure" (p. 169). Leisure, in fact, is "the epitome of freedom" (p. 170). Yet, "leisure is a condition for which the human species has been badly prepared. . . ." (p. 170).

Another telling sign that the time has come for leisure education is the outpouring of books and articles in that area (e.g., Brightbill and Mobley, 1977; Compton and Goldstein, 1977; Corbin and Tait, 1973; Edwards, 1977; Epperson et al., 1977; *Leisure Today*, March 1976, April 1977; McDowell, 1976; Mundy and Odum, 1979; Nahrstedt, 1975;

Overs et al., 1977; *Proceedings of the Third National Leisure Education Conference*, 1977). There is no doubt that these efforts represent a response to a widely perceived need for the development of leisure education programs and techniques.

Let us accept the fact that leisure education, in some form or other, has arrived and is here to stay. What does this mean and what are the implications?

Ebbinghaus, one of the founders of modern experimental psychology, is reported to have made the following statement: "psychology has a long past, but only a short history" (Boring, 1950, p. ix). The same may be said of leisure education or counseling.[1] For example, McDowell (1976, p. 5) states: "Leisure counseling, as a form of 'advice giving' probably has its most basic historical roots centuries ago." Nobody would want to argue with that. Both leisure and counseling are concepts as old as conscious awareness, thus taking us back at least to the days of antiquity. Therein, however, lies the strength of leisure education and counseling as well as their weakness, posing somewhat of a dilemma. The strong point is that leisure, ever since antiquity, had been recognized as one of our ultimate values; and counseling, understood as helping others to share in the good life, has been part of the human tradition no matter how negative our view of human nature may have been.

What is the dilemma, then? It is the following. Since issues of leisure and of counseling have been with us "ever since," we already have any number of well-established counseling techniques and orientations. We have approaches that deal with the issues from every possible angle and philosophical viewpoint. The only thing missing in these approaches is the word *leisure*. Up to very recently, they were not recognized for their role and importance in the context of leisure counseling. Given the general misconception of leisure (as a concept of time rather than a state of mind), this is not too surprising. We are, however, beginning to use the word *leisure* more and more in the psychological sense and as referring to the meaning and essence of life. The question is, is this reason enough to claim the need for a whole new discipline of leisure education and/or counseling? Furthermore, does adding the word *leisure* to the various already-existing techniques really turn them into leisure-counseling techniques?

Let me quote once more from Boring (1950, p. ix):

The modern history of psychology cannot, however, be written merely by adding chapters to the older history. Strange as it may seem, the present changes the past. . . .

This, I believe, is the way out of the dilemma. The present, and even more so the very near future, has changed and will change the past, particularly as it relates to leisure education and counseling. It is the recognition of that fact, plus the need to make these changes explicit and to modify existing techniques both in terms of content and process, that justify the development of a new discipline.

Recent Developments

The current stream of developing programs has its origin in therapeutic recreation services. Both O'Morrow (1977), a pioneer in leisure counseling, and McDowell (1976) trace this type of service to Olson and McCormick (1957), who were active in the psychiatric ward of Kansas City Veteran's Administration Hospital. They perceived leisure as recreation or play activity and, such activity in turn to be essential in the rehabilitation process.

Leisure counseling, however, is moving beyond the hospital setting and into the community. For example, Witt (1977, p. 5) states:

> At the community level, the impetus of institutional concern and the changing role of municipal recreation from that of an *activity provider* to that of an *activity enabler* has opened the door to the possibility of community based leisure counseling services.

Additional impetus is given to that development by the increasing tendency of hospitals to discharge psychiatric patients into the community as early as possible. Services are needed for "aiding the individual in the process of making transition from the institution to the community" (O'Morrow, 1977).

One survey made of leisure counseling orientations classifies them into three categories: *leisure resource guidance, leisure lifestyle counseling,* and *therapeutic-remedial counseling* (McDowell, 1976; 1977). McDowell sees the first of these as primarily an *information retrieval-dissemination service.* Such a service is activity-oriented and tries to match the individual with available community resources.

The second category, lifestyle counseling, involves a *developmental-education service.* It embodies counseling in a traditional sense, with emphasis on self-awareness, decision-making processes, and one's patterns of behavior.

Finally, therapeutic-remedial counseling is intended for people who are unable to function in certain leisure-related areas, on the basis of a physical or mental disability, block, or other inadequacy. It is the type of service traditionally carried out by therapeutic recreation workers in institutional settings.

Another way of looking at the major approaches in recent leisure-counseling techniques is that of Hitzhusen (1977). He distinguishes between the *group encounter-information* approach and the *testing-prescription* approach. The first of these uses group dynamics or group-encounter procedures, to increase self-awareness and insight into one's decision-making processes and behavior patterns. The second approach emphasizes instruments or testing procedures in obtaining information about the person involved, so as to enable the person to make appropriate choices about future leisure-related behavior. Fain (1977), for example, describes a method of establishing a real and an ideal leisure profile, and sees the counselor's role as bridging the gap between the two.

An important development in leisure education is the Leisure Education Advancement Project (LEAP), conducted by the National Recreation and Park Association under the original leadership of Peter J. Verhoven, Roger A. Lancaster, and Linda L. Odum. The initial focus of this project was to develop programs for kindergarten and elementary school (Woodburn and Cherry, 1978). "Future plans include not only the education target group but also recreationists and leisure service agencies" (Mundy and Odum, 1979, p. 26).

Yet another way of viewing recent developments is through the leisure education–leisure counseling distinction. As Connolly (1977) points out, there is considerable confusion in the field of therapeutic recreation concerning these terms. He suggests the following definitions:

> Leisure education involves awareness of, learning, and involvement in the total recreative experience including skills development and experiences in activities, as well as an awareness of leisure interests and available resources. Leisure counseling is a component of the total leisure education model that employs verbal facilitation techniques to discover and develop the client's leisure interests.

This position is in line with the distinction made by Epperson et al. (1977), who see "the *method* of leisure counseling as one means of achieving the *goal* of leisure education" (pp. viii–ix). Leisure counseling here implies a process; leisure education is presented as an end, a goal. While one might agree with this statement, it still does not clarify sufficiently the distinction between leisure education and leisure counseling, since the former also involves a method and is a process itself.

Even though there is no widely agreed-on definition of either term at this point, the two areas do seem to develop quite separately, as judged by separate publications and conferences regarding these topics. Thus, *Leisure Today* has published a special issue on leisure education (March 1976), and another on leisure counseling (April 1977).

The National Recreation and Parks Association has sponsored conferences on leisure education (e.g., *Proceedings of the Third National
Leisure Education Conference,* 1977) as well as on leisure counseling
(e.g., Compton and Goldstein, 1977). And the University of Maryland
held a national forum on leisure counseling in March 1979. Probably
the clearest practical distinction between the two areas is that leisure
education is primarily concerned with education in the traditional
sense, and is presently promoted through formal educational channels
(e.g., Walton, 1977; Lancaster, 1977); while leisure counseling is still
viewed as primarily a therapeutic process concerned to a larger degree with enabling rather than informative components.

The aspect that is missing in both approaches is a well-defined
theoretical underpinning anchored in the concept of leisure. That is
not to say that leisure counseling or education does not avail itself of
theoretical orientations. But the tendency is the following. The practitioner either chooses an already existing theoretical approach—like
reality therapy, transactional analysis and Gestalt awareness, values
clarification, assertiveness training, and so on—and simply links the
particular method to issues of leisure; or else, presents a step-by-step
procedure resembling a flow chart in computer programming as if it
constituted a theory or philosophy of leisure counseling. Neither approach comes to grips with the specific issues of leisure on either a
personal or societal level.

Content versus Process

Psychologists have traditionally emphasized process over content, or
to put it differently, dynamics over structure. Ever since the days of
Wundt (1873/74), the search has been on for general laws to the neglect of the individual case. Up to very recently, the tendency has been
to treat individual differences as error, particularly in experimental
social psychology. Personality psychologists and clinicians have of
course studied individual differences, but no generally accepted theory
or system of classification has emerged. Imagine a developing science
of chemistry without its having had at some point in its history a
periodic table of elements!

Tied in with the issue of content and structure is the fact that
these dimensions take on even more importance if we claim to engage
in interdisciplinary research or applied activity. There is no doubt that
the unique dynamics of the mind must be studied for their own sake;
but there is also no doubt that when we deal with complex forms of
human behavior and experience, we must understand these within the
context of the larger social and societal structures, giving content as
equal a share as process in the resulting interaction. One of the reasons

environmental psychology attempts to establish itself as a unit separate from social psychology is this very issue: the unwillingness of social psychologists to adopt truly an interdisciplinary approach that would give structure its deserved place in the study of human behavior (Proshansky, 1976).

Why this seeming digression? Because we seem to be heading toward the same neglect in the developing field of leisure education and counseling. Hardly anywhere in the many models mentioned do we see a concern for content. We hear of self-actualization, of raising consciousness, of increasing awareness, of improving communication skills, and so on. But what of the issues that brought about the very need for leisure education? What of the changes that are revolutionizing our society? Yes, we hear of values clarification. But what about the content of these values? Are we as educators pretending to be free of values? Do we not have values that we want to promote, that we need to promote? Have we not, through our thorough analyses of societal changes, discovered that certain values will be of greater adaptive potential than others? Do we not need to identify and make these values explicit?

There will be much disagreement on what these values should be. That is how it ought to be but that is not the point. The important issue is that as leisure educators we must have *some* values, and these must be an explicit and contributing part of the leisure education and counseling process. It is this content component, and this component only, which makes this process a unique discipline. If not for that, we might just as well continue with our present forms of education, counseling, and therapy.

What is this content that I am speaking of? It is information about the changing conditions of our society as we move into the postindustrial era; and it is values derived from and necessitated by these changes. It is the number, size, and ever-increasing rate of these changes which affect personal existence to a degree never before experienced. It is the unique task of leisure education and leisure counseling to deal with the impact of these changes on human lifestyles. This is the exciting challenge that we, as practitioners of a new discipline, must be willing to accept.

In the following pages I shall outline briefly some content issues of leisure education and leisure counseling. In light of what I just said, I hope that these issues will at least spark discussion and lead to a clarification of issues.

LEISURE EDUCATION

Leisure education is both different from and similar to (and overlaps with) leisure counseling. The content and the process of each will inevitably include some aspects of the other. One might extend this overlap to the content and process of leisure therapy, which may be placed at the far end of the continuum, beyond leisure counseling.

Education implies that both knowledge and development result from an educational process. The emphasis, however, is on knowledge and the conveying of knowledge, which then in turn is instrumental in bringing about the change. Leisure education thus implies foremost the imparting of knowledge that is relevant to the leisure domain—as it pertains to the individual, to the individual's immediate environment, and to society at large.

Since our knowledge is frequently the cognitive component of our attitudes, the previous statement implies that leisure education will be closely related to a process of attitude change (Neulinger, 1976b). Further, to the degree that a substantial proportion of leisure education consists of explicating new, more appropriate, and more adaptive attitudes and norms, it may overlap with, and become in some respects indistinguishable from, leisure counseling.

On a more concrete level, what kind of knowledge are we talking about? First and foremost, a clear understanding of what we mean by leisure, including an operationalizable conceptual model, becomes a *sine qua non*. If one is not clear whether one deals with free time, an activity, an attitude, or a state of mind, how can one hope to educate anyone else about these issues? [2] Each of these aspects has relevance to leisure education, but one is not the same as the other. At any given point an educator may wish to emphasize one aspect more than another, but at all times it should be clear to both the educator and the audience which aspect is being referred to.

Needless to say, we do have a model! Our model identifies leisure as a state of mind and considers two variables as critical for its coming about: *perceived freedom* and *intrinsic motivation*. Within this context, let us now look at what knowledge is relevant to the individual, the individual's environment, and society at large.

The Individual

The primary task of leisure education, at present, is to make the individual aware of what is meant by leisure within the context of leisure education. This is not a simple task. We must overcome the free time–leisure confusion that is so deeply embedded in all of our thinking. Unless we do so, neither teachers nor the students of leisure education will know what the subject matter is.

There will always be knowledge about free time that we need to be educated about: the amount and distribution of free time in various populations; the changing patterns of free time over time; the availability of activities and resources specifically relevant to free time; the very question of the conceptualization and delineation of free time; and many other factors. But all of these are ancillary to the task of leisure education.

Leisure education must make the individual aware of the conditions that bring about the state of mind referred to as leisure. We have identified these as perceived freedom and intrinsic motivation. Others may wish to add additional dimensions, or change them altogether. That is not the issue. What is important is that we keep searching for the dimensions that best describe the state of mind we are after: a state in which we feel fulfilled; for which the word *boredom* does not exist; which gives meaning to life; and as stated before, a state which may well be the criterion for the quality of life.

Having identified the conditions for leisure, leisure education will then elaborate on how they relate to the individual and what role they play in the person's life. This will inevitably involve environmental and societal settings, issues to which we turn next.

The Individual's Environment or Personal Setting

Perceived freedom and intrinsic motivation emerge from the interaction of the individual and the environment. People differ in what they perceive as freedom or as being intrinsically motivating. These factors will depend on each person's individual background and socialization history. As a result, an identical environment may be perceived quite differently by different people. This is an issue we discussed in chapter 5 when dealing with measurement problems. It becomes an issue again in leisure education when we come to realize that similar life settings may have quite different potentials for leisure, given the particular background and personality of the people involved. A person who lacks the satisfaction of very basic physiological needs (such as hunger or sufficient shelter) cannot be expected to avail him- or herself of an opportunity to the same degree as one who is not deprived in this respect. The quality of life, as represented by the physical aspects of our daily environment, varies tremendously among the various subgroups of our population,[3] and even more so of the populations of the world. We cannot educate for or about leisure without taking these differences into account.

How might this be done? The first step would be to develop a system of classification of the environment, perhaps based on a theoretical framework similar to that of Maslow's (1954) need hierarchies. Social indicators presently being developed would help in this enterprise. What might we achieve by this? Perhaps nothing more than the realization that, for the majority of the population of the world, leisure is still just a distant ideal, far too unreal to be thought reachable through a mere educational effort. Perhaps it would shock us into the realization that we cannot have a leisure society in one part of the world without sharing it with the rest. No matter how large our defense budget may be, neither our conscience (hopefully!) nor the rest of the world would let us get away with that.

Must all this really be part of leisure education? Does it sound overwhelming and somewhat depressing? If part of leisure education involves the promotion of a *leisure ethic*—a set of moral principles or values related to leisure—then leisure education must deal with these issues. Yes, enabling "the individual to identify and clarify his own leisure values and goals" (Mundy, 1976) is leisure education, but only if these values and goals are placed in perspective to others and the larger society. This is an extremely touchy topic. But we must confront it unless we wish to raise a generation of selfish and self-centered individuals. We cannot afford to pretend to be value-free, and, as I warned elsewhere, "beware of the professional who professes that 'no profession can justify teaching or imparting their own set of values, attitudes, and behavior to others . . .' (Mundy and Odum, 1979, pp. 8–9), particularly if that person is an educator or a member of a helping profession" (Neulinger, 1979b).

Society at Large

This brings us to the third area of crucial importance in leisure education, namely societal developments and values. It is not enough for a "leisure educated" person to be aware of one's own values and of issues related only to one's own quality of life. Such a person must be in touch with society at large: what are the current values and norms? How were they in the past? How are they holding up? How are they changing? What are the developments, both social and technological, that cause the meaning of so many concepts to become modified? Has the nature of work—that is, paid employment—remained the same over the years, or is it in a state of flux? Are the functions and potentials of "the job" what they used to be? How do technological developments affect the job market now, and in the future? What are the implications of the changes taking place in our population's age distribution? And perhaps most importantly, what do we mean by a new leisure ethic? How does it relate to the work ethic? What are the social, economic, political, and moral implications of our changing values?

It is only within the context of these larger issues that we can hope to understand and deal with the life of the individual. Leisure education is not a simple task. It faces the challenges of our rapidly changing society and must confront newly emerging values and norms.

It requires an interdisciplinary approach through the active involvement of members from all relevant disciplines. Its methods and techniques remain to be developed. But its goal is clear: examine and question the nature of the good life, and then promote it.

LEISURE COUNSELING

Leisure counseling, as a form of counseling, is a guidance and enabling process. To the degree that this involves getting to know oneself better—unlocking and channeling one's energies, becoming assertive, overcoming one's fears, anxieties, and internal barriers—traditional methods of counseling represent valuable and necessary tools for the leisure counselor. The better trained, more knowledgeable, and more artful the counselor is in these areas, the more effective will he or she perform counseling on issues of leisure, as well as on any other issues of life.

Let us now, however, look at *leisure* counseling, a guidance and enabling process that is specifically designed to help the individual overcome a syndrome we shall call *leisure lack,* the chronic absence or relative infrequency of a leisure experience (Neulinger, 1978). Note two distinctions from leisure education. (1) This process is directed primarily toward individuals (or at least groups of individuals), involving them in interaction as unique individuals. (2) The emphasis is on motivation rather than on information. On the other hand, leisure counseling shares with leisure education the need for a sound theoretical base anchored in an unambiguous understanding and integration of the concept of leisure.

Leisure Lack [4]

There are many reasons why a person might seek out a leisure counselor, just as there are many reasons why someone goes to a medical doctor. Nevertheless, we shall attempt next to identify a special condition, a syndrome that might be associated with those who are most appropriately served by leisure counseling. We have labeled this syndrome *leisure lack.*

Leisure lack is widespread in our society as well as the rest of the world. It besets the young and the old and the middle-aged, the poor and the rich, and members of the majority and all the different minorities. It knows no boundaries. It invades homes, schools, hospitals, prisons, industry, playgrounds, and even outer space. What is most threatening is that it is on the increase: the more progress we make on a technological level, the more this phenomenon seems to undermine the gains we otherwise would expect in the quality of our lives.

We shall take a preliminary look at leisure lack from the viewpoint of some traditional categories of approach. The remarks that follow are by no means meant to be definitive; consider them a first approximation.

Diagnosis. The first task of the leisure counselor is to identify the client's problem: Does the client really want or need leisure counseling? What are the symptoms to look for and what would indicate that the client might be better served by some other process?

Just for the record, let me raise two questions once more. Is leisure the problem? The answer, by definition, is no. It is the *lack* of leisure which is the problem, and quite to the contrary, an increase in the experience of leisure is the very goal of the counseling process.

Is free time the problem? For some it may represent a problem, and for others it is the lack of free time that is an issue. Thus free time in itself is not the critical factor. Whether the phenomenon manifests itself depends on the way time is used or, we might say, misused. The use of time depends on one's personal makeup, background, life history, personality, attitudes, values, and perception of self and others, as well as on one's social and societal environment. Does this sound very complex? It does, but wishing that it were not so does not make it less complex.

The problem then is a condition of the self as it functions in a particular environment. This may manifest itself in many different ways, any one or several of which may be present at any given time. The person may feel, but not necessarily express, a state of dissatisfaction, alienation, boredom, and at times, anxiety. There may be apathy or, on the other hand, frenzied and compulsive activity. Most of all, there will be a lack of goals, involvement, and ambition, combined with a sense of not achieving fulfillment or self-actualization. Life is experienced as meaningless: nothing seems to matter.

The person described above needs help: but is it the help of a leisure counselor or a psychotherapist? There is no easy answer to this. In part it will depend on the severity of the manifestations, the person's degree of functioning in other spheres of life, and most decisively, on the causal factors involved. We shall turn to those next.

Etiology. What brings about leisure lack? What are the causal factors of this condition? Personal malfunctioning is viewed by some (Freudian psychologists) primarily as a function of having acquired inappropriate ways of handling instinctual (*id*) demands, as a result of very early child-parent interactions and events experienced within the immediate family. Others emphasize coping mechanisms in dealing with reality (ego-psychology), giving the societal environment an equal share of the burden (social psychiatry). I suggest that the roots of leisure lack are to be found in the person's values, norms, and mores (the *super-ego*), but not only in terms of the dynamics of this component but primarily its content.

When we look for the causes of leisure lack, we must take into account personal structure and dynamics, but we are likely to find the origin of the problem in incongruencies between the person's and society's value systems. The values most involved will be the very ones that give meaning to life: the role of the job; the meaning of work; one's obligations to family, society, and the world at large; even questions of an afterlife; the right to play, to loaf, not to work; and so on. These are the values that are undergoing the greatest changes as we move from an industrial to a post-industrial society.

Note that leisure lack is likely to manifest itself mostly in later life, particularly at a point when an act of separation is involved. A set of standards that has been functional for some time is suddenly no longer appropriate. The person suddenly confronts an environment that is no longer what it used to be. An act of separation may make the person cruelly aware of how things have changed. A perfectly well-tempered superego, which would have harmonized beautifully if only the world would remain what it was when the superego was developed, is suddenly totally out of tune. But not because the strings of the instrument have weakened, but because a new orchestra has taken over with instruments tuned to a different key. Unfortunately, not only may persons be out of tune in this way, but whole institutions (run by persons!) may be so affected.

Prognosis. In making a prognosis, we shall have to keep in mind that we are dealing with the person as well as society. In general counseling and therapy, the emphasis is still on bringing about changes in the person. Leisure counseling must put equal emphasis on bringing about changes in the environment, or perhaps moving the person into a different setting. The prognosis will thus depend on possible changes envisioned in the person as well as on the social and societal setting involved.

Treatment. In light of what was just said, it is clear that we must treat both the person and society. Any of the methods developed for changing a person's values and attitudes may be appropriate, keeping in mind that one is interested not only in "values clarification," but also in influencing the direction and very nature of these values. Some may strongly disagree with this statement, but it is my conviction that neither leisure education nor leisure counseling is, or can be, value-free.[5]

But what is society and how do you treat it? Society is the world at large in which the person lives: the city, the neighborhood, the family, or the institution in which the person resides. This society is not only important in its physical reality, but also for the norms and values it promotes. Both of these aspects must be the concern of the leisure counselor, who must make it his or her task to bring them in line with the demands of post-industrial society.

Viewed from this larger perspective, it is clear that leisure counseling cannot be separated from leisure education. The content of leisure education must be part and parcel of any leisure-counseling program, or to restate Epperson et al.'s (1977, pp. viii–ix) phrase: the method of leisure counseling is one of the means of achieving the goal of leisure education. It is this goal or content, best described as the leisure ethic, which determines the processes that will be involved and necessary in leisure counseling, and which makes it a unique approach.

On the following pages we shall describe a leisure-counseling instrument as well as a hypothetical leisure-counseling program. The instrument is still in the developing stages and we are presently collecting baseline data and evaluating its practical usefulness. We would like to encourage others to participate in this effort.

A Leisure-counseling Instrument

The questionnaire *A Self-Exploration: "What Am I Doing?"* (WAID) is basically a time-budget instrument, to which are added variables that are relevant to the leisure experience (appendix 2). Let us take a brief look at the instructions and discuss the rationale for each item.

The instrument allows for the collection of information for a twenty-four-hour period. Obviously, the choice of day (i.e., weekday versus Sunday), and the number of days or administrations, will be a function of the particular program one is concerned with.

ACTIVITY. The choice of half hour as the time unit is intended to allow the respondent to be specific in describing activities, and yet not to become overwhelmed by detail. Longer-lasting activities present no problem: the respondent simply combines units. If there is more than one important event during any one half hour, the respondent has the option to indicate that. Also keep in mind that an eventual discussion and/or interview is implied with the respondent, where further details may be elicited and worked with. It is for this reason, and the practical aspect of not making the task too difficult, that no attempt is made to get at secondary activities.

WHERE. Knowing the context of an activity is essential for understanding its meaning. Reading a newspaper while commuting to your job has different implications than reading a newspaper on the job. Code numbers are used to simplify completion of the questionnaire.

WITH WHOM. The information obtained is restricted to the

number of others in one's life. During a follow-up interview one would probably inquire who some of the people were. To keep the issue of invasion of privacy to a minimum, it was deemed wise not to ask for that information in written form. The rationale for including the "WITH WHOM" dimension is the same as for the previous one. With whom an activity is carried out may make a considerable difference. To sleep with one's mate may have different implications than sleeping with one's neighbor's mate!

Note that another dimension of context, namely WHEN, the time of the activity, is derived from the method of data collection namely the half-hour intervals. It too has obvious implications. Having a cocktail at eight AM is different from having one at eight PM!

CHOICE. This is the first variable directly related to leisure, since it taps *perceived freedom*. The respondent is asked to estimate the degree of choice involved in the activity under scrutiny. It is not an easy question to answer. Life is complex; most activities involve several levels of choice, and one is often not clear on why one does something. For example, if I am at school or at a job, am I there because I want to be or because I have to be? Probably both; but the degree of choice will vary for individuals, and within individuals for particular activities within these contexts. The emphasis here is on particular activities and variations in these over time.

Answering these questions is difficult also because most of us have never thought about these matters in just this way. This, however, is precisely the task and potential of this instrument: to make one aware of this critical dimension. Completing this form may be like learning a new language: how to talk to and with oneself. It is something that will take time and practice.

REASON. This is the second critical variable, measuring the degree of *intrinsic* and/or *extrinsic* motivation. Responding to this question represents an equally difficult task and one literally needs to train oneself how to become aware of this dimension.

NEED. Respondents are asked to describe in their own words the need they see involved or being satisfied. Responses may be categorized and compared to independently obtained need profiles of the respondents. Or the responses might be compared to need-analyzed intentions of the respondents.

FEELING. Respondents are asked to describe in their own words their feelings. Thus a qualitative measure of affect is obtained.

FEELING TONE. This is a quantitative measure of affect experienced while engaged in the particular activity, ranging from extremely positive, through neutral, to extremely negative. The last two variables may be considered "outcome" or criterion variables.

So much for a brief description of the instrument and the information gathered from it. How can it be used? There are two distinct purposes for which it may be used. One is as a research instrument—and we shall hint at these uses only briefly. The other is as a leisure-counseling tool.

The research information gathered will be primarily inter-individual (*nomothetic*). in nature. Norms will be developed so that an individual's responses can be placed into perspective, and "unusual" responses identified. Differences among subpopulations will be established. Any number of before-and-after situations call for investigation. Nearly all the major milestones and crisis points in life need to be looked at in terms of changes in the perception of these variables. Thus information needs to be collected for the time periods before and after retirement, divorce, bereavement, the "empty-nest," job relocation, and many more.

Avenues of Approach

Now let us look at the use of the instrument as a leisure-counseling tool. There are any number of ways in which this instrument is relevant to this task.

First, it helps raise the respondent's awareness about conditions that are critical for a leisure experience. It makes the person look at him- or herself, as never before, in areas that have direct relevance to the achievement of leisure.

Second, it allows one to compare oneself to others (nomothetic information) in regard to leisure-relevant dimensions, as well as to oneself over time (idiographic information). One can establish one's own standard or baseline and study deviations therefrom. It provides a kind of self-confrontation, allowing oneself to come to grips with the validity of one's perceptions. For example, some respondents indicate that 100 percent of their activities are self-determined and based solely on their own choice; others state that they experience 100 percent positive affect throughout the total day. We let the reader ponder the implications of such responses!

Third, the instrument allows for both *retrospective* and *prospective* approaches. By a retrospective approach is meant examining the conditions that have brought about a certain affect. What were the conditions (i.e., degree of perceived freedom and kind of motivation) that were associated with the person feeling good or bad? Is positive affect indeed related to choice and instrinsic motivation? Does this relationship hold for all activities or only for some? If so, which ones? By a prospective approach is meant examining the same issues, but in the opposite direction. Starting with the degree of perceived freedom and intrinsic motivation, we examine whether the affect was as one would have predicted on the basis of the leisure model. If the predictions are not confirmed, what could be the reasons? [6] Might the person have problems handling freedom? Does this negative relationship hold consistently for all behavior patterns, or only for certain ones?

Fourth, the instrument not only allows, but certainly invites, periodic data collection, and thus a monitoring of the person's progress in any leisure-counseling program. At the same time, it could be used as the basis for an evaluation of any such program.

A Leisure-counseling Program [7]

There obviously has to be more to a counseling program than just an instrument, no matter how well thought through or effective it may be. First of all, there has to be a goal. Generally, the aim is to bring about a change in the person or to help the person achieve a desired outcome. (Parenthetically, I suggest that we have here another distinction between leisure education and leisure counseling. While the goal of the former may also involve changes in individuals, very frequently the desired outcome may be and ought to be changes in society, relating both to the physical and social environment.)

The goal of the leisure-counseling program will have to be tailored to the individual involved, or in a larger sense, to the target population in question. The differentiation among subpopulations will need to be made not only in terms of traditional distinctions such as health, age, or nature of institutionalization, but also in terms of societal variables, such as social class (income, area of residence, etc.) and cultural background. It cannot be repeated often enough: perceived freedom and intrinsic motivation are very much functions of the person's background and environmental setting. Effective leisure counseling must be both person- and environment-oriented.

The goal obviously will also vary as a function of the particular problem that brought the counselee to the program. Leisure plays an important role in all stages of the life cycle, as we have indicated in the last chapter. Specific programs need to be developed, each centered around one of the milestones or crisis points of life.

The program incorporates three phases. *Phase 1* deals with personal assessment and planning, in three ways:

1. The suitability of the counselee is assessed. Is the program appropriate for the problem presented? Is the problem a leisure-related one, or is it a health, economic, legal, or other kind of problem, which could be helped more efficiently by other means? Does the severity of the problem require leisure therapy or therapy in general rather than leisure counseling? These are some of the questions that need to be resolved at the very beginning of the program.

2. The nature of the program is explained to the counselee; goals and limits of the program are discussed and expectations are clarified. A contract is established.

3. Personal information relevant to the goal is obtained from the counselee. Such information will include a profile of the counselee's needs; a listing of actual and desired activities, both on and off the job; and background information, as well as information relating to the counselee's personal and societal environment.

Phase 2 of the program is the actual "work" phase. This may be carried out individually, in groups, or in combination. At this point, the WAID instrument will be introduced and counselees will be trained in completing it. Each counselee will maintain a personal record book and monitor his or her behavior and progress. Counseling sessions will first deal with the theoretical importance of the variables *perceived freedom* and *intrinsic motivation* as they apply to both personal and societal issues, and then begin to relate these dimensions to each individual's specific situation. At this point, use will be made of the information gathered in phase 1.

Phase 3 is the "action" phase. It is in line with Fromm's (1976, p. 170) admonition: *"Insight separated from practice remains ineffective."* Counselees test out behavior initiated on the basis of insights gained during phase 2. Their progress will be monitored through periodic WAID completions. Gradual separation from the program is initiated.

The success or failure of any leisure-counseling program will depend ultimately, of course, on the skills and quality of the leisure counselor. Computers, instruments, resource files, and whatever other gadgets we can come up with, are valuable but cannot eliminate the need for the ultimate integrator: the human mind.

LEISURE-RESOURCES INFORMATION

A major proportion of activities carried out presently under the name of either leisure education or leisure counseling is, in fact, providing leisure-resources information. At the moment, such information relates primarily to free-time activities, since the conceptualization of leisure as a state of mind has not yet been generally accepted by our society. Eventually, as this view catches on, such information will pertain to the employment situation as well as the nonemployment one.

The provision of such information is an essential and most necessary task. However, it may help to clarify and sharpen the nature of leisure education and counseling, if this task is kept separate from them or at least treated as a distinct component. It is the kind of task that can be highly mechanized; computers may be used to tremendous advantage. The size and the complexity of the problem clearly surpass the capacity of any individual counselor, even if we are dealing with only a small urban setting. Clearly, some government or private enterprise should organize such resource files and make them available to qualified leisure professionals.

Given modern technology, the scope of such information centers is practically limitless. We see modest examples of such services in the computerized dating organizations or the reservation devices for airlines and hotel chains. A system specifically designed for leisure counseling is the *Milwaukee Leisure Counseling Model,* based largely on the work of Drs. Robert Overs and George T. Wilson (Wilson et al., 1977).

The way these systems differ from mere information listings (such as the yellow pages of a phone book) is that they attempt to match the needs or wants of the person with the available resources. Given the complexity and multiplicity of our society, such systems certainly make the task of finding and selecting desired activities much easier. There is no doubt also that they may bring to the attention of the person resources he or she may otherwise never have become aware of.

We are obviously just beginning to see developments in this area. Yet it may not be too early to think about potential dangers. Things may be made too "easy" for us and in addition, we may be overwhelmed by the amount of choice given. Will the alternatives be *true* alternatives, or will they just reflect the contentions of our advertising agencies? Will we be losing the opportunity of discovering a satisfying experience all by ourselves? Will we have to miss the chance of becoming involved in the search, contributing to the eventual success and being an origin of our own behavior? Is our life going to become as automated off the job as on?

Perhaps it is really too early to worry about all of this. At the moment, systems of leisure-resources information are much needed and their development ought to be widely encouraged.

SUMMARY

In this chapter we looked at systematic and explicit methods of increasing the individual's leisure experience through leisure education and counseling. The need for such efforts was seen to be widely recognized as well as reflected in the large number of publications recently appearing in this area.

The concepts *leisure, education,* and *counseling* date back a long time ago. The point was made that developing the new disciplines of leisure education and leisure counseling requires more than just adding the label *leisure* to traditional education and counseling techniques.

Much of the present flow of activities in this area has its origin in therapeutic recreation services, going back to the late 1950s when these activities were centered primarily in institutional settings. More recently the trend has been to introduce leisure counseling into the community and leisure education into the formal school system.

Leisure-counseling methods have been classified in terms of their target population as well as approaches used. The former is one of the major distinguishing marks between leisure education and leisure counseling.

The issue of content versus process was seen as essential in delineating the unique disciplines of leisure education and leisure counseling. It is the content of these new disciplines, both in terms of variables considered and values espoused, that sets them apart from previous techniques and other disciplines. Another distinguishing feature must be their concern with both the person and society—equal partners in the processes we investigate and also attempt to influence. We need therefore to follow an interactionist and interdisciplinary approach.

Both leisure education and leisure counseling require explicitly stated conceptualizations of leisure, in order to be internally consistent, clear about goals, and translatable into action. Leisure education implies foremost the imparting of knowledge, which in turn, may result in attitude change. The knowledge conveyed may concern the individual, his or her environment or personal setting, and society at large. This implies primarily bringing about a clear understanding of the nature of leisure on the individual level; examining the personal setting in its role as an actualizer or inhibitor of leisure; and on the societal level dealing with the implications of our steadily advancing technology and the resulting changes in lifestyles and norms.

Present leisure-counseling approaches tend to use one or another of the various counseling techniques in vogue. Such techniques, however, need to be modified and extended so that they will specifically deal with both relevant content and process.

An attempt was made to identify a condition or syndrome that might be characteristic of the person for whom leisure counseling is most appropriate. That syndrome was labeled *leisure lack*. A very preliminary approximation of this condition was outlined within the context of diagnosis, etiology, prognosis, and treatment. The reduction of leisure lack in our society was seen as requiring the combined efforts of leisure education and leisure counseling.

A particular approach to leisure counseling was described. It makes use of an instrument of self-exploration designed to deal with variables that are specifically relevant to the leisure experience. Ways of using the instrument were illustrated, for both research and counseling. Three phases of a leisure counseling program were outlined: a personal assessment and planning phase, a "work" phase, and an

Table 9.1. Types of Professional Involvement in the Leisure Domain

Types	Ratio of informa-tional to motivational components	Suggested minimal education	Target populations	Approaches
Leisure resources consulting	5:1	B.A., B.S.	general population	Primarily information giving; raising awareness of options and opportunities for free time and employment opportunities. Provision of resources files. "Connecting" consumer and supplier interests.
Leisure education	4:2	B.A., B.S., through Ph.D.	general population	Educating about developments and changing conditions in post-industrial society, with emphasis on changing attitudes, values, and norms. Raising the awareness about the implications of these changes both for the individual and society.
Leisure counseling	2:4	M.A., M.S., M.S.W.	individuals experiencing *leisure lack*	Raising the awareness of personal needs and blocks, in the light of conditions necessary for experiencing leisure. Guiding individuals toward increasing their leisure experience, with due emphasis on environmental conditions.
Leisure therapy	1:5	Ph.D.	individuals experiencing *leisure lack* such that it interferes with adequate functioning	Helping individuals cope with *leisure lack*, when the problem is rooted primarily in the personal history of the individual rather than societal conditions.

*Certain groups can also be identified for whom leisure services are particularly relevant, for example, the retired, preretired individuals, the widowed, divorced or separated, the "empty-nest" housewife, the alcoholic or drug abuser, the institutionalized, the handicapped, and the elderly.

"action" phase. The importance of the counselor's skills for the ultimate success of any program was emphasized.

Finally, it was suggested that the task of providing leisure-resources information be treated as a separate component of leisure education and counseling. The task is an essential one, but represents special problems and may require a different level and type of training. The complexity of our society demands that this task be approached on a grand scale, too big for any one individual counselor or educator. The chapter closed with an ironic consideration: the ultimate leisure-resources information service might end up being detrimental, if not totally destructive, to the leisure experience.

We shall conclude this summary with a table that places leisure services along a continuum of informational-versus-motivational components (see Table 9.1). Leisure-resources consulting is seen as being (arbitrarily) five-sixths informational versus one-sixth motivational, compared to leisure therapy, which is viewed as one-sixth informational and five-sixths motivational. Suggested minimal education requirements are indeed only suggestive, permitting of appropriate exceptions. The rest of the items correspond to issues discussed in the chapter.

The main purpose of this table is to emphasize the fact that different backgrounds and training may be required within the possible range of leisure enabling services. This issue is an important consideration in terms of potential future licensing regulations for leisure professionals.

ENDNOTES

[1] At this point of the chapter we are dealing with issues of leisure education and leisure counseling at the same time. We shall make a distinction between the two very shortly, and then use the terms as defined.

[2] A new source of confusion has crept up lately among leisure counselors. Leisure is sometimes referred to as an attitude, when intending to refer to it as a state of mind. An attitude is indeed a state of mind, but as traditionally defined a very specific one. It is a disposition to respond in certain ways (i.e., cognitively, affectively, and conatively) *toward an object or event.* Thus, one has an attitude or attitudes toward leisure or aspects of leisure. But having an attitude toward leisure is not the same as being in a state of leisure!

[3] The reader is referred once more to the illuminating article relevant to this issue by Angus Campbell (1972).

[4] Some of the thoughts expressed in this chapter have been presented previously in a paper entitled "Leisure counseling: Process or content" (Neulinger, 1978).

[5] For those who are interested in the issue of value expression in the formulation of scientific theories, I recommend an article by Kenneth J. Gergen (1978), from which I quote the following:

> . . . *regardless of the traditional attempt to remain ethically neutral, the social theorist is inevitably favoring certain forms of social activity over others, certain strata of society as opposed to others, and certain values over their antitheses.*
>
> . . . *The theorist need not fear the expression of values in a given formulation; they are inevitable. (Pp. 1355, 1356.)*

[6] As a last resort we might even question the validity of our very model of leisure. To put it more positively, however, another research use of the instrument would certainly be for testing the basic hypotheses of the leisure model.

[7] This program was developed in cooperation with Gary Paluba, associate director of The Leisure Institute, New York, N.Y.

10

Leisure: a social-political issue

America is failing. We are building sports complexes and increasing our manufacture of luxury automobiles while failing to provide substance to the dreams we have told everyone to believe, the dreams of nothing more than shelter, clothes, food, and some occasional fun.
    Clayton Riley (1977).

We have reached the final chapter, you as the reader and I as the writer. Aside from a sigh of relief, some reflections are appropriate at this stage. Reflections on what it all means and more importantly on what the implications are.

Why start the chapter with a rather gloomy and pessimistic quote? Why not emphasize the positive, the strides forward we have made, the accomplishments we have achieved in this country? The answer is simple. Satisfaction and satiation lead to complacency, not to action, and it is the intention of this chapter to stir the emotions and provoke action. It is one of the ironies of our time that our success and affluence may well become the cause of our eventual downfall, particularly if that plenty is not shared with all members of our society and eventually the rest of the world.

A recent national survey of the quality of life of Americans came to the following conclusions:

> The findings from these surveys may be summarized by saying that most of the adults in this country report that their needs and wants are well met in the areas most important to their quality of life. (Flanagan, 1978.)

On the surface this sounds beautiful, and we shall not enter into a discussion of the validity of this study at this point; the author recognizes certain limitations himself. But even if an approximate 80 percent of our population does report that their needs are being met or that they are "satisfied," what about the other 20 percent (which is more than 40 million people)? And what of the millions of people in the rest of the world, which this survey did not cover?

One of the implications of accepting a state-of-mind definition of leisure is that it widens the scope of responsibility for the leisure professional. We are no longer restricted in our concerns to a section of the day, the so-called free time; nor to a section of the person, the "after work" component. We are dealing now with the whole person and his or her whole life. The recognition of this fact requires a tremendous shift in our thinking and in the necessary approaches we must take. We are suddenly involved in all of the complexity of both the individual and society. No wonder Kaplan (1975) had to propose a model of leisure with sixteen components giving practically an infinite number of possible combinations. But if we want to take our role as leisure professionals seriously, there is no escaping this complexity.

In this chapter, we shall first look at some ideal, perhaps utopian possibilities that are available to our society. There is always the hope of self-fulfilling prophecy, and predicting these conditions may help bring them about. We shall also consider some more down-to-earth possibilities that may help lay the foundation on which these utopian suggestions could be based.

THE IMPOSSIBLE DREAM

"Education for leisure in contemporary America is an impossible dream" (Sessoms, 1976). The author of this statement comes to this conclusion through the following reasoning. He correctly identifies leisure education as a process of teaching values and attitudes, rather than just skills or even knowledge. And he does not share the naive view of many Americans that values and attitudes can be taught within our formal educational system in the same manner we impart technical knowledge and develop operational skills. Our present societal values, still deeply rooted in the work ethic, will not succumb to even the most brilliant of lectures delivered in the classroom.

Does this mean we should forget about leisure education? Not according to Sessoms; we merely need to postpone it for a while. At present, "education for discretionary time use is possible." By this the author means instruction in the so-called nonproductive activities, such as the arts, music, sports, etc. Rather than addressing ourselves directly to changing values and attitudes, let us create the conditions that will make such changes more desirable and even necessary. Changes in values come about when the needs of a society demand them.

There are two aspects to this argument. On the one hand, one can readily agree with it. It would indeed be an impossible dream to attempt to promote values that are contradictory to the perceived goals and survival issues of a society, particularly through the formal educational system. On the other hand, one can also take a more optimistic point of view in regard to leisure education. Of foremost importance, of course, are the convictions that the promotion of a positive leisure ethic through leisure education is in line with the spirit of the times; that the conditions, in fact, have arrived that make such education appropriate now; and furthermore, that changing values requires prophets who see ahead, leading people in the direction appropriate for the given period. This touches on the unresolved question as to whether history makes great individuals, or great individuals make history.

However this may be, the leisure professional's task must be future-oriented, with an eye toward what is appropriate within the context of technological and societal developments.

Rather then dealing with leisure education per se, let us consider then some conditions that would make a leisure ethic not only more desirable but truly necessary. Let us picture our preferred utopia in terms of a minimal number of conditions that could bring about such a state. We shall not worry about how realistic these possibilities are; let that be the concern of economists and politicians. Let them find the means to achieve what society's values dictate to be the goals. Let us be demanding and follow the imperative so beautifully expressed by Obermeyer (1971):

> 'you *must*, therefore you can'; not, as our technological power is seductively whispering in our ears, 'You can, therefore you must—or why not?'

In other words, let our values and ideals determine our goals, rather than drift to wherever our next technological breakthrough will carry us.

A Guaranteed Health Service

To say that nothing is as important to life as life itself may sound slightly redundant. But it is still and always will be the most basic truth about our existence. Not that there have not been massive attempts to deny this truth. At the danger of being considered antireligious, I would say that all beliefs in an afterlife, whatever form they may take, are undermining the importance of life on earth. After all, how can a mere hundred or less years compete with an infinity of existence? Similarly, strong beliefs have led people to sacrifice their lives willingly, for their country, for their family, or for a good cause. These instances, however, while constituting a rejection of life, may be carried out for the sake of saving the lives of others, and may thus in fact be in line with a confirmation of life.

The fact remains that life, and by that we mean a relatively healthy life, is the very basis of existence. Conversely, the fear of losing this life or being seriously impaired is also the most serious worry that people have to face. Nevertheless, it is one of those things that one tends to appreciate less the more one has of it. The healthy person takes his or her health for granted. In our society, and in most post-industrial societies at least, the majority of people are relatively healthy. But at what cost is that health maintained, and what about those who are not healthy?

Unfortunately nobody can guarantee health. A society, however, could and should guarantee to everyone adequate and equal health-care services. Such services must include not only treatment but custodial care if necessary. The foremost and first condition of our utopia is freedom from the fear of the economic consequences of sickness.

The wish to bring about such a society rests on a basic belief: it is human nature to want to be healthy. This is not to deny that under certain conditions we may prefer to be sick or play the invalid. I remember being in the army and having hepatitis, a disease that required my resting in a comfortable bed for weeks, with entertainment provided by the Red Cross and similar organizations. The alternative meant being out on a bivouac in a sandy desert crawling with snakes. I made very little effort at getting better. On the contrary, I engaged in behavior that one might refer to as goldbricking. And it is equally possible and likely that whole sections of a society might prefer to suffer the consequences of ill health, if that type of behavior is perceived as the only way of getting a share of the benefits of society. We must not make the mistake of inferring from such behavior that people in general would not prefer to lead a healthy life given the chance to pursue a meaningful one.

Another point is important. We cannot resolve any one social problem in isolation. Health is just one of many issues, and even though it may be the most important one, it still must be considered within the context of others. Improvements in any one area cannot work unless related relevant ones are changing appropriately also.

For example, we often hear complaints about the selfishness of doctors in our society; they are said to enrich themselves and seek out medical practice not to heal but to gain a fortune. Such behavior is frowned on as unprincipled and wrong. But in this we are inconsistent. The pursuit of riches is considered a virtue and worthwhile goal in our society. Why should we expect a particular group to act contrary to the norms espoused by society at large? Instead, might we not have to reconsider the utility of the very norms in question?

It is for this reason that the advantages or disadvantages, or even the feasibility, of a national health service cannot be adequately judged in the light of the experience of countries that already have such a service. Such an evaluation must await the time when it can take place within the context of a totally new society, one with values in line with a leisure ethic.

A Guaranteed Income

People cannot live on health alone. Health is something we all strive for, and the amelioration of conditions brought on by disease is the problem that health services address themselves to.[1] The maintenance of health requires certain conditions that must be fulfilled. In Maslow's (1954) terms, people must satisfy certain basic physiological needs, such as hunger and thirst; they must have shelter from the elements; they must be safe from hurt. It is generally recognized that the healthy person also requires the satisfaction of psychological needs, such as the need for love and affiliation, and some degree of self-esteem and recognition. As we ascend this need hierarchy it becomes more and more difficult to imagine how any society can guarantee the satisfaction of these needs. An adequate guaranteed income, however, would furnish the basis for the fulfillment of at least the more primary of such needs. Such a guaranteed income represents the second condition of our utopia—the freedom from the economic burden of providing for subsistence needs.

The issue of a guaranteed income raises many questions and even more eyebrows; it tends to lead to emotional arguments. There are serious economic questions that need to be resolved; but as pointed out before, we shall leave those problems to the appropriate authorities. What is more relevant to our concerns is that the issue involves some deep-seated beliefs about human nature, beliefs that are intricately related to the value of work and leisure. I predict that the disentanglement of the work-leisure dichotomy will contribute directly to the chances of our seeing a guaranteed income coming about in our lifetime.

The argument against a guaranteed income goes something like this. A respectable citizen holds a job as long as he or she is physically fit to do so (mothers and some others are excepted). Why? Because it is the job that makes our lives meaningful, and really all of us ought to want to hold a job. But unfortunately, only some really want meaning in life. Others just want to fritter away their lives without goals or major commitments. A guaranteed income would make such people parasites of society and their lives would be wasted in an endless chain of meaningless pleasure seeking. We—the ones who have the right values, that is—understand that the meaning of life lies in paid employment, and so must do all we can to prevent this from happening.

There are two assumptions in this reasoning that may be seriously questioned. The first we have dealt with throughout this book, namely the belief that it is the job (i.e., paid employment) that is the primary and "natural" source of meaning in life. It should hardly be necessary to repeat our arguments all over again. This outdated belief may have had some validity in the past and may have some even now, under certain societal conditions. But it is no longer functional in a post-industrial society.

The second assumption to be questioned is that only some of us seek meaning in life. Questions of human nature are very difficult to resolve, but if there is one characteristic that distinguishes humans from other animals it is the need to find meaning in life. Once consciousness arises, once you know that you exist and you are aware of a past, present, and future, you start asking the question why and what for. The quest for meaning begins and we all share this need.

If we accept the fact that the desire for meaning, and thus meaningful activity, is universal, and realize that in the future such activity will have to be found primarily outside the employment sphere, we have the basis for accepting and wanting a guaranteed income. Such an income would not imply being without obligations to society or allowing people to lead parasitic lives. It simply means accepting the fact that our advanced technology is capable of providing for our subsistence needs with a minimal contribution of human toil, truly something to celebrate rather than be afraid of.

Our utopia, then, so far has two essential conditions: people are free from the fear of the economic consequences of sickness, and they are free from worry about subsistence needs.[2] It is time now to turn to issues of *freedom to* rather than *freedom from*.

A Guaranteed Education

Given the two conditions of our utopia so far described, what kind of society will it promote? That is hard to predict, even if we assume a benevolent or at least neutral human nature. Notwithstanding our previous statement about the universal need for meaning, it is possible that this need might eventually atrophy in a society that had all its subsistence needs taken care of. An organism is born with potentials for development; but these may never develop if the environment is not appropriately supportive. This is true of all organisms, but applies particularly to that most complex of all, the human being. Here, the social-societal-cultural environment becomes the most critical and decisive nurture that determines the degree and direction of growth. It is to those aspects that we now must turn.

The process by which people are shaped into functioning members of their society is usually referred to as socialization. Who are the agents of the socialization process? In some sense, every member of society contributes to the shaping of others' lives, but the degree to which this happens varies considerably.[3] The role of the parent and the family in the socialization process has always been a crucial one. The trend, however, is toward a decrease in this role as societies move from being agricultural to industrial and increasingly to post-industrial states. Concomitant with this trend is the general shift from an extended family (which may include all the descendants of a common great-grandparent with their wives and/or husbands), to a nuclear one (consisting merely of the parents and their children). More and more, institutions have taken on the function of socialization, some quite explicitly and for specific purposes (e.g., the army makes a soldier out of you); others carry out this socialization implicitly, within the context of their official functions. Note an interesting example. Banks' primary function is the facilitation of financial transactions. Yet banks also act as socialization agents. At one point, they used to promote the virtue of saving; today they are more likely to urge you to spend your money before it is even yours!

An institution that is intimately related to the socialization process is, of course, the educational system. Let us distinguish between socialization processes that are concerned with the transfer of values, attitudes, and norms (*values socialization*), and those that relate to knowledge and skills (*knowledge socialization*). The primary function of the formal educational system is knowledge socialization, although there are those who would argue that values socialization is just as much part of it, if not more so. The latter function, however, is probably achieved not so much in terms of what we teach but rather how we teach it.

If we wish to achieve a leisure society that will be enlivened by a prevailing leisure ethic, it is clear that an appropriate socialization process is an essential requirement. Knowledge socialization will be as important as ever, and in many respects, even more so. We shall need rigorous and highly specialized educational institutions to produce the experts who will not only run our highly technical and science-based society, but also advance further our knowledge and translate it into even more efficient labor-saving devices.

But there will be a shift of emphasis; vocational education will no longer be the prime purpose of our educational systems. We shall finally be able to return to a liberal arts education where knowledge and skills are taught for their own sake. The criterion for the selection of subject matters to be offered (aside from need for the maintenance and advancement of our technological society) will be their potential contribution to the person's self-actualization.

It is also clear that if a leisure society is to flourish, every member of society must have free access to this educational system, that is to say, freedom to participate unrestricted by any economic restraints. That is not to say that there may not be limitations on the freedom to participate, dictated by such factors as the person's skill and aptitude level, motivation and energy, and prior accomplishments. One of the major issues, as Kaplan (1975, p. 392) has pointed out, will be the question of selecting those who may be paid for going to some form of continuing education, to acquire the knowledge necessary to become our technological and professional "workers."

All of this makes it evident that values socialization will be of equal importance. We shall have to create a population that desires a leisure society; and once we shall have established this society, we shall have to work hard at maintaining it. The fate of all revolutionaries awaits us: we shall have to turn into conservatives! This, however, is a long way off, and we need not worry too much about it at the moment.

How will this values socialization be accomplished?

1. There will have to be an intensive commitment in this process by all the channels that have traditionally been involved, and particularly the mass media. We shall turn to that aspect in the next section; at this point we want to emphasize merely the importance of the media in getting the message across.

2. There must be a firm participation by the federal and local governments in promoting a leisure ethic. This sounds like a dangerous suggestion, arousing images of thought control and other authoritarian measures. However, we have reached a stage where the least government is no longer the best government; the problems facing post-industrial societies cannot be left to the whim of individuals, the profit motive, or wishful thinking. Why not at least assume the possibility that a government of the people and by the people could carry out the desires of the people?

Actually, however, we need more than that; we need a government that will lead our society. As Kaplan (1975, pp. 403–404) phrases it:

> Government is by no means, like business, exclusively a mechanism for *response*. Even the world of business has moved away from the traditional position of creating and selling what the public wants; it now *creates* consumer "wants" in every commercial on TV; it plans for change in attitudes at the same time that it plans new products.*

3. The formal educational system must get explicitly involved in values socialization. Given the conditions of our utopia we can be sure that the time will be ripe for such an effort. Leisure education, understood primarily as a process of value and attitude change, must become part of the curriculum of schools, from nursery to graduate school and beyond. At this point in time, the "beyond" is particularly important. The majority of our present population is already out of school. Yet they are even more in need of such education than those still in school. Thus, we shall have to institute adult leisure education and conceivably, such education will become mandatory just as other forms of education are now mandatory for the early years of life.

We shall limit the discussion of our utopia to these three aspects: a guaranteed health service, a guaranteed income, and a guaranteed education. Many questions remain unanswered, such as: what form of government would be optimal? What would be the people's obligations, and how would they contribute to the upkeep of society? What would be the system of rewards and punishments? But there is no point in pursuing these questions any further at this time. The three conditions listed are the primary and essential ones for any leisure society; all others will have to evolve so as to optimize the fulfillment of them.

Unfortunately, all of the above is still only "an impossible dream." The main obstacles to making this dream become a reality are the facts that the major portion of the world has not even reached a minimal subsistence level; that the resources and riches that exist are not evenly distributed throughout the world; and finally and most importantly, that our prevailing values and attitudes are not conducive to bringing about a leisure society. Yet there is hope. Sooner or later, inequalities will be eliminated or at least drastically reduced, and all of the world will share in a more economically secure life. Meanwhile we must prepare for that day, as well as do our best to make its arrival quicken.

POSSIBLE DREAMS AND LIMITED GOALS

Let us return to the present, with two more decades to go in the twentieth century, and more specifically, to the United States. As we look around us, one thing becomes evident: we are not now, nor have we ever been, a leisure society. I hate to think that we could add: nor shall we ever become one.

Several hundred thousand Americans die every year of cancer, the majority of them in extreme pain. For quite some time, heroin has been used for pain control of cancer in England; it has not even been seriously tested for that purpose in the United States. The reason, some pain specialists say, is that the puritanical belief that suffering is somehow good is still very much with us (*New York Times*, April 9, 1978, p. E9).

The Puritan ethic is a powerful force and it surfaces under many disguises. My reason for bringing up this rather gruesome example is to alert us to the fact that an argument against a method of improving the quality of life may, in fact, be motivated not by doubt about the effectiveness or suitability of the method, but rather by some underlying belief that an improvement of life is not really desirable.

The first issue, then, that we have to confront is the possibility of conscious or unconscious resistance to change, rooted in our cultural heritage of the work ethic. Confounded with this may be a concern about who will be doing all the work when the work ethic is gone. Do we not already see a decline in the quality of our products? Does not everything fall apart? Do we not recall thousands and thousands of cars every year? Are these not warning signs of what happens when the work ethic declines?

It would take a major study to answer these questions and document them with evidence. But it seems to me that good candidates for causes of these developments are the profit motive, worker alienation, mass production with an accompanying loss of pride in the product, and so on, rather than a decline of the work ethic per se. These are indeed questions that must be investigated and answered satisfactorily, if we wish to promote the leisure ethic in good conscience.

This is a good point, then, to list specific areas where work is needed. We shall start from within our profession, and then slowly move out into the public domain. The scientist has an important role to play in helping to improve the quality of life. But it is the citizen and the political system that carries the major burden. Values rooted in our society must become the guiding principle of our progress, rather than a technology that entices us in a new and uncharted direction with every breakthrough that happens to take place. We must learn to say no to scientific developments, at least until we have had the time to study their technological as well as social and psychological implications.[4]

Research

In light of what was just said, it is somewhat of a contradiction to start off with research as our first topic. Our position, however, is not anti-science; it is merely against the misuse of science. The very hope for a leisure society rests on the assumption that science will provide the technology to support such a society. We shall follow the imperative: "we *must*, therefore we can," and optimistically accept the premise that, indeed, we can.

The distinction between pure and applied research is often difficult to make. It is used here primarily for the purpose of bringing order into a listing of topics.

Pure Research. We have discussed various areas that need investigation throughout the book. The conceptualization of leisure and the components of the quality of life rank top on the list. Many of the issues involved are philosophical and ethical-moral ones, but require a scientific approach in order to be translated into researchable questions. The task of developing methods for measuring values, attitudes, and a broad spectrum of social indicators is a concomitant step of equal importance.

Leisure research and research into the quality of life are by nature interdisciplinary. This puts an added burden on the suggested tasks. Concepts and instruments developed must be suitable and acceptable to the many relevant disciplines involved. It has been customary for each discipline to develop its own language and its own methods. We must attempt to coin a universal language for a transcending leisure science.

Once testable theories of leisure and the quality of life have been developed, concepts clarified, and instruments for measurement exist, we can move into new areas. First we ought to spend a lot of effort on finding out "what is." What are the values and leisure attitudes that prevail in this country, throughout the world, in specific subpopulations and minority groups? Are they stable, or are they changing? At what rate, and in which direction? What seems to make them change? We so frequently hear statements about the decreasing work ethic, shifting values in regard to the job, and so on. But such statements are mostly based on guesses and intuition. There are as yet no firm baselines for comparisons.

An immediate corollary of such measurements will be the investigation of causal relationships, and these in turn will lead to further theoretical speculations.

Parallel research must address itself to theoretical issues from the very beginning. Variables identified as crucial to the leisure experience must be submitted to hypothesis testing and, if possible, experimental research. We suggested three such areas in chapter 5 (the perception of causality, individual differences in the perception of freedom, and intrinsic motivation); many others need to be added to this list.

The late 1930s saw the development of methods of studying leadership styles and group dynamics in field settings (Lewin et al., 1939). The time has come to study such issues as happiness, the good life, leisure, and the quality of life, in field settings and/or simulated societies. Since it is not too far-fetched to assume that we shall soon set up new societies in space, on the moon, or perhaps even on other planets, would it not be wise to consider what is essential and what is not for a happy life on such colonies? Must we export the follies of earth life into outer space? Do we really need toothpaste commercials on Mars?

Applied Research. Once we know what the facts are, we become concerned with either maintaining a status quo or changing it. In either case, we are then involved in applied research. Now that we know what the good life is, how can we bring it about? The areas of applied research are endless, just as our needs and wants seem to be. It is therefore so important to discover first what is really essential to our goals. We must continuously return to questions of pure research.

Social indicators will be crucial in identifying areas of needed applied research. Such indicators will help us decide what needs to be done, when, and where. Any such action research must be accompanied by extensive evaluation studies to check its effectiveness.[5]

Education

An immediate task that needs to be addressed by the leisure profession is the development and testing of sound programs of leisure education. It is at least equally important, however, to convince the public that they really want such programs. Leisure professionals must therefore become proselytizers for a while; they must speak with conviction of the need for such programs and do everything they can to help bring them about. To be able to do this, they must believe in the value of leisure education themselves. As I pointed out before, neither leisure education nor leisure counseling can be value-free. On the contrary, the new leisure ethic provides the very value we need in order to institute the imperative, "you must, therefore you can." Without a value we would not know what it is we must do!

Let me insert here an important point. While I am stressing that leisure is a value and implies a moral commitment, I would not like to see it become a religion or moral dogma. I would like to see our devotion to it be the outcome of an emotional commitment and not of a categorical imperative. The "must" can originate from either source. For example, consider the statements, "I love someone because I am told to love that someone," versus "I love someone because I feel that way, because I want to, because I desire to love that someone." "You must love thy parents" is about as far removed from leisure as "you must paint that fence." Our very premise is that there is no need to prescribe a love for leisure; we assume that to be part of the very essence of human nature.

The leisure profession, then, has three immediate tasks related to education. One is the development of leisure-education programs for the general educational system, from nursery school and kindergarten through elementary, undergraduate, graduate, postgraduate, and adult education. The second is a systematic and well-organized campaign to promote these programs and make leisure education a reality. The third task is the development of specific programs that cover certain areas relevant to the coming about of a leisure society and are addressed to the public in general and special groups in particular. Let us look at two such areas now; we shall treat them more fully in the next section, when we discuss needed political action.

Galloping Consumption.[6] One of the major obstacles to the coming of a leisure society is our consumption orientation. Our obsession with possessions, our concern with *having,* our need to own the latest and newest of everything—all of these devour much of the time we could spend *being.* To approach this problem on an individual level requires a differentiation between needs and wants. Such a distinction might help us decide how to spend our limited resources. Yet such a distinction is not easy to make and is highly subjective. Take the following attempt: a need is something I could not live without; a want is something I sometimes think I could not live without, but in fact could. This criterion is obviously too narrow for our purposes. Few of us would settle for only the things we absolutely need to survive. Where do you draw the line? We need food, but do we need caviar? We need means of transportation, but do we need Cadillacs? Besides, why should we strive for only the things we need? Is it not part of being human to strive for the things *we do not need?* Do we need art? Do we need beauty? We might answer yes, that they confirm that which makes us human. But beyond that, is it not arguable that we should have the right to want even that which we do not need for any reason whatsoever? Is that not the ultimate confirmation of the right to freedom?

The problem is that our wants are socially conditioned. We learn what to want. We are taught what to want long before we have any freedom to decide what we want to be taught. And throughout our life span we are exposed to a continuous, intensive conditioning process that attempts to shape our wants. Our system of advertising has made a science out of creating artificial wants. The task of leisure education is to make the consumer aware of the distinction between needs and wants, as well as between personally relevant wants and artificial ones. Every individual may have to draw the line him- or herself in terms of the distinction between these; but a distinction there is! And let the consumer become aware of the price to pay for accepting such artificial wants as real ones. How much unnecessary job time has to be expended to satisfy such wants? What could have been the alternatives? What will be lost for not giving in to these wants? Do *I* really need *this* product or *this* service to make me happy? The least we can attempt to do is create a self-questioning consumer.

The Right to Know. The political philosophers of the American Revolution considered an enlightened and literate electorate a necessary condition for the working of democracy. One can argue in a similar vein that a leisure society requires a populace that is aware of the "true state of things," be that in terms of the state of their society, or of the whole world; in terms of the advantages or disadvantages of a product or service, or of their own makeup and potentials. To become involved freely in activities for their own sake requires that one has accurate self-knowledge as well as an accurate assessment of what others or things can do for one. Making the distinction previously referred to between artificial and personally relevant wants requires accurate information. And understanding and overcoming the forces that will be directed against the establishment of a worldwide leisure society assumes information about the state of the world as it really is.

We cannot teach such information in leisure education; we have neither the means nor the power, nor is it really our task. What we must do, however, is create a demand for such knowledge. We must make it clear that it is our right to have that information, and that it is the obligation of society to see to it that we get it. We must protest the kind of "news" that is sold to us as news on radio and television. Who determines what we hear or see? What are the criteria for selection? We ought to be concerned, both as professionals and as citizens, with what is presented to us (and what is not!), and not let that be determined by the profit motive only. Once again, as in any issue of the quality of life, we end up asking for political action and it is to this that we turn next.

Political Action

Throughout this volume we have stressed the need for an interdisciplinary approach to the study of leisure. Once we include leisure within the context of the quality of life, such a step becomes an absolute necessity. And equally unavoidable becomes an intimate involvement in political issues and actions. No science and no subject matter is value-free; but leisure is by its nature more likely to be connected to things political than most other topics. It has been recognized since antiquity as a potential, ultimate goal of society, and of course every society must deal in one way or another with issues of the quality of life.

The odds against a leisure society in our lifetimes are tremendous. I see two major reasons for this. (1) The majority of the world has not yet reached a technological level of development that can make such a society a reality. (2) The minority of the world that has achieved this state does not seem to want a leisure society, or at least their political leadership does its utmost to prevent such a society from being realized.

What are the implications, particularly of the second reason? Does this mean that we must promote what nobody wants? Does this mean that we must preach, proselytize, tread on deep-rooted convictions and long-held beliefs, and be willing to take unpopular positions? Unfortunately, in many ways the answer to this must be yes.

I have stressed before that leisure education is not value-free, that its very essence is its content. It is not just value clarification; it is the clarification of certain values, and even the promotion of certain values. This needs to be repeated over and over again.

The fact that we, as leisure professionals, need take an unpopular stand faces us most immediately when we are confronting an elderly audience. Institutional staff predominantly feel, together with their clients, that the job is still the ultimate goal and salvation, and that nothing is more desirable than helping to find for their clients some gainful employment, no matter what. "You may be right, but our clients are just too old to change," is a frequently heard comment. We shall not try to analyze here whether such a statement is a projection or whether in fact, it may be true. In any case, it should be accepted only as a last resort and not be taken for granted. But we as a nation certainly must not accept this, unless we are really too old to change and are willing to be put aside so that "younger" and still-flexible nations can take over.

Let us now consider three areas of potential political action. There are innumerable others that call for active intervention, but the three depicted below should suffice to indicate to the reader the kind of approach we might take.

Consumer Advocacy. We have dealt with issues of consumption and "the right to know" in the previous section, there from the viewpoint of leisure education. Education, however, is not enough. As citizens we need to have the right to help determine which artificial wants we are taught—or at least which we do not want to be taught—and what information (including news) we are given.

> My life was empty. The phone never rang. Others had dates; I sat at home. Then I learned about ———. I bought ———; I used ———; and I became a new person. My life has changed: it is full now, the phone never stops ringing, I am popular, . . . I am happy. (From a fictional advertisement in *The Anti-Leisure Herald.*)

We all have seen ads like this, in many variations on the same theme: buy our product and your life will be changed instantly to one of greater happiness. Is anyone taking these messages seriously? Can we not shrug them off as harmless exaggerations? If we had one or two such experiences in a lifetime, a year, a month, or even a week, perhaps yes. But we are exposed to such messages day in, day out, from all directions. And an industry whose ultimate gospel is "the bottom line," would not spend millions on an effort that does not pay off.

The above example, however, illustrates only one of the many evils of advertising as it prevails. Add to this, creating the illusion of choice where the alternatives are not really significantly different; preventing real choice by not informing the consumer of the really significant differences between products (if there are any!); promoting products and people through purely emotional and irrational approaches; and throughout and foremost, promoting a lifestyle where happiness is guaranteed through possessions. And since acquiring possessions requires money, riches, and power, this kind of advertising (supported in style and orientation by most of our television programming) contributes to making the profit motive the determining guideline of our value system.

Have you ever, in your wildest dreams, considered what would happen if the money and effort spent on all those ads were suddenly turned to altruistic goals, such as telling us how we can help others, how we can build a society in which there are no poor, in which all share equally in the benefits of society? Or, on a milder level, how about consumer-sponsored advertisements telling us *not* to buy all these things, because we really do *not* need them? Or that inform us that there are no real differences between the less and more expensive products offered?[7] It could not work? Why? Do we hear anywhere serious discussions why it could not work? Is it really a waste of time even to discuss such possibilities?

There is a growing consumer movement in this country, and some efforts in our government to support such a movement. However, such undertakings have been rather halfhearted and quite unproductive so far. For example, only recently a bill designed to create a consumer protection agency was defeated in Congress, due to an intensive lobbying effort by the business community. Attempts to give the consumer a voice at the government level are vehemently being fought under any and all pretexts.

If we wish to bring about a leisure society, we must be willing to question certain basic beliefs of our society. We must raise questions that are never seriously discussed, no matter how obvious they are. For example: is it in the interest of the consumer to build products that do not last? To have "new" car models every year? To sell the same product under different labels? To introduce fashion changes with every season? And so on, and so on. Or perhaps just as a minimal condition, would it not be of tremendous help to have a government agency that would give us objective and trustworthy evaluations of both goods and services available?

The United States will never have a revolution of the workers, because the majority of them are too well-off. But let us have at least a revolution of consumers, because as consumers we certainly are not well-off; we are being taken in. Consumers of the world, unite!

Technological Innovations and the Public Good. A free-time conception of leisure has its political implications. It leads to a concern with
increasing the amount of free time available and the use of this free
time to the best benefit of both the individual and society. Labor and
union movements, as well as organizations such as the National Recreation and Parks Association, have been active in these areas for a
long time.

A state-of-mind conception of leisure also has political implications, but much more far-reaching ones. Leisure, in this sense, can only
be experienced when certain conditions of life have been fulfilled.
Leisure is no longer an either/or affair (free time versus non-free time);
it is an ideal state of mind which we attempt to reach but of which
there are many degrees. It now becomes the task and obligation of
society to maximize for each and every one of its members the opportunities for reaching this state.

As we have stressed throughout this book, the prime condition
for reaching this state is perceived freedom, *freedom from* as well as
freedom to. At this point, we wish to reassert society's obligation to
maximize its members' freedom from the need to be concerned with
providing subsistence and existence needs. Does this sound like socialism? Let us not be blinded or turned off by labels that have acquired
bad connotations in our society. Let us remember that *welfare* means
first of all the state of doing well, especially in respect to happiness and
well-being; only secondarily does it imply relief or the handing out of
help to the needy.

The implications of the demanded freedom are not that members
of a leisure society will be without obligations. There will always be
jobs that must be done; there will always be goals to strive for,
achievements to be accomplished, criteria by which one person can
outrank another. But why must these criteria be economic ones? Why
can they not be educational, artistic, athletic, or altruistic ones? The
answer used to be the fact that the conditions of life were such that
economic considerations had to come first for all but a very small minority. But modern science and technology have provided the chance
to change this and to make economic considerations secondary for
all people.

To accept this fact as a real possibility requires a tremendous
change in our thinking. It constitutes the most radical change in the
history of mankind, and makes all previous political philosophies obsolete.

It is not the task of the leisure professional to figure out how technological improvements can be translated into social good. For example, a factory installs a new machine producing ten times more
shoes per week than before. How can this achievement be translated

into the workers having to work less and share in the benefit of the machine, that is, increased production? Given enough innovations of this kind, the necessary goods might be produced with workers on the job for only one day a week, or perhaps ten years out of a life span. These are details that economists and politicians must work out. The leisure professional, however, must provide the philosophy that will enable the politicians to get the economists to solve the problem. And the leisure professionals must stir up the public so it will demand that its politicians seek and pursue that leisure society.

Political Platforms and Leisure. We have come a long way from the days when a politician could campaign on a slogan like "a chicken in every pot. . . ." Today we want a steak prepared in a computerized micro-oven! But have we really come a long way? What is it we ask of our politicians? What promises do we settle for? What issues are being discussed, and what is left out? Are there still politicians who address themselves to basic problems, rather than to topics guaranteed by their public relations experts to catch the voters? We heard about a "war on poverty" and a "war on cancer"—both powerful phrases. But did we confront the real issues of poverty or health care? Did we hear discussions of the obligations a society has in these respects? Politics and politicians have become yet more commodities to be sold to the public through whatever the most efficient advertising techniques.

We need a change in the process of selecting our political leaders. Bringing about a leisure society requires new approaches and new thinking: a lot of thinking and a lot of discussion.

None of us has the answers at this point; but let us at least raise the questions and demand that our politicians discuss them and take positions on them. The wish that our country be run by philosophers may be an idle dream, but the thought that it is run by bankers and businessmen is a nightmare. If we are serious in wanting to achieve a leisure society we must confront the fact that the profit motive cannot be the guiding principle in such a society. At the moment that may sound to us very threatening; instead we must come to realize the beauty of that thought. Therein, after all, lies the strength we need to push toward a leisure society.

Perhaps it is all too late. The super-national corporations have a firm grip on our political processes, and unfortunately may see the coming of a universal leisure society in conflict with their own interests. But is their power greater than that of the emperors and kings of old? And is not the force of an idea whose time has come greater than any other? And we are not even asking for a revolution; only an evolution into the necessary modes of a new society that takes full advantage of the potentials of a never-before-existing technology for the benefit of all.

The reader may feel that I am pushing too hard or that I am drawing the picture in extreme shades. But we are fighting for high stakes. We have heard it said many times: peace is a dangerous thing; it is obviously more difficult to achieve than war. It is even more difficult to maintain and no nation has yet succeeded in maintaining it forever. Yet we are reaching the point where we, the people of this planet, can no longer afford the folly of wars, and where by necessity we must settle for peace. In peace, however, lies the very condition for leisure, and with peace may finally come the Age of Leisure.

SUMMARY

This final chapter stressed the interface between leisure and the quality of life on the one hand, and political questions and issues on the other. The conceptualization of leisure as a state of mind increases the scope of responsibility of leisure professionals, and they will inevitably find themselves involved in politics, both as professionals and as citizens. For some this will mean no more than voting relevantly on leisure-related issues. For others it could take the form of active leadership in a local club or city organization, or participation in state-level decision-making processes. Some, however, should attempt to have an impact on the federal government.

Within the context of wishful thinking, we considered three developments that could move our society closer to an Age of Leisure. The first was a guaranteed health service. Although no society can guarantee freedom from sickness, it should guarantee freedom from the economic consequences of it and adequate treatment for all. Given the present conditions of our society, some sections of our population may prefer to be "sick" rather than healthy; it is our assumption that such would not be the case in a leisure society. It was also stressed, however, that improvements in any one area of our society cannot be expected to materialize without concomitant, relevant changes in others.

The second development required for our utopia was a guaranteed income: the freedom from the economic burden of providing for subsistence needs. Objections to such a policy tend to be based on the fear that people will just fritter away their lives and accomplish nothing meaningful, given such an income. The fallacy of this argument consists in equating meaningful activity with paid employment and in doubting the universality of the need for meaning.

The third necessary condition envisioned was a guaranteed education. Every organism needs an optimal environment to develop to its greatest potential. For humans, this means primarily the social-societal-cultural environment. The process through which this environment

interacts with the developing organism is usually referred to as socialization. We distinguish between knowledge socialization and values
socialization. The former is primarily the task of the formal educational institutions. In a leisure society, these will be able to emphasize
liberal arts rather than professional or vocational skills. Educational opportunities must be freely available to all those qualified.

Values socialization will have the task of creating a population
that desires a leisure society, that is, of transmitting the leisure ethic.
At least three segments of society must be actively involved in this
process: the mass media, the government, and once again the educational system.

We next addressed ourselves to more down-to-earth issues that
require attention if we wish to promote a leisure society. A number
of topics were outlined for both pure and applied research. Leisure
education programs need to be developed and the public must be
convinced that such programs are indeed needed. Two areas of education were singled out for particular emphasis: consumption behavior
and the right to know. Educational goals in the first involve making
people aware of the distinctions between needs and wants, and between personally relevant and artificial wants. The second area relates
to the fact that freedom—that is, making meaningful choices—requires
a knowledge of the true nature of the available alternatives. The right
to know is thus an essential component of any leisure society.

Finally, we turned to political action and the fact that our task
may not always be a popular one. We dealt with three issues. First, we
emphasized the need for consumer advocacy. The growing consumer
movement must be strengthened and must be given at least an equal
voice in our government to that of industry. Second, we highlighted
the need to find ways to make technological innovations benefit the
worker and consumer rather than industry and big business. This will
require a tremendous shift in our thinking, with many political implications and overtones involved; but nothing less will suffice. Third,
we pointed out the need to *demand* of our politicians that they desist
from waging campaigns in terms of public relations slogans. Make
them discuss basic political-philosophical-moral problems and issues,
and address themselves explicitly and concretely to issues of leisure
and the quality of life. A leisure society will not come to us through
empty slogans and hollow gestures. We shall have to work hard to
achieve such a society, but that work will be our leisure.

ENDNOTES

[1] In actuality, of course, modern health services also address themselves
to the prevention of disease before it sets in.

[2] The reader might ponder the fact that many of our highest political leaders in the United States originate from a background where these two conditions, in fact, prevail.

[3] Note the recent emphasis in the psychological literature on the child as a socializing agent of the parent!

[4] This, of course, is the intent of the so-called environmental impact statements, now required for all major federally sponsored construction projects.

[5] The term *action research* was coined by Lewin (1948) to describe research that has as its purpose the understanding or solution of social problems.

[6] A phrase I used elsewhere to describe how our society, through advertising, attempts to make us use our free time primarily for the consumption of goods and services (Neulinger, 1974a, p. 144).

[7] Comparative price listings of consumer items on cable television in New York City represent a step in that direction.

Appendix 1

TO THE READER:

Please complete these forms only *after* you have read the introductory remarks to chapter 8 (up to "Time out for completing appendix 1"). Thank you.

Experience 1. *Your "Lifeline"*

Birth • Death

Imagine that the line above represents your life span. You are presently somewhere along this line, between birth and death.

Put a check mark at the point on this line where you see yourself *now*, at this moment in your life.

For comparison purposes and possible further analyses, complete the information below:

Sex: male _____ ; female _____ ;   Age: _____ ;   Marital Status: _____ ;

Religion: _____ ;   Ethnic Background: _____ ;

Experience 2. *Milestones in Your Life*

(2a) List, in rank order, the three events that you consider to be the most outstanding *milestones* in your life. Also indicate your age (in years) when the event took place.

*Most important: _____ Age:_____

*Second most important: _____ Age:_____

*Third most important: _____ Age:_____

(2b) List, in rank order, the three events in your *future life* that you expect to be the most outstanding *milestones*. Also indicate at what age you expect these events to take place.

*Most important: _____ Age:_____

*Second most important: _____ Age:_____

*Third most important: _____ Age:_____

227

Appendix 2

A SELF - EXPLORATION

WHAT AM I DOING ?

A systematic method of finding out

WHERE YOU ARE ...

WHERE YOU WERE ...

and WHERE YOU ARE GOING

John Neulinger

THE LEISURE INSTITUTE

145 EAST 92nd STREET, NEW YORK, N.Y. 10028

WHAT AM I DOING?

The purpose of the enclosed forms is to help you look at yourself and to get to know yourself better. You may know yourself quite well already, but you probably have not taken account of yourself in just this manner ever before.

What you are about to do will take some time and effort. And to be worthwhile, it needs to be done right. You will have to take your time and consider things carefully. But remember, you are doing this for a purpose: to help yourself.

The way of looking at yourself, suggested by our method, is based on certain assumptions about what is important in life.* The method is not designed to guarantee happiness; it is designed to identify critical dimensions that relate to how satisfied you are with your life. It is designed to help you work through, in cooperation with a trained counsellor or through feedback from us, certain difficulties you may experience in finding meaning in your life.

What can you expect from completing these forms? Perhaps nothing more than having spent some pleasant hours exploring yourself, your way of life, your particular life style. Perhaps more than that. Perhaps you will achieve a new sense of yourself, of who you are and what you want. This will involve work, but this work may be your leisure.

---

*The philosophy underlying this method is fully described in The Psychology of Leisure, by John Neulinger (Charles C. Thomas, Publisher).

WHAT AM I DOING?
================

<u>INSTRUCTIONS</u>

There are four pages per day: two for AM and two for PM. Start with the AM page, marked *Midnight*. Complete both sides of that sheet and then continue on the PM page, marked *Noon*. Proceed until you have completed the full twenty-four hours.

COMPLETE THE FORMS AS FOLLOWS:

ACTIVITY: For each 30 minute interval, list your <u>primary</u> activity, that is, the most important thing you did during that interval. If the activity lasted more than 30 minutes (for example, sleep), simply draw an arrow to when the activity ended.

WHERE: Use the following code ...

0 – in my home;
1 – at my place of employment;   3 – commuting;
2 – at school;   4 – other; specify!

WITH WHOM: Use the following code ...

0 – alone;   3 – with three others;
1 – with one other;   4 – with four others;
2 – with two others;   5 – with 5 or more others;

CHOICE: Who made you do it? Do you feel that you had a choice in what you were doing? Were you an "Origin" of your actions, or did you do it because you had to? To what degree was it a matter of one or the other? Use the numbers FROM ZERO TO 100 to reflect your feeling!

0 100
Not my choice   Totally
   at all;   my choice;
Had to do it;   I decided

REASON: What did you do it for? Did you do the activity for its own sake, because you like doing it? Just for the pleasure and satisfaction you get out of doing it? Or did you do it for a pay-off, a consequence? To what degree was it a matter of one or the other? Use the numbers FROM ZERO TO 100 to reflect you feeling!

0 100
For pay-off only;   For its own sake;
No satisfaction   Satisfaction from
from activity itself;   activity only;
If your feelings were mixed, pick an appropriate middle point!

NEED: Which of your needs was involved or satisfied by this activity? Describe the need in your own words.

FEELING: What feeling was involved? Describe it in your own words.

INSTRUCTIONS, continued

F/T: FEELING TONE: Rate your feeling while engaged in the activity, from good to bad, or from positive to negative.

      100 – extremely good or positive;
       50 – neutral; so-so; no feeling; some good, some bad
        0 – extremely bad or negative;

Pick any value between 100 and zero that best reflects your feeling.

PLEASE LEAVE THE LAST TWO COLUMNS BLANK, UNLESS OTHERWISE INSTRUCTED!

BACKGROUND INFORMATION

Please provide the information requested below. This will help us in giving you meaningful feedback about your responses, and also enable us to use the data for research purposes. Of course, ALL INFORMATION WILL BE KEPT CONFIDENTIAL AND ANONYMOUS.

Sex: male _____(1)   Age: _____   Religious preference: (4)
(1) female _____(2)   (2, 3)   Protestant _____(1)
                          Catholic _____(2)
What is (or was) your occupation   Jewish _____(3)
or profession: Other _____(4)
(5, 6) _____ None _____(5)

Marital status: (7)   Ethnic Background: (8)

    single, never married _____(1)   American Indian _____(1) White _____(6)
    married _____(2)   Black _____(2) Other _____(7)
    separated, divorced _____(3)   Oriental _____(3)
    widowed _____(4)   Puerto Rican _____(4)
                          Other Hispanic _____(5)

What was the last grade you completed in school? (9)

    to 6 years _____(1)   12 years (high School graduate) _____(4)
    7-9 years _____(2)   13-15 years (some college) _____(5)
  10-11 years _____(3)   16 years (college graduate) _____(6)
                  17 years or more (graduate work) _____(7)

Adding up the income from all sources, what was your total family income last year? (Under family include only people you actually lived with) (10)
under $5,000 _____(1) $11,001 – 13,000 _____(5)
$5,001 – 7,000 _____(2) $13,001 – 15,000 _____(6)
$7,001 – 9,000 _____(3) $15,001 – 20,000 _____(7)
$9,001 – 11,000 _____(4) $20,001 or over _____(8)

What is your present work status? (11)
    work full-time _____(1)   unemployed _____(4)
    work part-time _____(2)   housewife _____(5)
    student _____(3)   retired _____(6)
                    other _____(7)

TIME A.M.	ACTIVITY	WHERE	WITH WHOM	CHOICE You—100 Other—0	REASON Own sake— 100 Other—0	NEED	FEELING	F/T +100 =50 —0
Mid-night								
12:30								
1:00								
1:30								
2:00								
2:30								
3:00								
3:30								
4:00								
4:30								
5:00								
5:30								

Date: _____

Source: J. Neulinger, Form 1977–2; © The Leisure Institute, 1977.

234

TIME A.M.	ACTIVITY	WHERE	WITH WHOM	CHOICE You–100 Other–0	REASON Own sake– 100 Other–0	NEED	FEELING	F/T +100 =50 –0
6:00								
6:30								
7:00								
7:30								
8:00								
8:30								
9:00								
9:30								
10:00								
10:30								
11:00								
11:30								

Date: _____

Source: J. Neulinger, Form 1977–2; © The Leisure Institute, 1977.

235

TIME P.M.	ACTIVITY	WHERE	WITH WHOM	CHOICE You—100 Other—0	REASON Own sake—100 Other—0	NEED	FEELING	F/T +100 = 50 − 0														
Noon																						
12:30																						
1:00																						
1:30																						
2:00																						
2:30																						
3:00																						
3:30																						
4:00																						
4:30																						
5:00																						
5:30																						

Date: _____

Source: J. Neulinger, Form 1977–2; © The Leisure Institute, 1977.

TIME P.M.	ACTIVITY	WHERE	WITH WHOM	CHOICE You—100 Other—0	REASON Own sake—100 Other—0	NEED	FEELING	F/T +100 =50 -0
6:00								
6:30								
7:00								
7:30								
8:00								
8:30								
9:00								
9:30								
10:00								
10:30								
11:00								
11:30								

Date:_____

Source: J. Neulinger, Form 1977–2; © The Leisure Institute, 1977.

Bibliography

Adler, Mortimer J. Education in a democracy: Should we give liberal schooling to all, and can we succeed in doing so? *American Educator*, 1979, *3*, no. 1, 6–9.

Albee, G.W. The uncertain future of psychology. *American Psychology Association Monitor*, 1973, *4*, no. 3, 10.

Allport, G.W. The historical background of modern social psychology. In G. Lindzey and E. Aronson (eds.), *The handbook of social psychology*, vol. 1. 2d ed. Reading, Mass.: Addison-Wesley, 1968.

American Psychological Association Publication Manual Task Force. Publication manual change sheet 2, June 1977. *American Psychologist*, 1977, *32*, 487–494.

Anderson, N. *Work and leisure*. New York: Free Press, 1961.

Andrews, F.M., and Withey, S.B. *Social indicators of well-being: Americans' perceptions of life quality*. New York: Plenum, 1976.

Aquinas, T. Treatise on active and contemplative life, the *Summa Theologica* (vol. 2). Trans. Fathers of the English Dominican Province, rev. D.J. Sullivan. Chicago: Encyclopaedia Britannica, 1952.

Asher, J. Flexi-time, four-day weeks thrive despite recession. *American Psychological Association Monitor*, 1975, *6*, no. 4, 5.

Ball, C. New sport gives ski slopes a piece of summer action. *New York Times*, July 10, 1977, sec. 10, pp. 1, 20.

Beisser, A.R. *The madness in sports*. New York: Appleton, 1967.

Bem, D.J. Self-perception theory. In L. Berkowitz (ed.), *Advances in experimental social psychology*, vol. 6. New York: Academic, 1972.

Bengtsson, A. *Adventure playgrounds*. New York: Praeger, 1972.

Berg, C., and Neulinger, J. The alcoholic's perception of leisure. *Journal of Studies on Alcohol,* 1976, *37,* no. 11, 1625–1632.

Berger, B.M. The sociology of leisure: some suggestions. In E.O. Smigel (ed.), *Work and leisure.* New Haven: College and University Press, 1963.

Berlyne, D.E. The vicissitudes of aplopathematic and thelematoscopic pneumatology (or the hydrography of hedonism). In D.E. Berlyne and K.B. Madsen (eds.), *Pleasure, reward, and preference.* New York: Academic, 1973.

Bishop, D.W. Stability of the factor structure of leisure behavior: Analyses of four communities. *Journal of Leisure Research,* 1970, *2,* 160–170.

Bishop, D.; Jeanrenaud, C.; and Lawson, K. Comparison of a time diary and recall questionnaire for surveying leisure activities. *Journal of Leisure Research,* 1975, *7,* 73–80.

Bolgov, V.I., and Kalkei, G.A. *The structure and organisation of spare time under socialism.* Institute of Sociological Research of the USSR Academy of Sciences, Moscow, 1974.

Borgatta, E.F., and Lambert, W.E. (eds.). *Handbook of personality theory and research.* Chicago: Rand McNally, 1968.

Boring, E.G. *A history of experimental psychology.* 2d ed. New York: Appleton, 1950.

Boyack, V.L. (ed.). *Time on our hands: The problem of leisure.* Los Angeles: Ethel Percy Andrus Gerontology Center, University of Southern California, 1973.

Bradburn, N.M., and Caplovitz, D. *Reports on happiness.* Chicago: Aldine, 1965.

Brayfield, A., and Crockett, W. Employee attitudes and employee performance. *Psychological Bulletin,* 1955, *52,* 396–424.

Brightbill, C.K. *The challenge of leisure.* Englewood Cliffs, N.J.: Prentice-Hall, 1960.

Brightbill, C.K., and Mobley, T.A. *Educating for leisure-centered living.* 2d ed. New York: Wiley, 1977.

Brim, Jr., O.G.; Glass, D.C.; Neulinger, J.; and Firestone, I.J. *American beliefs and attitudes about intelligence.* New York: Russell Sage, 1969.

Bruner, J.S. *Processes of cognitive growth: Infancy.* Worcester, Mass.: Clark University, 1968.

Bühler, C. The developmental structure of goal setting in group and individual studies. In C. Bühler and Massarik (eds.), *The course of human life.* New York: Springer, 1968.

Bull, N.C. Comments on two panel discussions concerned with the future of the sociology of leisure. *Society and Leisure,* 1973, *5,* no. 1, 145–148.

Burdge, R.J. The state of leisure research as reflected in the *Journal of Leisure Research. Journal of Leisure Research,* 1974, 6, 312–317.

Burt, C. *The factors of the mind.* London: University Press, 1946.

Burton, T.L. Identification of recreation types through cluster analysis. *Society and Leisure,* 1971, *1,* 47–64.

Calder, B.J., and Staw, B.M. The self-perception of intrinsic and extrinsic motivation. *Journal of Personality and Social Psychology,* 1975, *31,* 599–605.

Campbell, A. Aspiration, satisfaction, and fulfillment. In A. Campbell and and P.E. Converse (eds.), *The human meaning of social change.* New York: Russell Sage, 1972.

Campbell, A., and Converse, P.E. (eds.). *The human meaning of social change.* New York: Russell Sage, 1972.

Campbell, A.; Converse, P.E.; and Rodgers, W.L. *The quality of American life.* New York: Russell Sage, 1976.

Cantril, H. *The pattern of human concerns.* New Brunswick, N.J.: Rutgers University, 1965.

Caplan, N., and Barton, E. *Social indicators 1973; a study of the relationship between the power of information and utilization by federal executives.* Ann Arbor: Institute for Social Research, University of Michigan, 1976.

Capon, R.F. Is leisure the hollandaise of life? Some saucy reflections. *Travel and Leisure* (American Express Publishing Corp.), September 1976, 6, no. 9, 24–25.

Carlson, R.E.; MacLean, J.R.; Deppe, T.R.; and Peterson, J.A. *Recreation and leisure: The changing scene.* 3d ed. Belmont, Calif.: Wadsworth, 1979.

Caro, F.G. (ed.). *Readings in evaluation research.* New York: Russell Sage, 1971.

Charter for leisure, *Leisure Today,* March 1972, *1,* 16–17.

Chein, I. The problems of inconsistency: A restatement. *Journal of Social Issues,* 1949, *5,* 52–61.

————. Notes on a framework for the measurement of discrimination and prejudice. In J. Jahoda, M. Deutsch, and S.W. Cook (eds.), *Research methods in social relations: Basic processes,* pt. 1. New York: Dryden, 1951.

Cherry, G.E. Leisure and the community: research and planning. In J.T. Haworth and A.J. Veal (eds.), *Leisure and the community.* Birmingham, England: University of Birmingham, 1976.

Clawson, M. How much leisure, now and in the future? In J.C. Charlesworth (ed.), *Leisure in America: Blessing or curse?* Philadelphia: American Academy of Political and Social Science, 1964.

Cohen, A.R. *Attitude change and social influence.* New York: Basic, 1964.

Compton, D.M., and J.D. Goldstein (eds.), *Perspectives of leisure counseling.* Arlington, Va.: National Recreation and Park Association, 1977.

Connolly, M.L. Leisure counseling: A values clarification and assertive training approach. In A. Epperson, P.A. Witt, and G. Hitzhusen (eds.), *Leisure counseling: An aspect of leisure education.* Springfield: Thomas, 1977.

Converse, P.E. Time budgets. *International Encyclopedia of the Social Sciences,* vol. 16. New York: Macmillan, 1968.

Corbin, D.H., and Tait, W.J. *Education for leisure.* Englewood Cliffs, N.J.: Prentice-Hall, 1973.

Council on accreditation lists first accredited departments. *Parks & Recreation,* 1979, *14,* No. 1, 8–9.

Crandall, R., and Lewko, J. Leisure research, present and future: Who, what, where. *Journal of Leisure Research,* 1976, *8,* 150–159.

Crook, W. Adventure playground tribulations and successes. *Recreation Canada,* 1974, *32,* no. 5, 45–49.

Csikszentmihalyi, Mihaly. *Beyond boredom and anxiety.* San Francisco: Jossey-Bass, 1975.

deCharms, R. *Personal causation, the internal affective determinants of behavior.* New York: Academic, 1968.

deCharms, R.; Carpenter, V.; and Cuperman, A. The "origin-pawn" variable in person perception. *Sociometry,* 1965, *28,* 241–258.

Deci, E.L. Effects of externally mediated rewards on intrinsic motivation. *Journal of Personality and Social Psychology,* 1971, *18,* 105–115.

———. Intrinsic motivation, extrinsic reinforcement and inequity. *Journal of Personality and Social Psychology,* 1972, *22,* 113–120.

———. *Intrinsic Motivation.* New York: Plenum, 1975.

De Grazia, S. *Of time, work and leisure.* New York: Doubleday-Anchor, Twentieth Century Fund, 1962.

Dember, W.N., and Earl, R.W. Analysis of exploratory, manipulatory, and curiosity behaviors. *Psychological Review,* 1957, *64,* 91–96.

Disraeli, B. Speech to the conservatives of Manchester, April 3, 1872.

Ditton, R.B.; Goodale, T.L.; and Johnsen, P.K. A cluster analysis of activity, frequency, and environment variables to identify water-based recreation types. *Journal of Leisure Research,* 1975, *7,* 282–295.

Driver, B.L. Potential contributions of psychology to recreation resource management. In J.F. Wohlwill and D.H. Carson (eds.), *Environment and the social sciences: Perspective and applications.* Washington, D.C.: American Psychological Association, 1972.

Dumazedier, J. *Toward a society of leisure.* London: Collier, 1967.

————. Leisure. *International Encyclopedia of the Social Sciences,* 1968, pp. 248–254.

————. Leisure and post-industrial societies. In M. Kaplan and P. Bosserman (eds.), *Technology, human values, and leisure.* Nashville: Abingdon, 1971.

————. *Sociology of leisure.* Amsterdam: Elsevier, 1974a.

————. Prominent recreationist defines "leisure." Interview in *Recreation Canada,* 1974b, *32,* no. 5, 55–57.

Duncan, O.D. Social Indicators, 1973: Report on a conference. In R.A. Van Dusen (ed.), *Social indicators, 1973: A review symposium.* Washington, D.C.: Social Science Research Council, 1974.

Dunn, D.R. Intentional futures: Space age developments for leisure research and resource management. *Society and Leisure,* 1973, *5,* no. 3, 5–28.

————. Book review of *The use of time* by Szalai. *Journal of Leisure Research,* 1974, *6,* 84–86.

Edwards, A.L. *Manual for the Edwards Personal Preference Schedule.* New York: Psychological Corporation, 1953.

Edwards, P.B. *Leisure counseling techniques, individual and group counseling step-by-step.* 2d ed. Los Angeles, Calif.: University Publishers, 1977.

English, H.B., and English, A.C. *A comprehensive dictionary of psychological and psychoanalytical terms.* New York: Longmans, 1958.

English, O.S. Leisure time program for a community without psychiatric leadership. In P.A. Martin (ed.), *Leisure and mental health: A psychiatric viewpoint.* Washington, D.C.: American Psychiatric Association, 1967.

English, P.W., and Mayfield, R.C. *Man, space, and environment.* New York: Oxford University Press, 1972.

Epperson, A.; Witt, P.A.; and Hitzhusen, G. *Leisure counseling: An aspect of leisure education.* Springfield: Thomas, 1977.

Erikson, E.H. *Childhood and society.* New York: Norton, 1950.

————. The roots of virtue. In J. Huxley (ed.), *The humanist frame.* New York: Harper & Row, 1961.

————. *Identity: Youth and crisis.* New York: Norton, 1968.

————. *Toys and reasons.* New York: Norton, 1977.

Ewald, Jr., W.R. Planning for the new free time. In E.J. Staley and N.P. Miller (eds.), *Leisure and the quality of life.* Washington, D.C.: American Association for Health, Physical Education and Recreation, 1972.

Fain, G.S. Leisure counseling: Translating needs into action. In A. Epperson,

P.A. Witt, and G. Hitzhusen (eds.), *Leisure counseling: An aspect of leisure education.* Springfield: Thomas, 1977.

Fain, G., and Hitzhusen, G. *Therapeutic recreation state of the art.* Arlington: National Recreation and Park Association, 1977.

Faris, R.E.L., and Dunham, H.W. *Mental disorders in urban areas: An ecological study of schizophrenia and other psychoses.* Chicago: University of Chicago, 1939.

Faught, M.C. The 3-day revolution to come: 3-day workweek, 4-day weekend. In R. Poor (ed.), *4 days, 40 hours.* Cambridge, Mass.: Bursk and Poor, 1970.

Ferenczi, S. Sunday neurosis (1918). In Ferenczi, S. *Further contributions to the theory and technique of psycho-analysis.* 2d ed. New York: Basic, 1950.

Festinger, L. *A theory of cognitive dissonance.* Stanford: Stanford University, 1957.

Fiss, B.L. Flexitime. In *Alternative work patterns: Changing approaches to work scheduling.* Scarsdale, N.Y.: Work in America Institute, 1976.

Flanagan, J.C. A research approach to improving our quality of life. *American Psychologist,* 1978, *33,* 138–147.

Ford, J.D., and Foster, S.L. Comment: Extrinsic incentives and token-based programs; a reevaluation. *American Psychologist,* 1976, *31,* 87–90.

Ford, R.N. Job enrichment lessons from A.T.&T. In K.N. Wexley & G.A. Yukl (eds.), *Organizational behavior and industrial psychology.* New York: Oxford University, 1975.

Friedman, M., and Rosenman, R.H. *Type A behavior and your heart.* Greenwich, Conn.: Fawcett, 1975.

Friedmann, G. Leisure and technological civilization. *International Social Science Journal,* 1960, *12,* no. 4, 509–521.

Fromm, E. *Escape from freedom.* New York: Holt, 1941.

———. *To have or to be?* New York: Harper & Row, 1976.

Gallup, G.H. Statement to the United States Senate Foreign Relations Committee Hearing, Washington, D.C., September 20, 1976. In *Human needs and satisfactions (A global survey),* A report conducted for The Charles F. Kettering Foundation by Gallup International Research Institutes, June 1977, pp. 54–60.

———. Human needs and satisfactions: A global survey. *Public Opinion Quarterly,* 1977, *41,* Winter 1976–1977, 459–467.

Gardell, B. Technology, alienation and mental health in the modern industrial environment. In L. Levi (ed.), *Society, stress and disease,* vol. 1. London: Oxford University, 1971.

————. *Quality of work and non-work activities and rewards in affluent societies.* Report from the Psychological Laboratories, University of Stockholm, no. 403, December 1973, pp. 1–17.

————. *Technology, alienation and mental health: Summary of a social psychological research programme on technology and the worker.* Report from the Department of Psychology, University of Stockholm, no. 456, October 1975, pp. 1–11.

Gergen, K.J. Social psychology as history. *Journal of Personality and Social Psychology,* 1973, *26,* 309–320.

————. Toward generative theory. *Journal of Personality and Social Psychology,* 1978, *36,* 1344–1360.

Godbey, G. Time deepening and the future of leisure. *Leisure Today: Journal of Physical Education and Recreation,* October 1976, pp. 16–18.

Goldhammer, H., and Marshall, A.W. *Psychosis and civilization: Studies in the frequency of mental disease.* Glencoe, Ill.: Free Press, 1953.

Goodey, B. Environmental perception and planning provision for recreation and tourism. Working paper 14, Centre for Urban and Regional Studies, University of Birmingham, July 1974.

Gray, D.E. This alien thing called leisure. Speech delivered at Oregon State University, Corvallis, Oregon, July 8, 1971.

Gray, D., and Greben, S. The future of the recreation movement. A scenario prepared for the National Park and Recreation Association Congress, 1973.

————. Future perspectives. *Parks and Recreation,* July 1974, *9,* no. 6, 26–33.

Gray, G. Leisure studies: An area of research for sociologists. *Society and Leisure,* 1973, *1,* 181–188.

Green, T.F. *Work, leisure, and the American schools.* New York: Random House, 1968.

Guide to information resources programming for persons with handicapping conditions through physical education, recreation, and related disciplines; Appendix in D.A. Pelegrino (ed.), *What recreation research says to the recreation practitioner.* Washington, D.C.: American Alliance for Health, Physical Education, and Recreation, 1975.

Gurin, G.; Veroff, J.; and Feld, S. *Americans view their mental health.* New York: Basic, 1960.

Gutentag, M., and Streuning, E. (eds.), *Handbook of evaluation research.* Beverly Hills: Sage, 1975.

Hall, C.S., and Lindzey, G. *Theories of personality,* (2d ed.). New York: Wiley, 1970.

Haun, P. Leisure. In P.A. Martin (ed.), *Leisure and mental health: A psy-*

chiatric viewpoint. Washington, D.C.: American Psychiatric Association, 1967.

Hebb, D.O. Drives and the c.n.s. (conceptual nervous system). *Psychological Review,* 1955, *62,* 243–254.

———. What psychology is about. *American Psychologist,* 1974, *29,* 71–79.

Heberlein, T.A., and Black, J.S. Attitudinal specificity and the prediction of behavior in a field setting. *Journal of Personality and Social Psychology,* 1976, *33,* 474–478.

Heider, F. Social perception and phenomenal causality. *Psychological Review,* 1944, *51,* 358–374.

———. The psychology of interpersonal relations. New York: Wiley, 1958.

Hendricks, J., and Burdge, R.J. The nature of leisure research: A reflection and comment. *Journal of Leisure Research,* 1972, *4,* 216.

Herbert, W. Quality of working life: Congress tackles the job. *American Psychological Association Monitor,* 1977, *8,* no. 11, 6–7.

Herzberg, F.; Mauner, B.; Peterson, R.O.; and Capwell, D.F. *Job attitudes: Review and opinion.* Pittsburgh: Psychological Service of Pittsburgh, 1957.

Hitzhusen, G. Introduction. In A. Epperson, P.A. Witt, and G. Hitzhusen (eds.). *Leisure counseling: An aspect of leisure education.* Springfield: Thomas, 1977.

Hobbs, C.L. *Wanted . . . a philosophy of leisure.* Toronto: Recreation Education, Sports and Recreation Bureau, 1973.

Hodge, R.W.; Siegel, P.M.; and Rossi, P.H. Occupational prestige in the United States, 1925–1963. *American Journal of Sociology,* 1964, *70,* 286–302.

Holleb, D. Social statistics for social policy. In American Society of Planning Officials (ASPO) (eds.), *Planning: 1968.* Chicago: ASPO, 1968.

Hollingshead, B.B., and Redlich, F.C. *Social class and mental illness: A community study.* New York: Wiley, 1958.

Homans, G.C. Group factors in worker productivity. In H. Proshansky and L. Seidenberg (eds.), *Basic studies in social psychology.* New York: Holt, 1965.

Horney, K. *The neurotic personality of our time.* New York: Norton, 1937.

How Americans pursue happiness, *U.S. News & World Report,* May 23, 1977, p. 62.

Hunt, J. M. Intrinsic motivation and its role in psychological development. *Nebraska symposium on motivation,* 1965, *13,* 189–282.

Hutchins, R. News summaries, January 2, 1954. *International Thesaurus of Quotations,* New York: Crowell, 1970, p. 349.

Ibrahim, H. The future of leisure studies. In D.A. Pelegrino (ed.), *What recreation research says to the recreation practitioner.* Washington, D.C.: American Alliance for Health, Physical Education, and Recreation, 1975.

Insko, C.A. *Theories of attitude change.* New York: Appleton, 1967.

Iso-Ahola, S.E. *The social psychology of leisure and recreation.* Dubuque: Brown, 1980.

Iso-Ahola, S.E. (ed.), *Social psychological perspectives on leisure and recreation.* Springfield: Thomas, 1980.

Jones, E.E., and Davis, K.E. From acts to dispositions. In L. Berkowitz (ed.), *Advances in experimental social psychology,* vol. 2. New York: Academic, 1965.

Kando, T.M. *Leisure and popular culture in transition.* Saint Louis: Mosby, 1975.

Kaplan, M. *Leisure in America: A social inquiry.* New York: Wiley, 1960.

———. Aging and leisure. Speech delivered at a meeting of the American Psychological Association, Washington, D.C., September 4, 1971.

———. *Leisure: Theory and policy.* New York: Wiley, 1975.

———. *Leisure: Lifestyle and lifespan.* Philadelphia: Saunders, 1979.

Katzman, M.T. Social indicators and urban public policy. In American Society of Planning Officials (ASPO) (eds.), *Planning: 1968.* Chicago: ASPO, 1968.

Kelley, H.H. Attribution theory in social psychology. In D. Levine (ed.), *Nebraska Symposium on Motivation,* Lincoln: University of Nebraska, 1967.

———. The process of causal attribution. *American Psychologist,* 1973, *28,* 107–128.

Kelly, J. Work and leisure: a simplified paradigm. *Journal of Leisure Research,* 1972, *4,* 50–62.

———. Two orientations of leisure: Processual theory-building. Paper presented at the American Sociological Association meeting, New York, August 1976.

Kelman, H.C. Attitudes are alive and well and gainfully employed in the sphere of action. *American Psychologist,* 1974, *29,* 310–324.

Kerlinger, F.N. *Foundations of behavioral research: Educational and psychological inquiry.* 2d ed. New York: Holt, 1973.

Kerr, W. *The decline of pleasure.* New York: Simon & Schuster, 1962.

Kiesler, C.A.; Collins, B.E.; and Millter, N. *Attitude change.* New York: Wiley, 1969.

Kimmel, D.C. *Adulthood and aging.* New York: Wiley, 1974.

Kluckhohn, C., and Murray, H. *Personality in nature, society and culture.* 2d ed. New York: Knopf, 1962.

Kornhauser, A. *Mental health of the industrial worker.* New York: Wiley, 1965.

Kraus, R. *Recreation and leisure in modern society.* 2d ed. Santa Monica, Calif.: Goodyear, 1978.

Kuebler-Ross, E. *On death and dying.* New York: Macmillan, 1969.

Kulpinska, J. Workers' attitudes towards work. In M.R. Haug and J. Dofny (eds.), *Work and technology,* Beverly Hills, Calif.: Sage, 1977.

Laird, D.A., and Laird, E.C. *How to get along with automation.* New York: McGraw-Hill, 1964.

Lancaster, R.A. LEAP progress report. In *Proceedings of the Third National Leisure Education Conference,* Arlington Va.: National Recreation and Park Association, 1977.

Lawler, E. *Pay and organizational effectiveness: A psychological view.* New York: McGraw-Hill, 1971.

Lazarsfeld, P.F. Notes on the history of quantification in sociology: Trends, sources and problems. In H. Woolf (ed.), *Quantification: A history of the meaning of measurement in the natural and social sciences,* Indianapolis: Bobbs-Merrill, 1961.

Lefcourt, H.M. The function of the illusions of control and freedom. *American Psychologist,* 1973, *28,* 417–425.

Leisure Sciences, New York: Crane, Russak, 1977, *1,* no. 1.

Leisure Today, Journal of Physical Education and Recreation. March 1976, April 1977.

Lepper, M.R.; Greene, D.; and Nisbett, R.E. Undermining children's intrinsic interest with extrinsic reward: A test of the "overjustification" hypothesis. *Journal of Personality and Social Psychology,* 1973, *28,* 129–137.

Leuba, C. Toward some integration of learning theories: The concept of optimal stimulation. *Psychological Reports,* 1955, *1,* 27–33.

Levine, F.M., and Fasnacht, G. Token rewards may lead to token learning. *American Psychologist,* 1974, *29,* 816–820.

————. Comment. *American Psychologist,* 1976, *31,* 90–92.

Levy, J. Leisure module: An objective-subjective model for leisure-time planning. Ph.D. dissertation, University of Waterloo, Faculty of Environmental Studies, 1975.

Lewin, K. *Field theory in social science.* New York: Harper & Row, 1951.

———. *Resolving social conflicts.* New York: Harper, 1948.

Lewin, K.; Lippitt, R.; and White, R. Patterns of aggressive behavior in experimentally created "social climates." *Journal of Social Psychology,* 1939, *10,* 271–299.

Likert, R. *The human organization: Its management and value.* New York: McGraw-Hill, 1967.

Lime, D.W. Behavioral research in outdoor recreation management: An example of how visitors select campgrounds. In J.F. Wohlwill and D.H. Carson (eds.), *Environment and the social sciences: Perspectives and applications,* Washington, D.C.: American Psychological Association, 1972.

Linder, S.B. *The harried leisure class.* New York: Columbia University, 1970.

Lindzey, G., and Aronson, E. (eds.). *The handbook of social psychology.* 2d ed. Reading, Mass.: Addison-Wesley, 1968.

Lipsey, M.W. Research and relevance, a survey of graduate students and faculty in psychology. *American Psychologist,* 1974, *29,* 541–553.

Lundberg, G.; Komarowski, M.; and McInerny, M. *Leisure: A suburban study.* New York: Columbia University, 1934.

Macarov, D. *Incentives to work.* San Francisco: Jossey-Bass, 1970.

McDowell, Jr., C.F. *Leisure counseling: Selected lifestyle processes.* Eugene, Ore.: University of Oregon, 1976.

———. Leisure counseling: A review of emerging concepts and orientations. In A. Epperson, P. Witt, and G. Hitzhusen (eds.), *Leisure counseling: An aspect of leisure education.* Springfield: Thomas, 1977.

McGregor, D. *The human side of enterprise.* New York: McGraw-Hill, 1960.

McGuire, W.J. The nature of attitude and attitude change. In G. Lindzey and E. Aronson (eds.), *The handbook of social psychology,* vol. 3. 2d ed. Reading, Mass.: Addison-Wesley, 1969.

———. The Yin and Yang of progress in social psychology: seven Koan. *Journal of Personality and Social Psychology,* 1973, *26,* 446–456.

Machlowitz, M.M. Working the 100-hour week—and loving it. *New York Times,* October 3, 1976, sec. F., p. 3.

McKechnie, G.E. The psychological structure of leisure: Past behavior. *Journal of Leisure Research,* 1974, *6,* 27–45.

Marans, R.W. Outdoor recreation behavior in residential environments. In J.F. Wohlwill and D.H. Carson (eds.), *Environment and the social sciences: Perspectives and applications.* Washington, D.C.: American Psychological Association, 1972.

Marcuse, H. *One-dimensional man.* Boston: Beacon, 1964.

Martin, F.W. Therapeutic recreation research: A content analysis of subject areas and methodologies. *Recreation Review,* 1974, *4,* no. 1, 25–30.

Martin, F.W., and Bigness, D.R. 1974 catalogue of Ontario recreation and leisure research. *Recreation Review,* 1975, suppl. no. 4.

Martin, P.A. Introduction to P.A. Martin (ed.), *Leisure and mental health: a psychiatric viewpoint.* Washington, D.C.: American Psychiatric Association, 1967a.

————. The psychiatrist's role in free time and its uses. In P.A. Martin (ed.), *Leisure and mental health: A psychiatric viewpoint.* Washington, D.C.: American Psychiatric Association, 1967b.

Maslow, A.H. *Motivation and personality.* New York: Harper, 1954.

————. Some basic propositions of a growth and self-actualization psychology. In G. Lindzey and C.S. Hall (eds.), *Theories of personality: Primary sources and research.* New York: Wiley, 1965.

Mead, M. The pattern of leisure in contemporary American culture. *The Annals of the American Academy of Political and Social Science,* September 1957, vol. 313.

Meriwether, J.M., and Millgate, M. *Lion in the garden: Interviews with William Faulkner, 1926–1962.* New York: Random House, 1968.

Meyer, H.D.; Brightbill, C.K.; and Sessoms, D.H. *Community recreation, a guide to its organization.* 4th ed. Englewood Cliffs, N.J.: Prentice-Hall, 1969.

Meyersohn, R. Television and the rest of leisure. *Public Opinion Quarterly,* 1968, *1,* 111–112.

————. The sociology of leisure in the United States: Introduction and bibliography, 1945–1965. *Journal of Leisure Research,* 1969, *1,* 53–68.

Morgan, C.D., and Murray, H.A. A method for investigating fantasies. *Archives of Neurological Psychiatry,* 1935, *34,* 289–306.

Muir, K. Book review of *The Psychology of Leisure. British Journal of Psychology,* 1975, *66,* pt. 2.

Mullen, E.J., and Dumpson, J.R. *Evaluation of social intervention.* Washington, D.C.: Jossey-Bass, 1972.

Mundy, J. A conceptualization and program design. *Leisure Today: Journal of Physical Education and Recreation,* March 1976, pp. 17–19.

Mundy, J., and Odum, L. *Leisure education, theory and practice.* New York: Wiley, 1979.

Murphy, J.F. *Concepts of leisure.* Englewood Cliffs, N.J.: Prentice-Hall, 1974.

————. *Recreation and leisure service.* Dubuque, Ia: Brown, 1975.

Murphy, J.F.; Williams, J.G.; Niepoth, W.E.; and Brown, P.D. *Leisure service delivery system: A modern perspective.* Philadelphia: Lea & Febiger, 1973.

Murphy, P.E. The role of attitude in the choice decisions of recreational boaters. *Journal of Leisure Research,* 1975, *7,* 216–224.

Murray, H.A. (and collaborators). *Explorations in Personality.* New York: Oxford, 1938.

Nahrstedt, W. *Die Entstehung der Freizeit.* Gottingen: Vandenhoeck & Ruprecht, 1972.

————. *Freizeitberatung? Animation zur Emanzipation?* Gottingen: Vandenhoeck & Ruprecht, 1975.

Neff, W.E. *Work and human behavior.* New York: Atherton, 1968.

Neulinger, J. The psychology of individual similarities: The use of the self as an independent variable. Paper presented at the New York State Psychological Association meeting, Buffalo, May 1967.

————. Perceptions of the optimally integrated person: A redefinition of mental health. *Proceedings of the American Psychological Association,* 1968, pp., 553–554.

————. Leisure and mental health: A study in a program of leisure research. *Pacific Sociological Review,* 1971, *14,* 288–300.

————. *The psychology of leisure.* Springfield: Thomas, 1974a.

————. Into leisure with dignity: Social and psychological problems of leisure. *Society and Leisure,* 1974b, *6,* no. 3, 133–137.

————. *Leisure, tourism, and the quality of life.* Hearings of the U.S. Senate Subcommittee on Foreign Commerce and Tourism, Serial no. 93–75, S. Res. 281. Washington, D.C.: U.S. Government Printing Office, 1974c, pp. 38–42.

————. Leisure or free time. In R. Crandall and J. Neulinger (eds.), *Leisure Information Newsletter,* October 1975, *2,* no. 3.

————. The need for and the implications of a psychological conception of leisure. *Ontario Psychologist,* 1976a, *8,* no. 2, 13–20.

————. Education for leisure: An issue of attitude change. *Leisure Today: Joural of Physical Education and Recreation,* March 1976b, *47,* no. 3, 5–6.

————. Book review. *Journal of Leisure Research,* 1977, *9,* 55–57.

————. Leisure counseling: Process or content? Paper presented at the Dane County Recreation Coordinating Council Conference on Leisure Counseling, Madison, Wisconsin, September 27, 1978.

————. Creative free time: Yes; Creative leisure: No. Paper presented at the International Congress of the World Federation of Mental Health, Salzburg, Austria, July 1979a. (Monograph series; Dordrecht, Holland: Reidel Publishing, *in press.*)

————. Leisure education: A serious task, not self-delusion nor child's play. Paper prepared for the Fourth Annual Leisure Education Conference, The Pennsylvania State University, University Park, Pennsylvania, April 24, 1979*b*.

Neulinger, J., and Breit, M. Attitude dimensions of leisure. *Journal of Leisure Research*, 1969, *1*, 255–261.

————. Attitude dimensions of leisure: A replication study. *Journal of Leisure Research*, 1971, *3*, 108–115.

Neulinger, J., and Brok, A.J. Reflections on the 1973 American Psychological Association symposium on leisure. *Journal of Leisure Research*, 1974, *6*, 168–171.

Neulinger, J., and Crandall, R. The psychology of leisure: 1975. *Journal of Leisure Research*, 1976, *8*, 181–184.

Neulinger, J., and Raps, C.S. Leisure attitudes of an intellectual elite. *Journal of Leisure Research*, 1972, *4*, 196–207.

Notz, W.W. Work motivation and the negative effects of extrinsic rewards: A review with implications for theory and practice. *American Psychologist*, 1975, *30*, 884–891.

Obermeyer, C. Challenges and contradictions. In M. Kaplan and P. Bosserman (eds.), *Technology, human values and leisure*. Nashville: Abingdon, 1971.

Olson, W.E., and McCormick, J.B. Recreation counseling in the psychiatric service of a general hospital. *Journal of Nervous and Mental Diseases*, 1957, *25*, no. 2, 237–239.

O'Morrow, G.S. Recreation counseling: A challenge to rehabilitation. In A. Epperson, P.A. Witt, and G. Hitzhusen (eds.), *Leisure counseling: An aspect of leisure education*. Springfield: Thomas, 1977.

Ossowski, S. Z zagadnien psychologii spolecznej [From the problems of social psychology]. *The Works*, vol. 3. Warsaw: Scientific Editions, 1967.

Overs, R.P.; O'Connor, E.; and Demarco, B. *Avocational activities for the handicapped*. Springfield: Thomas, 1974.

Overs, R.P.; Taylor, S.; and Adkins, C. *Avocational counseling manual*. Washington, D.C.: Hawkins, 1977.

Packard, V. *The status seekers*. New York: McKay, 1959.

Parker, S.R. *The future of work and leisure*. New York: Praeger, 1971.

————. *The sociology of leisure*. London: Allen and Unwin, 1976.

Parks and Recreation, 1974, *9*, no. 5, 22–28.

Perlis, L. Leisure: Opportunity for public service. Address before the 25th Anniversary Conference of the Public Affairs Committee, New York City, March 24, 1961.

Piaget, J. *The language and thought of the child.* New York: Harcourt, 1926.

————. *The judgment and reason in the child.* New York: Harcourt, 1928.

————. *The child's conception of physical causality.* London: Routledge, 1930.

————. *The psychology of intelligence.* London: Routledge, 1950.

————. *The moral judgment of the child.* New York: Macmillan, 1955.

Piaget, J., and Inhelder, B. *The growth of logical thinking from childhood to adolescence.* New York: Basic, 1958.

Pieper, J. *Leisure, the basis of culture.* New York: New American Library, 1963.

Poor, R. (ed.). *4 days, 40 hours.* Cambridge: Bursk and Poor, 1970.

Proceedings of the Third National Leisure Education Conference. Arlington Va.: National Recreation and Park Association, 1977.

Proctor, C. Dependence of recreation participation on background characteristics of sample person in the September 1960 National Recreation Survey. *Outdoor Recreation Resources Review Commission.* Study report no. 19, 1962, pp. 77–94.

A Program for Outdoor Recreation Research. Report on a study conference, conducted June 2–8, 1968, by the National Academy of Sciences for the U.S. Department of the Interior, Bureau of Outdoor Recreation. Washington, D.C.: National Academy of Sciences, 1969.

Proshansky, H.M. Comment on environmental and social psychology. *Personality and Social Psychology Bulletin,* 1976, 2, no. 4, 359–363.

Proshansky, H.M.; Ittelson, W.H.; and Rivlin, L.G. Freedom of choice and behavior in a physical setting. In J.F. Wohlwill and D.H. Carson (eds.), *Environment and the social sciences: Perspectives and applications.* Washington, D.C.: American Psychological Association, 1972.

Proshansky, H.M.; Ittelson, W.H.; and Rivlin, L.G. (eds.). *Environmental psychology: Man and his physical setting.* New York: Holt, 1970.

Puner, M. Retirement and leisure. In S.H. Zarit (ed.), *Readings in aging and death: Contemporary perspectives.* New York: Harper & Row, 1977.

Quinn, R. and Cobb, Jr., W. *What workers want: Factor analyses of importance ratings of job facets.* Ann Arbor, Mich.: Survey Research Center, 1971.

Raskin, A.H. Trying the four day week. *New York Times,* January 15, 1978, sec. E, p. 9.

Reich, C. *The greening of America.* New York: Random House, 1970.

Riley, C. Time is no longer running out: It's gone. *New York Times,* July 17, 1977, sec. E, p. 21.

Ritchie, J.R.B. On the derivation of leisure activity types: A perceptual mapping approach. *Journal of Leisure Research,* 1975, 7, 128–140.

Robinson, D. *Alternative work patterns: Changing approaches to work scheduling.* Report of a conference by the National Center for Productivity and Quality of Working Life and the Work in America Institute, Scarsdale, N.Y.: Work in America Institute, 1976.

Robinson, J.P., and Converse, P.E. Social change reflected in the use of time. In A. Campbell and P.E. Converse (eds.), *The human meaning of social change.* New York: Russell Sage, 1972.

Robinson, J.P., and Shaver, P.R. *Measures of social psychological attitudes.* Ann Arbor: Institute for Social Research, 1972.

Rokeach, M. *The nature of human values.* New York: Free Press, 1973.

Rosenberg, B. & White, D.M. (eds.). *Mass culture.* New York: Free Press, 1957.

Rossi, P., and Williams, W. (eds.). *Evaluating social programs.* New York: Seminar, 1972.

Rotter, J.B. Generalized expectancies for internal versus external control of reinforcement. *Psychological Monographs,* 1966, *80,* no. 609, 1–28.

Russell, B. In praise of idleness. In E. Larrabee and R. Meyersohn (eds.), *Mass leisure.* New York: Free Press, 1958.

Scheuch, E.K. Die Problematik der Freizeit in der Massengesellschaft. In E.K. Scheuch and R. Meyersohn (eds.), *Soziologie der Freizeit.* Koeln: Kiepenheuer and Witsch, 1972a.

———. The time-budget interview. In A. Szalai (ed.), *The use of time.* The Hague: Mouton, 1972b.

Scheuch, E.K., & Meyersohn, R. (eds.). *Soziologie der Freizeit.* Koeln: Kiepenheuer and Witsch, 1972.

Schumacher, E.F. *Small is beautiful.* New York: Harper & Row, 1973.

Sessoms, D.H. The impossible dream. *Leisure Today: Journal of Physical Education and Recreation,* March 1976, pp. 15–16.

Sessoms, D.H.; Meyer, H.D.; and Brightbill, C.K. *Leisure services, the organized recreation and park system.* 5th ed. Englewood Cliffs, N.J.: Prentice-Hall, 1975.

Shafer, Jr., E.L., and Mietz, J. Aesthetic and emotional experiences rate high with Northeast wilderness hikers. In J.F. Wohlwill and D.H. Carson (eds.), *Environment and the social sciences: Perspectives and applications.* Washington, D.C.: American Psychological Association, 1972.

Sheldon, E.G., and Moore, W.E. (eds.). *Indicators of social change.* New York: Russell Sage, 1968.

Sherwood, C.C. Issues in measuring results of action programs. *The Research Letter,* October 1967, p. 1.

Siegel, L., and Lane, I.R. *Psychology in industrial organizations.* Homewood, Ill.: Irwin, 1974.

Skinner, B.F. *Beyond freedom and dignity.* New York: Bantam, 1971.

Slater, P.E. Some social consequences of temporary systems. In W.G. Bennis and P.E. Slater, *The temporary society.* New York: Harper & Row, 1968.

Smith, M.B. Is psychology relevant to new priorities? *American Psychologist,* 1973, *28,* 463–471.

Social Indicators, 1973. Washington, D.C.: U.S. Office of Management and Budget, 1973.

Social Indicators, 1976. Washington, D.C.: U.S. Department of Commerce, 1977.

Social Indicators Newsletter, April 1977, no. 11.

Solzhenitsyn, A. *One day in the life of Ivan Denisovich.* New York: Praeger, 1963.

Sorokin, P., and Berger, C. *Time-budgets of human behavior.* Cambridge: Harvard University, 1939.

Spreitzer, E.A., and Snyder, E.E. Work orientation, meaning of leisure and mental health. *Journal of Leisure Research,* 1974, *6,* 207–219.

Srole, L.; Langner, T.S.; Michael, S.T.; Opler, M.K.; and Rennie, T.A. *Mental health in the metropolis: the midtown Manhattan study.* New York: McGraw-Hill, 1962.

Stein, M.I. Explorations in typology. In R.W. White (ed.), *The study of lives.* New York: Atherton, 1963.

Stein, M.I., and Neulinger, J. A typology of self-descriptions. In M.M. Katz, J.O. Cole, and W.E. Barton (eds.), *The role and methodology of classification in psychiatry and psychopathology.* Washington, D.C.: Government Printing Office, 1968.

Steiner, I.D. Perceived freedom. In L. Berkowitz (ed.), *Advances in experimental social psychology,* vol. 5. New York: Academic, 1970.

Stephenson, W. *The study of behavior: Q-technique and its methodology.* Chicago: University of Chicago, 1953.

Stoddard, S. *The hospice movement: A better way of caring for the dying.* New York: Vintage, 1978.

Suchman, E.A. *Evaluative research: Principles and practice in public health, service and social action programs.* New York: Russell Sage, 1967.

Swados, H. Less work—less leisure. In E. Larrabee and R. Meyersohn (eds.), *Mass leisure.* New York: Free Press, 1958.

Szalai, A. Trends in comparative time-budget research. *American Behavioral Scientist,* May 1966, *9,* no. 9, 3–8.

———. Trends in contemporary time-budget research. In *The Social Sciences; Problems and Orientations.* The Hague: Mouton/UNESCO, 1968, pp. 242–251.

————. Introduction: Concepts and practices of time-budget research. In A. Szalai (ed.), *The use of time*. The Hague: Mouton, 1972a.

Szalai, A. (ed.). *The use of time: Daily activities of urban and suburban populations in twelve countries*. The Hague: Mouton, 1972b.

Thomas, W.I., and Znaniecki, F. *The Polish peasant in Europe and America*. 5 vols. Boston: Badger, 1918–1920.

Thurstone, L.L. Attitudes can be measured. *American Journal of Sociology*, 1928, *33*, 529–554.

Thurstone, L.L., and Chave, E.J. *The measurement of attitude*. Chicago: University of Chicago, 1929.

Tinsley, H.E.A.; Barrett, T.C.; and Kass, R.A. Leisure activities and need satisfaction. *Journal of Leisure Research*, 1977, *9*, 110–120.

Toffler, A. *Future shock*. New York: Bantam, 1970.

Tosi, H.L., and Carroll, S. Management by Objectives. In K.N. Wexley and G.A. Yukl (eds.), *Organizational behavior and industrial psychology*. New York: Oxford University, 1975.

Tourism is everybody's business, *Canada Weekly*, August 31, 1977, p. 6.

U.S. Department of Health, Education, and Welfare. *Toward a social report*. Washington, D.C.: U.S. Government Printing Office, 1969.

U.S. Department of Labor. *Job satisfaction: Is there a trend?* Manpower research monograph no. 30. Washington, D.C.: U.S. Government Printing Office, 1974.

Van Dusen, R.A. (ed.). *Social indicators, 1973: A review symposium*. New York: Social Science Research Council, 1974.

Veal, A.J. Recreation and environmental perception: A preliminary discussion paper. Centre for Urban and Regional Studies, University of Birmingham, Birmingham, England, January 1973.

Veblen, T. *The theory of the leisure class*. New York: New American Library, 1953 (copyright 1899).

Vroom, V. *Work and motivation*. New York: Wiley, 1964.

Walton, R. Leisure education advancement project. In *Proceedings of the third national leisure education conference*. Arlington, Va.: National Recreation and Park Association, 1977.

Weidner, G., and Matthews, K.A. Reported physical symptoms elicited by unpredictable events and the Type A coronary-prone behavior pattern. *Journal of Personality and Social Psychology*, 1978, *36*, 1213–1220.

Weigel, R.H., and Newman, L.S. Increasing attitude-behavior correspondence by broadening the scope of the behavioral measure. *Journal of Personality and Social Psychology*, 1976, *33*, 793–707.

Weiss, C.H. *Evaluation research: Methods of assessing program effectiveness.* Englewood Cliffs, N.J.: Prentice-Hall, 1972a.

Weiss, C.H. (ed.). *Evaluating action programs: Readings in social action and education.* Boston: Allyn and Bacon, 1972b.

Welkowitz, J.; Ewen, R.B.; and Cohen, J. *Introductory statistics for the behavioral sciences.* 2d ed. New York: Academic, 1976.

White, R.W. Motivation reconsidered: the concept of competence. *Psychological Review,* 1959, *66,* 297–333.

White House Conference on Aging: Toward a national policy on aging, 1971, vols. 1 and 2. Washington, D.C.: U.S. Government Printing Office, 1971.

Wicker, A.W. Attitudes versus action: The relationship of verbal and overt behavioral responses to attitude objects. *Journal of Social Issues,* 1969, *25,* no. 4, 41–78.

Wilcox, L.D.; Brooks, R.M.; Beal, G.M.; and Klonglan, G.E. *Social indicators and societal monitoring: An annotated bibliography.* San Francisco: Jossey-Bass, 1972.

Wilson, G.T.; Mirenda, J.J.; and Rutkowski, B.A. Milwaukee leisure counseling model. In A. Epperson, P.A. Witt, and G. Hitzhusen (eds.), *Leisure counseling: An aspect of leisure education.* Springfield: Thomas, 1977.

Wilson, J.A.; and Byham, W.C. (eds.). *The four-day workweek: Fad or future?* Proceedings of a conference conducted by the Graduate School of Business, University of Pittsburgh, 1973.

Witt, P.A. Factor structure of leisure behavior for high school age youth in three communities. *Journal of Leisure Research,* 1971, *3,* 213–219.

————. Introduction. In A. Epperson, P.A. Witt, and G. Hitzhusen (eds.), *Leisure counseling: an aspect of leisure education.* Springfield: Thomas, 1977.

Wolfenstein, M. The emergence of fun morality. *Journal of Social Issues,* 1951, *7,* 3–16.

Wolman, B.B. (ed.). *Handbook of clinical psychology.* New York: McGraw-Hill, 1965.

Woodburn, R., and Cherry, C. Leisure: A resource for educators. Toronto: Ministry of Culture and Recreation, 1978.

Wundt, W. *Principles of physiological psychology.* 2 vols. New York Macmillan, 1873–74.

Yadov, V.A., and Kissel, A.A. Job satisfaction: Analysis of empirical data and attempt at their theoretical interpretation. In M.R. Haug and J. Dofny (eds.), *Work and technology.* Beverly Hills, Calif.: Sage, 1977.

Yutang, L. *The importance of living.* New York: Day, 1937.

Zlutnick, S., and Altman, I. Crowding and human behavior. In J.F. Wohlwill and D.H. Carson (eds.), *Environment and the social sciences: Perspectives and applications.* Washington, D.C.: American Psychological Association, 1972.

Author index

Adler, M. J., 1
Albee, G. W., 179
Allport, G. W., 95
Altman, I., 71
Anderson, N., 48
Andrews, F. M., 68
Aquinas, Saint Thomas, 45
Aristotle, 7, 18, 33, 44, 45
Aronson, E., 112
Asher, J., 124

Ball, C., 148
Barrett, T. C., 101
Barton, W. E., 72
Beisser, A. R., 10
Bem, D. J., 108
Bengtsson, A., 153
Berg, C., 7, 138
Berger, B. M., 85
Berger, C., 75
Berlyne, D. E., 109
Bigness, D. R., 84
Bishop, D. W., 83, 101
Black, J. S., 95
Bolgov, V. I., 39, 133
Borgatta, E. F., 112
Boring, E. G., 180
Boyack, V. L., 9
Bradburn, N. M., 93
Brayfield, A., 119
Breit, M., 7, 74, 137
Brightbill, C. K., 179

Brim, Jr., O. G., 108
Brok, A. J., 60
Bruner, J. S., 109
Bühler, C., 157
Bull, N. C., 85
Burdge, R. J., 20, 73
Burt, C., 101
Burton, T. L., 101
Byham, W. C., 124

Calder, B. J., 109, 110
Campbell, A., 70, 93, 102, 199
Cantril, H., 93
Caplan, N., 72
Caplovitz, D., 93
Capon, R. F., 55–57
Carlson, R. E., 60
Caro, F. G., 87
Carroll, S., 123
Chave, E. J., 67
Chein, I., 95, 112
Cherry, C., 182
Cherry, G. E., 85
Clawson, M., 23
Cobb, Jr., W., 130
Cohen, A. R., 112
Compton, D. M., 179, 183
Connolly, M. L., 182
Converse, P. E., 70, 74–77
Corbin, D. H., 179
Crandall, R., 60, 74
Crockett, W., 119

Subject index